Paths to the Past

**HISTORY HIKES THROUGH
THE HUDSON RIVER VALLEY,
CATSKILLS, BERKSHIRES, TACONICS,
SARATOGA & CAPITAL REGION**

Published by
Black Dome Press Corp.
PO Box 64, Catskill, NY 12414
blackdomepress.com
518.577.5238

First Edition Paperback 2021

Copyright © 2021 by C. Russell Dunn & Barbara A. Delaney

Without limiting the rights under copyright above, no part of this publication may be reproduced, stored in or introduced into a retrieval system, or transmitted, in any form, by any means (electronic, mechanical, photocopying, recording, or otherwise), without the prior written permission of the publisher of this book.

ISBN: 978-1-883789-97-8

Library of Congress Control Number: 2021938061

CAUTION: Outdoor recreational activities are by their very nature potentially hazardous and contain risk. See Caution: Safety Tips, p . xiv

Front cover: Thomas Cole (American, born England, 1801–1848).
A View of the Two Lakes and Mountain House, Catskill Mountains, Morning, 1844.
Oil on canvas, 35 13/16 × 53 7/8 in. (91 × 136.9 cm). Brooklyn Museum, Dick S. Ramsay Fund, 52.16 (detail view)

Back cover (left to right): View from Dibble's Quarry looking out across Platte Clove to the northern mountains; Cohoes Falls, from William Cullen Bryant's 1874 *Picturesque America*; Thomas Cole House, photo by Zio & Sons, courtesy of Thomas Cole National Historic Site and the Olana Partnership.

Photographs by the authors unless otherwise noted.

Chapter maps created using Google Earth.

Map and key created by Toelke Associates.

Design: Toelke Associates, www.toelkeassociates.com

Printed in the USA
10 9 8 7 6 5 4 3 2 1

HISTORY HIKES THROUGH
THE HUDSON RIVER VALLEY,
CATSKILLS, BERKSHIRES, TACONICS,
SARATOGA & CAPITAL REGION

Paths to the Past

RUSSELL DUNN & BARBARA DELANEY

BLACK·DOME

BLACKDOMEPRESS.COM

Cohoes Falls.

This book is dedicated to:

Adam Dunn & Alice Berke
Daniel & Lanita Canavan
Michael & Christine Canavan
Matthew & Catherine Canavan

Family forever.

CONTENTS

FOREWORD BY MARK KING, EXECUTIVE DIRECTOR,
   MOHAWK-HUDSON LAND CONSERVANCY … VIII
INTRODUCTION … XI
A USER'S MANUAL … XIII
CAUTION: SAFETY TIPS … XIV
MAPS … XVI–XVII

PART ONE: HUDSON RIVER VALLEY & CATSKILL REGIONS

1. NORTH & SOUTH REDOUBT (GARRISON) … 1
2. BOWDOIN PARK ROCK SHELTERS (NEW HAMBURG) … 8
3. WALKWAY OVER THE HUDSON &
   CEDAR GLEN RUINS (POUGHKEEPSIE) … 13
4. VAL-KILL (HYDE PARK) … 23
5. VANDERBILT MANSION & BARD ROCK (HYDE PARK) … 30
6. SLABSIDES (WEST PARK) … 38
7. DOVER STONE CHURCH CAVE (DOVER PLAINS) … 45
8. ICE CAVES & SAM'S POINT (CRAGSMOOR) … 49
9. FALLING WATERS (GLASCO) … 55
10. DIBBLE'S QUARRY (PLATTE CLOVE) … 62
11. OLD STAGE ROAD TO CATSKILL MOUNTAIN HOUSE SITE
    (PALENVILLE) … 69
12. HIGH FALLS (PHILMONT) … 82
13. HUDSON RIVER SKYWALK: THOMAS COLE HOUSE TO OLANA
    (CATSKILL & HUDSON) … 90
    MAWIGNACK PRESERVE (CATSKILL) … 99
14. R. & W. SCOTT ICEHOUSE RUINS (NUTTEN HOOK) … 101
15. JORALEMON MEMORIAL PARK (RAVENA) … 107

Part Two: Capital Region

16. Washington Park (Albany)	116
17. Hollyhock Hollow Sanctuary (Feura Bush)	126
18. John Boyd Thacher State Park	136
Section I: High Point & Hang Glider Cliff (Altamont)	136
Section II: Upper Minelot Creek (New Salem)	142
19. Johnson Hall State Historic Site (Johnstown)	150
20. Christman Sanctuary Preserve (Delanson)	160
21. Normanskill Farm (Delmar)	167
22. Schuyler Flatts Cultural Park (Watervliet)	178
23. Erie Canal Ruins (Cohoes)	184
Section I: Cohoes falls and Lock 18, 17, 16, 15 and 14	187
Section II: Locks 9 & 10 and the old Juncta	195
Section III: Weighlock, Maplewood Historic Park	198
Section IV: Cohoes Mastodon	200

Part Three: Saratoga Region

24. Shenantaha Creek Park (Round Lake)	203
25. Lester Park (Saratoga Springs)	210
26. Victory Woods (Schuylerville)	216

Part Four: Taconic & Berkshire Regions

27. Dickinson Hill Fire Tower (Grafton)	224
28. Dyken Pond (Grafton)	231
29. Mattison Hollow (Cherryplain)	236
30. Snow Hole (Petersburg Pass)	241
31. Field Farm & McMasters Caves (South Williamstown)	250

Acknowledgments	255
About the Authors	257
Index	258

FOREWORD

Reading and walking at the same time turns out to be ill-advised. I realize this as I wander the Hollyhock Hollow Preserve and trip over a log while skimming the pages of this wonderful book. Almost immediately it was obvious to me that there is so much more to know about localities I had thought I already knew well. In *Paths to the Past*, Russell Dunn and Barbara Delaney have once again presented us with a series of richly detailed, step-by-step, hikes through history.

As the Executive Director of a land trust that operates more than twenty preserves in the Hudson and Mohawk valleys, I am on a constant quest to provide more in-depth history and information about the sites we protect. Often people visit a park or preserve and go for a nice walk, then hop back in their cars or on their bikes having not truly understood or appreciated the many stories each place has to tell.

Our shared public spaces are not unlike art museums. One can walk through the gallery of any museum and see beautiful images, yet not know the stories they tell. Land is no different, especially in regions like the Hudson and Mohawk valleys where thousands of years of human history have shaped what we see today. As with artworks, the more we know about what we are observing in nature, the more we are drawn into a deeper appreciation of the experience. It is this quest for knowledge about communities and landscapes that encourages the drive to preserve our natural world and ultimately influences the decisions we make about the future of these lands.

An important thread within the various adventures described in these pages is this passion for natural areas and their history that has motivated people to preserve and share these special places. Behind each location there is often one passionate individual, group, or organization that initiated and carried through the very challenging work of land conservation. The Mohawk Hudson Land Conservancy and the numerous other land trusts and preservation organizations in our region are intimately familiar with these challenges. Thanks to a supportive public, we can all enjoy their successes.

Within these struggles to preserve historically and ecologically important places is a significant piece of local history that I feel is not always recognized. The pioneering conservation work of creating the Adirondack and Catskill Parks is widely known, but the Hudson Valley region's influence on conservation extends well beyond that.

The Storm King Mountain decision, which gave citizens legal standing in environmental disputes, dramatically changed how we approach development and conservation, setting the stage for the National Environmental Policy Act (NEPA) and New York's State Environmental Quality Review Act (SEQRA)—legislation that affects many of our major development decisions. Passionate conservationists and philanthropists have worked and fought to protect the many important places included in this book and beyond. John Burroughs, Teddy Roosevelt, and Ver Plank Colvin are all major figures in the environmental movement who spent time exploring the natural wonders of the Hudson Valley region and helped shape our shared conservation ethic. The post–World War II era of rapid growth and environmental change led to the creation of consequential and influential conservation organizations that began as local grass roots groups. The Nature Conservancy, now the largest environmental conservation organization, began in the Hudson Valley, as did Scenic Hudson and River Keeper.

Individuals who had an impact include William Christman, whose story is told in this book. Christman was a once widely read Helderberg poet who created one of the first nature preserves and authored four books of poetry on his beloved location—perhaps a record for the most poetry written about a single preserve. The work and influence of many others at the sites described in these pages and beyond have helped shape our national environmental ethic, resulting in park systems and preserves that set an example for the world.

The Covid-19 pandemic that thankfully appears to be waning as this foreword is being written created a classic case of how opportunity can arise from adversity. In the fear and uncertainty of the initial stages of the pandemic, something amazing happened—people looked to nature for solace, recreation, and even spiritual connections. When so many of our previous escapes and pleasures—restaurants, movies, sporting and musical events—were no longer available, people sought alternatives and discovered, or rediscovered, open spaces in or near their own communities. For the Mohawk Hudson Land Conservancy, our preserve parking lots, with normally ample available parking, were suddenly packed to overflowing. Similar experiences occurred across the state and the country as people were rediscovering natural areas and all the benefits they have to offer.

Now, as we cautiously emerge from the restrictions of the pandemic, this tremendous newfound enthusiasm for nature and history shows no sign of diminishing. A lesson from this experience is that we need natural areas to enhance our lives. These places should be safe, interesting, and accessible to everyone. Our national and state parks are some of the best in the world, but for most of us a visit requires planning, travel and, increasingly, reservations. Local parks and preserves, on the other hand, are nearby and more easily enjoyed. While they might not always span thousands or even hundreds of acres, a public space of even a few acres can still offer a great deal, especially if we have guidebooks such as *Paths to the Past* to accompany us. After all, how else would you learn where

King George had his first hot dog or what *Muhheakantuck* refers to? You'll have to read on to find out.

These stories of the land and its history are not stagnant. History is being made every day. Organizations, including land trusts and government entities, continue to work diligently to preserve threatened and sometimes forgotten places. The move to connect and expand parks and preserves is offering exciting new possibilities for outdoor adventures and learning. Projects such as the Empire State Trail, which will traverse all of New York State—east to west and north to south—connect us to history and remind us of an earlier time when trails were New York's transportation system.

Addressing climate change is strengthening our understanding of the need to protect natural areas and is building support for trail networks to connect people with open spaces. With the simple act of walking or riding a bike, rather than driving, we are slowing down transportation to human speeds that allow us to truly observe our surroundings. We are also awakening to the need to maintain connections between places to ensure ecological and genetic diversity. Conservation is moving toward preservation at a landscape scale—creating linkages between systems such as the Adirondacks to the Catskills.

Paths to the Past, along with Russ and Barbara's many other guidebooks, offers us a window into the past, deepening our understanding of these wonderful places and the forces that created them. It offers us a view to what the eyes of the past might have seen and experienced. Reading about these destinations will make you want to head out to explore new places or revisit familiar places armed with new perspectives and insights. For those living in the regions explored by Dunn and Delaney, or for visitors who can tour and explore the fascinating sites found throughout this historically and ecologically rich part of the Northeast, this guidebook needs to be off the shelf and in your backpack. So grab a copy and begin discovering the adventures beyond your doorstep!

Mark King
Executive Director, Mohawk Hudson Land Conservancy
May 2021

INTRODUCTION

This book takes the adventurous hiker on paths that lead to the discovery of a wondrously rich past.

You may think of a hike as a quiet road under a leafy canopy in a bucolic setting with only birdsong to accompany your footsteps—a respite from busy lives and the constant everyday noise of the modern world—but a hike can be all of that and yet much more. The crumbling wall or derelict building spotted through the brush might be a puzzling clue to events and lives of another time—perhaps it is an abandoned icehouse, a long-gone mill, or a former grand estate that belonged to a forgotten luminary. We pass these relics while hiking and usually think of them as just something curious whose secrets will remain unknown to us.

With this book in hand, however, you will be able to "see" the past as you walk through the present and you may even find yourself intrigued enough to research on your own and delve further into the history of the sites you pass. Some of the historical sites explored in this book have been rescued from neglect and decay by conservationists and historians. Others, sadly, are well on their way to oblivion. But for the moment, while they still last, you can walk in these public spaces and envision them as they were.

Our society has only recently begun to cherish and preserve the historic structures of our culture. Today there are specialized professions motivated by the guiding interest of saving our heritage from vanishing forever. But earnest attempts at preserving historical buildings did not begin in the United States until well into the twentieth century. Up until then, the old was often considered obsolete and simply demolished to make room for the new. Then, in 1966, Congress passed the National Historic Preservation Act. This act authorized the Secretary of the Interior to expand and maintain a National Register of Historic Places, to administer a program of grants to aid in the preservation of places listed on the National Register, and to establish professional standards for those who are involved in the preservation of historic properties. Much earlier, a 1916 act of Congress signed into law by President Woodrow Wilson had created the National Park Service, which also became heavily vested in historic preservation and today employs architects, archaeologists, curators, landscape architects, historians, and other resource professionals to ensure that historic preservation is carried out both within and outside of the National Park system.

As authors and hikers, we feel fortunate to be living in an age when the past is increasingly valued—even prized. This has inspired us to encourage people to venture out into the great outdoors to experience history first-hand in places where it actually happened rather than solely experiencing the artifacts of history within the confines of a museum or gallery. We make no claim to be academicians or historians. We are hikers who, like so many others today, have an abiding love for history and a desire to see it kept alive. Our book is intended for hikers who enjoy history and for history lovers who enjoy hiking.

And so begins *Paths to the Past*—the third in a series of history-oriented hiking guidebooks published by Black Dome Press, beginning with *Trails with Tales: History Hikes through the Capital Region, Saratoga, Berkshires, Catskills, and Hudson Valley* (2006) and followed by *Adirondack Trails with Tales: History Hikes through the Adirondack Park and the Lake George, Lake Champlain & Mohawk Valley Regions* (2009). With *Paths to the Past* we return to the Hudson Valley, Greater Capital Region, Taconics, and Berkshires for our material, with chapters ranging as far south as Garrison (the North & South Redoubt), as far east as South Williamstown (the Field Farm), as far north as Schuylerville (Victory Woods), and as far west as Johnstown (Johnson Hall).

High Falls, Philmont. Postcard circa 1910.

We now invite you to walk outside with us and step back into the past.

Happy trails!

Russell Dunn and Barbara Delaney
May 2021

A USER'S MANUAL

New York State Atlas & Gazetteer—The Delorme *New York State Atlas & Gazetteer* is a valuable tool for plotting driving routes, particularly if you are going from one site to the next. The coordinates listed in each chapter of this book start with the page number of the *Atlas* followed by the row and ending with the column. Thus, "p. 82, A4" instructs the reader to turn to page 82, look across row A (horizontal axis) and then down column 4 (vertical axis) to find the intersection of these coordinates.

We have listed GPS coordinates for both the Tenth Edition as well as the earlier edition of the *Atlas & Gazetteer*. The reason for this is that when Delorme published their Tenth Edition, they flipped all of the numbers around so that those that were at the bottom of the page were now at the top of the page. Be sure to match up your edition of the *Atlas* with the correct version.

GPS Coordinates—Whenever possible, Google Earth–created GPS coordinates have been used for parking locations and for hiking destinations. Enter the GPS coordinates into Google Earth (a program that can be downloaded into your computer) and you can see where the hike begins and where the various points of interest are relative to your starting point. It is an opportunity to reconnoiter the area before actually hiking it.

Readers should take into consideration that the Google Earth GPS coordinates listed may not always coincide precisely with ones that are taken on-site with a hand-held GPS unit. Because Google Earth had to stitch together thousands of individual maps in order to create one large, worldwide map, minor compromises had to be made here and there. For the most part, however, the differences created by such compromises are insignificant.

In our two previous books of history hikes, GPS coordinates were not included, but over the last decade much has changed, with both hikers and authors having become considerably more technologically sophisticated.

Mileages—Driving mileages were determined primarily by car odometer readings and secondarily by Google Earth measurements. Readers should be mindful that odometer readings will vary from one vehicle to another and expect slight discrepancies.

Hiking mileages were obtained from a variety of sources including Web sites, other hiking guidebooks, Google Earth, and personal estimates. The mileages as listed are one-way only unless otherwise indicated by RT (round-trip).

A USER'S MANUAL

Degree of Difficulty—We realize that this category is arbitrary. What is easy for one person may prove to be difficult for another. Such factors as general health, age, and level of fitness all come into play and cannot be disregarded. Generally, the longer the hike, the greater the degree of difficulty assigned to it, particularly if significant changes in elevation are encountered.

CAUTION:

Nature is inherently wild, unpredictable, and uncompromising. Outdoor recreational activities are by their very nature potentially hazardous and contain risk. All participants in such activities must assume the responsibility for their own actions and safety. No book can replace good judgment. The outdoors is forever changing. The author and the publisher cannot be held responsible for inaccuracies, errors, or omissions, or for any changes in the details of this publication, or for the consequences of any reliance on the information contained herein, or for the safety of people in the outdoors.

Remember: the real destination is not the site being hiked to. The real destination is home, and the goal is getting back there safely.

SAFETY TIPS

1. **Always hike with two or more companions.** If one person becomes incapacitated, a second person can remain with the victim while another goes for help.
2. **Carry a day pack complete with emergency supplies**—compass, whistle, flashlight, dry matches, raingear, power bars, extra layers, snacks, duct tape, lots of water (at least twenty-four ounces per person), mosquito repellent, emergency medical kit, sunblock, and a device for removing ticks.
3. **Your skin is the largest organ in your body.** To protect it, wear sunblock when exposed to sunlight for extended periods of time, especially during the long days of summer, and apply repellents when you know that you are going into an area where there are likely to be mosquitoes, black flies, and other insects that view you as mealtime. Wearing a hat with a wide brim to keep out the sun is always helpful, too. Remember that even on a cloudy day you can still get burned. Wear long pants and a long-sleeved shirt to protect yourself from both the sun and biting insects.
4. **Hike with ankle-high boots—always!** High-ankle boots provide traction, gripping power, and ankle support that your sneakers and other shoes cannot provide.

SAFETY TIPS

Wearing loafers, sandals, or flip-flops is especially asking for trouble. Wear liners under wool socks to reduce the likelihood of blisters forming on long hikes.

5. **Be cognizant of the risk of hypothermia, and stay dry.** The air temperature doesn't have to be near freezing for you to become overly chilled. Of equal concern is the danger of hyperthermia (overheating). Drink plenty of water when the weather is hot and muggy. Stay in the shade whenever possible and use a nearby stream to cool off in if you begin to feel overheated.
6. **Stay out of designated hunting areas during hunting seasons.** If you do enter the woods during these periods of time, wear an orange-colored vest and make periodic loud noises to draw attention to the fact that you are a human and not a wild animal.
7. **Stay on trails whenever possible to avoid becoming disoriented and lost.** Off-trail hiking also causes more damage to the environment than on-trail hiking. Do not consider bushwhacking through dense woods unless you: are an experienced hiker; have a compass or GPS unit (including spare batteries) and know how to use them; are prepared to spend several days in the woods if forced to by circumstances; and are with a group of similarly prepared hikers.
8. **Be flexible and adaptive to a wilderness environment that can change abruptly.** Trails described in this book can become altered by blowdown, beaver dams, avalanches, mudslides, and forest fires.
9. **Always let someone know where you are going, when you will return, and what to do if you have not shown up by the designated time.**
10. **Avoid any creature acting erratically.** If an advancing animal cannot be frightened off, assume that it is either rabid or in a predatory mode.
11. **Use good judgment (something that is easier said than done) and avoid impulsive actions.** Unless you are in an immediate crisis and need to react at once and decisively, stop for a moment and think through what your options are. The old sports adage "the best offense is a good defense" applies to hiking. It's far better to defuse a problem early on than to wait until it has reached crisis proportions.
12. **Leave early in the morning if you are undertaking a long hike.** A late start could cause you to be caught in the woods with daylight dwindling and a long way still to go. Allow for even more extra time if the hike is in the winter when night arrives hours earlier than in the summer.
13. **Be mindful of ticks, which have become more prevalent and virulent as their range increases.** Check yourself thoroughly after every hike and remove any tick immediately. The longer the tick remains in contact with you, the greater the risk that you will contract Lyme disease.

MAPS

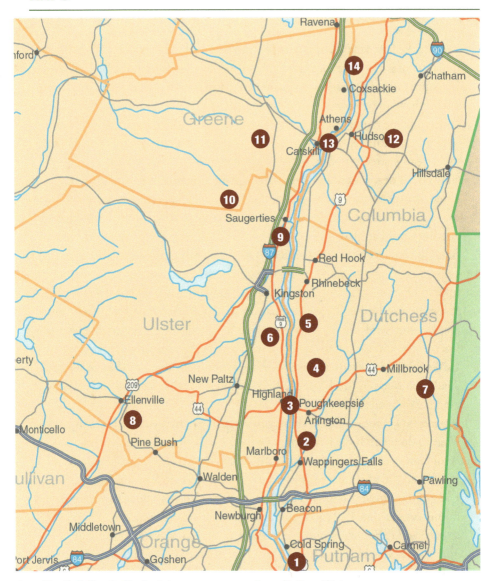

1. North & South Redoubt
2. Bowdoin Park Rock Shelters
3. Walkway over the Hudson & Cedar Glen Ruins
4. Val-Kill
5. Vanderbilt Mansion & Bard Rock
6. Slabsides
7. Dover Stone Church Cave
8. Ice Caves & Sam's Point
9. Falling Waters
10. Dibble's Quarry
11. Old Stage Road to Catskill Mountain House Site
12. High Falls
13. Hudson River Skywalk: Thomas Cole House to Olana and Mawignack Preserve
14. R. & W. Scott Icehouse Ruins

MAPS

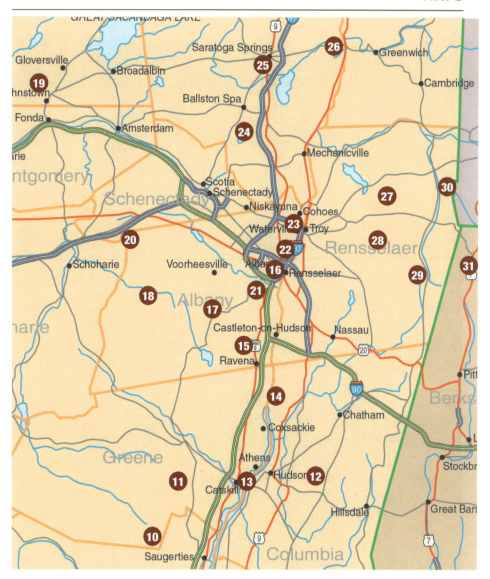

15. Joralemon Memorial Park
16. Washington Park
17. Hollyhock Hollow Sanctuary
18. John Boyd Thacher State Park
19. Johnson Hall State Historic Site
20. Christman Sanctuary Preserve
21. Normanskill Farm
22. Schuyler Flatts Cultural Park
23. Erie Canal Ruins
24. Shenantaha Creek Park
25. Lester Park
26. Victory Woods
27. Dickinson Hill Fire Tower
28. Dyken Pond
29. Mattison Hollow
30. Snow Hole
31. Field Farm & McMasters Caves

PART ONE
HUDSON RIVER VALLEY & CATSKILL REGIONS

1. NORTH & SOUTH REDOUBT

Location: Garrison (Putnam County)
NYS Atlas & Gazetteer, Tenth Edition, p. 108, B2–3; **Earlier Edition,** p. 32, A4
GPS Parking: *North Redoubt*—41.385533, –73.930396:
South Redoubt—41.381184, –73.923341
GPS Destinations: *North Redoubt*—41.383363, –73.928511;
South Redoubt —41.376081, –73.928692
Hours: Dawn to dusk
Fee: None
Restrictions: Removal of artifacts prohibited
Accessibility: *North Redoubt*—0.4-mile-hike; *South Redoubt*—0.5-mile-hike
Degree of Difficulty: Moderate

Directions: From I-84 in Beacon, take Exit 41, turn right onto Route 9D, and drive south for ~11.5 miles (or 3.2 miles from the junction of Routes 9D & 301 in Cold Spring). Turn left onto Snake Hill Road/Route 11 (earlier known as Philips Brook Road) and head east.

From south of Garrison (junction of Routes 9D & 403), drive northeast on Route 9D for 0.8 mile, turn right onto Snake Hill Road/Route 11 and head east.

- → *North Redoubt parking*—After 0.2 mile (just past Avery Road on your left), turn right into a parking area next to an open field at a sign for "North Redoubt Trail."
- → *South Redoubt parking*—After 1.0 mile, turn right onto a tiny unnamed dirt road at the end of a golf course. Immediately cross over a little bridge spanning a creek and proceed south for 0.1 mile, heading toward a private residence. At a fork, turn left away from the private residence onto a second unmarked dirt road and follow it for 0.05 mile to a small parking area.

Description: The North and South Redoubts were primitive earthen fortifications that were part of a greater ring of forts and batteries in the Hudson Highlands built to defend the valley from the advancement of British warships and troops up the Hudson River.

Highlights: Revolutionary War breastworks • Excellent views of West Point, the Hudson River, and Hudson Highlands • Historic Cannon Trail

Hike: *North Redoubt*—From the parking area follow the North Redoubt Trail into the woods, paralleling Snake Hill Road to your left for >0.1 mile. Look for a large rock on your left not far from the start of the hike—by far the largest rock that you will see along the hike. The trail then veers right and begins following an old tote road (a road that was built for hauling supplies) along the side of a ravine. You will occasionally notice stone wall supports on the left that help shore up the road/trail. After 0.3 mile you will come to a junction where one sign points the way to the North Redoubt and the other to the South Redoubt. Turn right and follow the North Redoubt trail uphill for >0.1 mile to reach the top of the 537-foot-high promontory. Although the views to the west are limited by a dense forest of trees, the terrain falls away steeply on all sides of the promontory, graphically illustrating why this spot was chosen for a defensive position. When the leaves are fairly sparse, you can make out Constitution Island to the northwest (named after a British outpost called Fort Constitution) and, even farther northwest, Storm King Mountain, easily identified by a gash on its southeast side that was created when the Storm King Highway was constructed in 1922.

Despite the fact that the breastworks are not as clearly defined as they are on the South Redoubt, you can still see a six-foot-high rise of earth on the east side of the knoll.

Alternative Approach—You can also hike to the North Redoubt from the parking area for the South Redoubt. From the northwest end of the South Redoubt parking area, follow an old road/path northwest for >0.3 mile. At a junction indicated by two trail signs, take the trail to the left that leads to the top of the North Redoubt promontory in >0.1 mile. The trail straight ahead leads to the North Redoubt Trail parking area in 0.3 mile.

South Redoubt—From the southwest end of the parking area, follow the red-marked Cannon Trail into the woods. You will immediately come to a sign on your right that states "Garrison School Forest," followed by a kiosk on your left that contains a map of the preserve. Continue hiking uphill on the Cannon Trail for >0.5 mile, essentially heading southwest. When you finally reach the top of the hill, you will come to a kiosk that displays a map showing the position of the main redoubt, the two south batteries, the north battery, and a number of other points of interest including the location of the former Sloan's Tower (75 feet to the left of the kiosk) and the locations of other forts and redoubts along the Hudson River.

The South Redoubt is less than 100 feet away from the kiosk and in an area kept open for its views of the Hudson River and West Point (the oldest continuously occupied military post in the United States). The redoubt is an impressive breastwork surrounded by a trench (moat). It is best visited early in the season before the

1. NORTH & SOUTH REDOUBT

underbrush partially obscures the earthen ruins. We visited too late in the season to get a decent photograph of the breastworks for this book. A path behind the picnic table takes you up and over the oval-shaped breastworks into the inner section. Another path takes you around the breastworks through the trench.

Take time to explore the site; see if you can locate the various batteries and other artifacts depicted on the map at the kiosk. This is also a great spot to enjoy wonderful views of the Hudson Highlands scenery.

If you happen to hear a "pop, pop, pop" sound echoing through the woods and wonder if you're having an auditory hallucination emanating from the distant past, you may actually be hearing artillery fire coming from the U.S. Military Academy at West Point.

History: The North and South Redoubts at one time were part of the outermost (third and highest) ring of fortifications that rose up along the Hudson River. Both forts on the eastern side of the Hudson River were constructed by Chief Engineer Brigadier General Louis Lebègue Duportail in 1779 at the direction of General George Washington. Duportail was a French military leader who rose to become the chief engineer for the Continental Army during the Revolutionary War. Credit is also given to two French volunteers in the Continental Corps of Engineers for completing the task of building the redoubts—Lieutenant Colonel Jean Baptiste Gouvion and Captain Etienne Bechet de Rochefontaine. Although the Marquis de

North Redoubt breastworks.

Lafayette may be the name best remembered for France's involvement in the Revolutionary War, many other Frenchmen made important contributions, as attested to by these three men.

The South Redoubt boasted a bomb-proof magazine and three external batteries containing three 18-pounders and three 12-pounders. The fort included a raised parapet on its north side that faced the North Redoubt, set up to provide protection in the event that the North Redoubt fell to the British. A total of 150 men were stationed at the two forts.

A third redoubt on the east side of the Hudson River south of the other two, named Sugar Loaf Hill, was also planned but never developed into a full-fledged redoubt with exterior batteries. Sugar Loaf Hill, 785 feet in elevation, would have made an excellent site because of its long summit ridge, proximity to the river, and its conical southwestern shoulder. It was named for its resemblance to a sugarloaf (in colonial times, prior to the advent of granulated sugar, sugar was packaged in solid cone shapes).

South Redoubt—The South Redoubt was constructed to defend the area from British forces advancing from the south, coming up the Hudson River, or marching from the east along the road from Continental Village in Putnam County.

The land was originally part of the Philipse Patent, a large tract of land along the east side of the Hudson River that was given to Adolphus Philipse by King William III of England in 1697.

By the time of the American Revolution, the land belonged to Beverley Robinson, a Loyalist who had acquired the property by marrying Philipse's great-niece, Susannah Philipse Frederick. When Robinson returned to the safety of England after the Revolutionary War, his estate was confiscated by the victorious Americans and then later auctioned off.

A large piece of the land—Water Lot 1—was purchased by William Denning who, at a later date, sold it to the Nelson family. Denning's name, however, lives on at Denning's Point, a peninsula that extends into the Hudson River at Beacon.

In 1803 Cornelius Nelson sold 125 acres of farmland to Harry Garrison. This land, in turn, was later inherited by Harry's son, John Garrison, a county judge, sheriff, and legislator. The Garrisons were industrious people who also established a ferry to West Point in the early 1800s. They live on in name today through the village of Garrison's Landing, which includes the Garrison Landing Historic District.

In 1863 John Garrison sold around 83 acres of land, including Fort Hill (aka Redoubt Mountain), where the South Redoubt is located, to Samuel Sloan, a nineteenth-century railroad magnate and 32-year-long president of the Delaware,

1. NORTH & SOUTH REDOUBT

The S-shaped curve of the Hudson River is clearly visible from the South Redoubt.

Lackawanna & Western Railroad. Sloan was interested in the Hudson Highlands because he wanted a healthier environment for his children than New York City. Between 1881 and 1882 Sloan built a road up to the South Redoubt, where a skeletal observation tower was erected. Sloan's carriage road, however, which came up from the south, is not the Cannon Road that modern visitors take to reach the redoubt today.

In 1956 Sloan's grandson, Samuel Sloan Duryee, and his neighbor, General Frederick Henry Osborn (a philanthropist, military leader, and eugenicist), donated 135 acres of Sloan Mountain, including the South Redoubt, to the Garrison Union Free School District, a school that had been established in 1793. Over time other family members donated additional units of land, bringing the total aggregate of land in the parcel to 181 acres.

As time went on, the land around the fort became overgrown and more difficult to access. A slice of history was beginning to disappear as an expanding forest reclaimed it. In 2001–2002, Tim Donovan and Robert Dodge, working along with Colonel Allan Biggerstaff through the South Redoubt Reclamation Project, surveyed the land and then began to strip away the brush and trees that had obscured the South Redoubt and its views of the Hudson Valley. In this enterprise they were assisted by a number of volunteers, as well as support provided by the Garrison School Forest Committee and the Garrison Union Free School District Board of Education.

Today, the land is well cared for and offers hikers the opportunity to visit a vital, living part of American history.

North Redoubt—Much like the South Redoubt, the North Redoubt was built on a promontory where it could provide commanding views of the area and be well-positioned to repel British forces from any direction. The North Redoubt was 220 feet lower than the South Redoubt; this meant that if the North Redoubt fell to British forces, it could be easily bombarded by batteries from the South Redoubt.

The word "redoubt" has its origins in the French word *redoute* and the Latin word *reductus*, and refers to "a refuge, stronghold, or hidden place." Typically, a redoubt consisted of an interior defensive position protected by an outer wall that was most often a breastwork made of earth, sod, and timber. The South Redoubt is an excellent example of a defensive fortification of this type.

Soldiers through the centuries were required to make Herculean efforts. Visualize hacking out the primitive Cannon Road that leads up to the South Redoubt. Then imagine cutting down thousands of trees and bushes to clear a swath both wide and long enough for oxen and wagons to drag cannons up to the summit. Huge tree stumps had to be pulled out in order for the heavily loaded wagons to proceed unimpeded.

And that was only to reach the summit. Then, battalions of men had to clear away the trees and brush over a wide area for construction of the redoubt and batteries, and to create unobstructed views of the river and valley below. The breastworks, in turn, had to be dug, and an earthen wall built.

One can imagine George Washington, an imposing 6-foot-3-inch figure on horseback, riding up to the redoubts on September 25, 1780, to inspect the progress being made on the forts while Benedict Arnold was simultaneously making good his escape from West Point, which he had conspired to surrender to the British. Arnold escaped via an obscure lane now called Arnold's Path and was rowed out to the British ship the *Vulture*, which earlier had been driven downriver to Teller's Point by cannon fire from a battery on Verplanck's Point. The irony is that Washington was scheduled to meet with Arnold for breakfast earlier that morning. If Washington hadn't decided to inspect the two redoubts on his way from Fishkill to West Point, he would have been at West Point that morning when Arnold received word that his co-conspirator, Major John André (a British intelligence officer), had

1. NORTH & SOUTH REDOUBT

been captured with the plans for the West Point fortress hidden in his boot. Such are the fortunes of war.

Fortifications—The network of fortifications around the Hudson Highlands was built to prevent British naval and land forces from splitting the colonies in half by seizing control of the Hudson River, Lake George, and Lake Champlain waterways, which would have severed New England from the other colonies. Military strategists believed that the fortifications along the Hudson River could delay the British long enough for the Continental Army and militia reinforcements to arrive.

The fortress at West Point, which Washington considered to be "the most important Post in America," was built from 1778 to 1779. In itself, however, it was insufficient. To bolster West Point's strength against assault, sixteen enclosed positions and ten major battery sites were constructed on both sides of the Hudson River in three rings of ascending height, linked together by overlapping artillery ranges and positioned on points of high lands that defied easy assault by the enemy.

In addition, a massive iron chain that weighed 65 tons was extended across the Hudson River from Constitution Island on the east side to a small cove between Horn Point and Love Rock on the west side of the river. The chain was constructed of two-foot-long iron links, each weighing 114 pounds, and was 1,800 feet long. It was kept afloat by rafts made out of 16-foot lengths of timber. The great chain was strategically placed where the Hudson River narrows and changes direction momentarily, creating an S-curve. British ships would be forced to tack here, losing momentum and becoming sitting ducks exposed to heavy cannon fire from multiple locations along the shoreline.

Over the course of four years, the chain was dutifully laid across the river each spring and then disassembled each winter because the frozen Hudson River, thickened with ice, was sufficient in itself to discourage the British Navy from mounting an upriver attack.

The fortifications were such a deterrent that West Point and its many preparations for war never needed to be battle-tested. ■

PART ONE • HUDSON RIVER VALLEY & CATSKILL REGIONS

2. BOWDOIN PARK ROCK SHELTERS

Location: New Hamburg (Dutchess County)
NYS Atlas & Gazetteer, Tenth Edition, p. 103, D7; **Earlier Edition,** p. 36, D4
GPS Parking: 41.602310, –73.940760
GPS Destinations: *North Rock Shelter*—41.605520, –73.941031 (estimated); *South Rock Shelter*—41.597250, –73.939517
Hours: Daily; hours adjusted seasonally (consult park Web site for details)
Fee: None
Restriction: Removal of artifacts prohibited
Accessibility: *North Rock Shelter*—0.2-mile walk followed by a 100-foot uphill trek; *South Rock Shelter*—0.4-mile hike to top of bluff; <150-foot bushwhack to base of escarpment and rock shelter (bushwhack not recommended unless you are physically fit, sure-footed, and are with a companion)
Degree of Difficulty: *North Rock Shelter*—easy to side path; moderate to rock shelter; *South Rock Shelter*—moderate to rocky promontory; moderate to difficult to rock shelter at base of overlook, which involves a scramble/bushwhack
Additional Information: Bowdoin Park, 85 Sheafe Road, Wappinger Falls, 12590; *Trail map*—dutchessny.gov/Departments/Parks

Directions: From west of Spackenkill (junction of Routes 9 & 113/Spackenkill Road), drive south on Route 9 for ~1.7 miles. Turn right onto Sheafe Road and continue south for another ~2.6 miles, then turn right into the entrance for Bowdoin Park near the historic Ellessdie Chapel (part of Bowdoin Park) and follow the main road downhill for 0.2 mile to a mid-level parking area.

Description: Bowdoin Park, encompassing 301 acres, contains two historically significant rock shelters in addition to athletic fields, pavilions, and a handicapped-accessible playground area. Both rock shelters have formed at the base of a rocky escarpment, and both have downslopes that lead from their base to the floor of the valley.

Highlights: Two Native American rock shelters within <1.0 mile from one another • Scenic views of the Hudson River

Hike: *North Rock Shelter*—From the parking area walk north to the four-way intersection from which you just turned left. Cross the road and continue past a red-colored sign that says "Private. No Vehicles Allowed," following a dirt road north for ~0.2 mile. When trees are leafless, you will notice an old road to your right that gradually gets closer and closer to the dirt road until it merges. At that point you will see a faint path to your right that leads uphill in 100 feet to the rock shelter.

South Rock Shelter—Walk east uphill from the parking area for 50 feet to reach the trailhead. You will initially be following the red-blazed Edna C. Macmahon Hiking Trail that was dedicated in 1978. The trail is named for an educator who taught economics at Vassar College from 1942 to 1966 and who became involved in environmental planning in Poughkeepsie and elsewhere in Dutchess County.

Follow the trail south for >0.2 mile. In addition to the rectangular-shaped red blazes, you will also see white-colored Wappinger Greenway Trail circles. At a fork across from a bench, bear right and continue south along the top of the escarpment on the now yellow-blazed trail for another <0.2 mile. Eventually the trail will dip, come back up, and then dip for a second time. When you come up from the second dip you will reach a bare, rocky prominence, called Indian Rock, that overlooks the valley. The rock shelter is directly below this overlook.

From Indian Rock you can see the Danskammer Energy Center across the river to the southwest on Danskammer Point. *Danskammer* is Dutch for "Devil's Dance Chamber." In "The Romance of the Hudson," written in 1876, an unidentified

The park's northern rock shelter as it may have looked when occupied by Native Americans.

author explains, "On that spot, for a century after the discovery of the Hudson, the Indians held their *kinte-kayes*—fearful orgies, in which they danced and yelled around great fires on the eve of an expedition for war or the chase. They appeared more like fiends than human creatures, and the Dutch skippers called the place the Devil's Dance Chamber. There it was, according to the veracious Knickerbocker, that Peter Stuyvesant's crew was 'most horribly frightened by roistering devils.'"

There is no path that leads down to the rock shelter. For those who don't mind a brief bushwhack, backtrack down to the dip and from there make your way over to the rock shelter. Expect a fairly demanding descent over blowdown and loose rock. Most people will probably be content just to enjoy the view of the Hudson River from the top of the rocky promontory.

History: Bowdoin Park contains over four miles of trails and has become a favorite recreational area for locals. In the 1920s the Children's Aid Society received the Bowdoin estate as a bequest. The land was purchased by Dutchess County and opened to the public in 1975.

The North Rock Shelter, roughly 6–7 feet high, lies at the bottom of a 30-foot-high escarpment. Four feet of debris and earth had to be removed from the entrance in order to restore the shallow cavity to its original state when it provided shelter for Native Americans thousands of years ago. It's possible that the rock shelter may also have been wider at one time. This can only be determined, however, if further excavations take place in the future. Equally possible is that the overhang may have extended out farther from the cliff and some of it broke off, but no one really knows for certain.

Millennia ago this land was not as devoid of food as it is today. Game was more plentiful and chestnut trees, which were abundant throughout the region until wiped out by the chestnut blight in the early 1900s, also provided plenty of nourishment.

Archaeological digs have been performed at the rock shelters, and several thousand years of early Native American history have been uncovered. In 1978 the Bowdoin Park Historical and Archaeological Association was formed.

It's likely that Native Americans lived much closer to the river during the warmer months, retreating to the rock shelter seasonally when weather conditions became less hospitable. Part of the North Rock Shelter is presently covered with a wooden frame thatched with reed grass in order to replicate how Native Americans created an enclosure to keep out the harsh weather.

The South Rock Shelter, at the opposite end of Bowdoin Park, is located at the bottom of a 40-foot-high bluff. It has considerably more rock face showing as well

2. BOWDOIN PARK ROCK SHELTERS

as more of an overhang than its northern counterpart. Despite this, the rock shelter evidently gets fewer visitors, for no discernible path leads down to it.

In *Walks & Rambles in Dutchess and Putnam Counties*, Peggy Turco refers to the rocky overlook from above the South Rock Shelter as "Indian Rock," where you can "… walk out to the edge of the cliff for an open view of the river."

In their book *Poughkeepsie Halfway up the Hudson*, Joyce C. Ghee and Joan Spence mention that the rock shelters historically were easily accessible from the Hudson River and provided inhabitants with an unobstructed view of the river for defensive purposes. The views today are not quite as unobstructed.

It is believed that a Native American village may have occupied the site where the park's soccer fields are located today.

The white and gray rock that you see throughout the park is called Pine Plains Dolomite. This rock is similar to limestone except that calcium carbonate has been replaced by calcium magnesium carbonate.

The *Ellessdie Chapel* at the entrance to Bowdoin Park dates back to the early 1800s. It was founded by James Lennox and his sister, Mary Lennox Scheafe. According to the "Wappinger Greenway Trail brochure," the name of the church is based on the initials of James and Mary and a third sibling.

Peeling back layers of the past, the genesis for Bowdoin Park began with the birth of George Bowdoin in 1833. Bowdoin, who was the great-grandson of Alexander Hamilton, became a successful Wall Street broker and in 1862 married Julia Grinnell. This proved to be a fortuitous arrangement, for George became good friends with Julia's brother, Irving Grinnell, who introduced him to the Wappinger Falls/New Hamburg area where Irving owned land. Grinnell called his property "Netherwood." It essentially encompassed what would become Bowdoin Park in the future. Spurred on, George started purchasing land in the area as well and established a retreat that he and his family could travel to from New York City. Ten years later, in 1872, Bowdoin also purchased, from Grinnell, the part of Netherwood located on the west side of Sheafe Road.

In 1863 George and Julia had a son, Temple, who married Helen Kingsford in 1894. It was through Helen that the Bowdoins became involved with the Children's Aid Society. Helen, who served on a local board, was able to get her father-in-law to make annual donations to the institution.

In 1907 the Bowdoin family established a country home in New Hamburg where ill children could go to recuperate. They called the home "Kinderfold."

Temple and Helen had a son, George Temple Bowdoin, who also became involved in banking and finances and who continued to support the home for children in Dutchess County.

George Temple was able to acquire the rest of the Netherland estate from Irving Grinnell before Grinnell's death in 1921. He was also able to obtain the John Fisher Sheafe estate's land, as well as land owned by his grandfather.

In 1925, after joining the Board of Directors of the Children's Aid Society, George Temple Bowdoin donated the family property in New Hamburg to the Children's Aid Society in memory of his parents. This was followed by a series of nine land transfers between 1927 and 1949 that brought the property held by the Children's Aid Society up to a total of 312 acres. At that time the home was called the Bowdoin Memorial Farm.

Despite all efforts, the children's home went into decline and was forced to close in the early 1970s, and the society refocused on urban challenges that were closer to home. In 1975 Dutchess County purchased the property, delineating 11 acres to be used by the Tri Municipal Sewer Plant. The remaining 301 acres became Bowdoin Park, which has been a popular town park ever since. ■

View from Indian Rock above the park's southern rock shelter.

3. WALKWAY OVER THE HUDSON & CEDAR GLEN RUINS
WALKWAY OVER THE HUDSON STATE HISTORIC PARK & FRANNY REESE STATE PARK

Location: Highland/Poughkeepsie (Ulster/Dutchess Counties)
NYS Atlas & Gazetteer, Tenth Edition, p. 103, C7; **Earlier Edition,** p. 36, C4
GPS Parking: *Walkway over the Hudson: East End*—41.712017, –73.926217; *Walkway over the Hudson: West End*—41.710400, –73.957023; *Johnson-Iorio Memorial Park*—41.704398, –73.951670; *Bob Shepard Highland Landing Memorial Park*—41.715948, –73.948463; *Franny Reese State Park*—41.700370, –73.962945
Franny Reese State Park Destinations: *Cedar Glen Ruins*—41.702375, –73.954568 & 41.702101, –73.953795; *Blue Trail Overlook*—41.703716, –73.953471
Hours: *Walkway over the Hudson*—daily, 7 AM to dusk; *Franny Reese State Park*—daily, dawn to dusk
Fee: None
Restrictions: *Walkway over the Hudson*—pets must be leashed; smoking not allowed; rules & regulations posted at both ends of the bridge. *Franny Reese State Park*—pets must be leashed
Accessibility: *Walkway over the Hudson*—1.3-mile walk; *Cedar Glen Ruins*—0.3–0.6-mile hike
Degree of Difficulty: *Walkway over the Hudson*—easy; *Cedar Glen Ruins*—easy to moderate
Information: *Walkway over the Hudson*—restrooms at each end of the bridge. *Franny Reese State Park Trail map*—parks.ny.gov
Directions: *General directions to Highland*—From the New York State Thruway (I-87) take Exit 18 for New Paltz and drive east on Route 299 for ~5.2 miles. Turn right

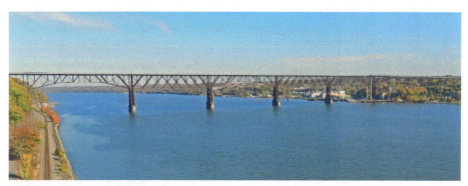

Walkway over the Hudson.

onto Route 9W and proceed south for ~1.8 miles until you come to the junction with Route 44/55, to your right. The directions to the following parking areas all start from this junction:

→ *Parking area at the west end of the Walkway over the Hudson*—Continue southwest on Route 9W/44/55 for 0.4 mile. Turn left onto Haviland Road and proceed east for 0.4 mile, turning left into the parking area for the rail trail.

→ *Parking area at the east end of the Walkway over the Hudson*—Continue southwest on Route 44/55/9W for 0.5 mile and then turn right off Route 9W to follow Route 44/55 as it takes you east across the Mid-Hudson Bridge. At the Poughkeepsie end of the Mid-Hudson Bridge, drive past the right turn for Route 9/Hyde Park/Wappinger Falls and continue east on Route 44/Church Street for 0.4 mile. When you come to Market Street (a one-way street), turn left and proceed north on Market Street/Civic Center Plaza for 0.4 mile. Turn right onto Mansion Street, go east for 0.1 mile, and then bear left onto Garden Street. After heading northeast for 0.4 mile, turn sharply left onto Parker and proceed west for 0.1 mile, turning right at the Walkway sign onto a paved road that leads immediately into a parking area for the Walkway over the Hudson State Historic Park.

→ *Parking for Johnson-Iorio Memorial Park*—Continue southwest on Route 9W/44/55 for 0.4 mile. Turn left onto Haviland Road and proceed southeast for 0.9 mile, turning left into a small parking area just before the end of the road.

→ *Parking for Bob Shepard Highland Landing Memorial Park*—*Option #1*: Turn right onto Route 44/55 and drive northeast for >0.1 mile into the village of Highland. Bear right onto Vineyard Avenue and head northeast for 0.3 mile. As soon as you pass under the Route 9W Bridge, turn right onto River Road and follow it downhill through a deep ravine for 0.8 mile. Immediately after crossing over railroad tracks, turn left into the parking area for Highland Landing. *Option #2*: From the west end parking area for Walkway over the Hudson, drive southeast on Haviland Road for >0.2 mile. Turn sharply left onto Ransom Road and go downhill, heading north for 0.1 mile. In doing so you will pass directly under the Walkway. When you come to Mile Hill Road, turn right and proceed northeast for >0.2 mile. Then turn left onto River Road and drive north for >0.2 mile, bearing right into the parking area for Highland Landing.

→ *Parking for Franny Reese State Park*—*South entrance*: Drive south on Route 9W for ~1.5 miles. Turn left onto Macks Lane and head northeast for <0.3 mile. As Macks Lane veers right, look for the sign for Franny Reese State Park and follow a dirt road north for 0.1 mile to a small parking area. *North entrance*: At Johnson-Iorio Memorial Park, walk toward the end of the road. Just as you reach the west end of the Mid-

3. WALKWAY OVER THE HUDSON & CEDAR GLEN RUINS

Hudson Bridge, follow a flight of stairs that takes you down to a lower level by the river. At the bottom, to your left is an old road that dead-ends at a barricade in 100 feet (an offshoot of Oakes Road). Take note of a 10-foot cascade choked with blowdown that descends next to the abandoned road.

To your right is an enormous stone archway that is part of the Mid-Hudson Bridge. This is the north entrance to Franny Reese State Park. Walk through the archway, taking note of the various informational plaques on its wall, and follow an old carriage road into the interior of the park.

Description: *Walkway over the Hudson*—The 212-foot-high, 1.3-mile-long walkway provides a thrilling walk over the Hudson River between the village of Highland and the city of Poughkeepsie.

Bob Shepard Highland Landing Memorial Park, located along the west shore of the Hudson River, provides views of the Walkway over the Hudson and Poughkeepsie.

Johnson-Iola Memorial Park, located directly next to the northwest end of the Mid-Hudson Bridge, provides views of the Walkway over the Hudson, Mid-Hudson Bridge, and Poughkeepsie.

Franny Reese State Park offers great views of the Hudson River, Mid-Hudson Bridge, and Poughkeepsie, and contains the ruins of one of the Hudson Valley's great estates.

Highlights: *Walkway over the Hudson*—the second-longest elevated pedestrian bridge in the world • Views of the Hudson River and shoreline upriver and downriver from both sides of the river and both ends of the Walkway over the Hudson • Ruins of Cedar Glen, an old Hudson River estate in Franny Reese State Park

Historic 1915-vintage caboose at west end of the Walkway.

PART ONE • HUDSON RIVER VALLEY & CATSKILL REGIONS

Hike: *Walkway over the Hudson*—The walk we describe starts from the west end of the pedestrian bridge and takes you across to the east end of the bridge and back. This can also be a one-way trip if you place a second car on the east side of the river. The hike can just as easily be taken from the parking area at the east end of the bridge, of course, walking west and then back.

Leaving the Haviland Road parking area, walk east past the 1915-vintage caboose, which the Ulster County Chamber of Commerce previously used as a visitor kiosk. In 100 feet you will pass a large rocky protuberance to your left. Next to this rock is a spur path that leads downhill, then across a small stream via a footbridge, to Mile Hill Road. This unmarked but well-maintained path is unknown to most bridge walkers. It is there for hikers who wish to reach the Bob Shepard Highland Landing Memorial Park on foot. From the spur path, Mile Hill Road leads down to River Road in 0.3 mile and, from there, north on River Road for 0.2 mile to Highland Landing Memorial Park.

Bypassing this spur trail for now, continue east on the Rail Trail, passing by the power station to your right. It is a walk of only <100 feet to reach the Welcome Center, where restrooms and outdoor tables can be found. The Welcome Center opened in 2018 and can be a hub of activity. A similar, but slightly smaller, Welcome Center awaits at the east end of the bridge.

Look for a 7-foot-high statue of Sojourner Truth, created by Vinnie Bagwell. The statue was installed on the southeast side of the Center's open space in 2020. Despite having reached the Welcome Center, you are still 0.3 mile away from the Hudson River. Continuing east you will quickly find yourself suspended high above the ground. Ransom Road, followed by River Road (close to the river) appears tiny far below.

Sojourner Truth (1797–1883) was a woman's rights activist and abolitionist. Born into slavery in Swartekill (a small hamlet in New York at the confluence of Swartekill Creek and the Wallkill River), Sojourner managed to escape with her infant daughter in 1826 after already being sold three times. She became a free woman and changed her name from Isabella Baumfree to Sojourner Truth. In 1828 she went back to gain custody of her son and prevailed legally. She was the first black woman to win such a case against a white man.

Truth gave a well-received extemporaneous speech at the Ohio Women's Rights Convention in Akron, Ohio, and during the Civil War she helped recruit black troops for the Union Army.

3. WALKWAY OVER THE HUDSON & CEDAR GLEN RUINS

Once you are at the river's edge, there are many points of interest to take in. To your left (north) on the west side of the bridge is the 1.7-acre Bob Shepard Highland Landing Memorial Park, 0.2 mile upriver. An oil storage facility once operated here from the mid-1900s to 2003, at which time the abandoned tanks were dismantled. For a shorter time, from 1897 to 1925, a trolley line operated here. There were factories and warehouses, but they are long gone.

A local businessman named Matthew Smith was the first to envision turning the property into a riverfront park. He was joined by a group of Highland citizens and they formulated a plan for acquiring and developing the park. Bob Shepard, the town supervisor as well as a local businessman, became involved in the project at this point and was instrumental in helping the citizen group become authorized by the Town of Lloyd as the Highland Landing Park Association. Shepard also advised the association in its support of a town-wide referendum to purchase the land, which was approved by voters by a 2–1 margin. For his fervent support, the association decreed that the park would be named to memorialize Bob Shepard.

Closer to the bridge, 0.1 mile downriver from the Highland Landing Memorial Park, is the site of the former Mariners Harbor Marina & Restaurant.

The train tracks that you see running along next to the river belong to CSX Railroad (formerly Conrail). The tracks on the eastern shoreline belong to Amtrak, the National Railroad Passenger Service.

Look to your right (south) along the west side of the river and you will see part of Franny Reese State Park.

Across the river and along the shoreline directly south of the east end of the Walkway is the Mid-Hudson Children's Museum, followed by 9-acre Victor C. Waryas Park, named after a Poughkeepsie mayor who served from 1960–1964.

0.5-mile farther downriver, by the east end of the Mid-Hudson Bridge, is Kaal Rock, also known as Caul Rock and Call Rock—a huge, 50-foot-high buttress of rock that fronts Kaal Rock Park. In early times it provided a vital point of reference for sailors navigating the Hudson River. It was also from here that the early burghers of the town would sit and hail passing sloops to receive news of local and world events.

North of the Walkway along the east side of the Hudson River, 0.7 mile upriver, is the 12-acre Longview Park that was created in 2007. Look closely and you will easily make out the renovated, historic, two-story-high Cornell Boathouse used by the Marist College rowing teams. Directly behind the park is Marist College, founded in 1905 by the Marist Brothers, an international Catholic Brotherhood.

But the main sight from the Walkway is the Mid-Hudson Bridge, 0.5 mile downriver, which endlessly teems with cars going to and from Poughkeepsie.

PART ONE • HUDSON RIVER VALLEY & CATSKILL REGIONS

The last 0.7 mile of the Walkway takes you first past the 21-story-high elevator rising from Upper Landing Park, then over railroad tracks, city streets, and between neighboring houses where trees line both sides of the Walkway, creating the illusion during the summer that you have entered a more rural area.

Cedar Glen ruins at Franny Reese State Park—South End approach: Pause for a moment at the kiosk next to the parking area. Three trails are described: the 0.9-mile-long Yellow Trail; the 1.8-mile-long White Trail; and the 0.3-mile-long Blue Trail. For this hike you will only need to follow the Yellow Trail for <0.6 mile to reach the Cedar Glen ruins.

From the kiosk follow the Yellow Trail, a wide, old road, north, heading downhill. After >0.5 mile, the Upper White Trail junction is reached. Turn left here, continuing northeast on the Yellow Trail for 250 feet to reach the ruins, which are on your right at the Lower White Trail junction (which forms a 1.8-mile loop with the Upper White Trail). Turn right onto the White Trail for frontal views of the partially intact ruins of the Cedar Glen mansion with its stone construction and cement facing. A tall, red-brick fireplace chimney is particularly noticeable.

Continue along the White Trail for several hundred feet to see other fairly intact ruins of buildings on your left and then on your right.

North End approach: From the archway under the west end of the Mid-Hudson Bridge (see Johnson-Iorio Memorial Park for trailhead information), follow the old carriageway southwest for 0.3 mile to reach the junction with the White Trail where the ruins begin.

Just before reaching the White Trail, you will encounter the Blue Trail, leading off to your right next to an old, filled well. If you wish to do a very short, spur-trail hike, follow the Blue Trail uphill for <0.05 mile to reach an impressive overlook of the Hudson River and Mid-Hudson Bridge (you will be looking down at the bridge). Fourteen 3-foot-high stone pillars that are connected in a row by a long,

> **The Mid-Hudson Bridge** is 3,000 feet long and 135 feet above the river at its highest point. Ralph Modjeski, a Polish-American civil engineer who worked on strengthening the Walkway over the Hudson Bridge at a time when it was still the Poughkeepsie Railroad Bridge, was the chief engineer of the Mid-Hudson Bridge.
>
> The Mid-Hudson Bridge was officially named the Franklin Delano Roosevelt Mid-Hudson Bridge in 1994 in honor our 32nd president, who along with his wife Eleanor had attended the bridge's opening ceremony in 1930.

3. WALKWAY OVER THE HUDSON & CEDAR GLEN RUINS

Ruins of the Cedar Glen Mansion.

Cedar Glen is the name of a nineteenth-century, seven-building estate (including a stone house and windmill) that was built by Dr. Charles H. Roberts (1821–1909), a medical doctor who turned to dentistry and became a pioneer in the use of anesthesia for "painless" dentistry. Roberts married in 1866. In 1868, he built his great estate and called it "Cedar Glen" after the numerous cedars that populated the site. The couple went on to have six children.

Roberts retired from dentistry at age 47—around the same time that he built Cedar Glen—and then proceeded to become a successful railroad magnate, acquiring additional wealth in the process.

After Roberts died in 1909, his wife, Catharine Freeman, held onto the property until her death in 1946. By then Dr. Robert's fortune had dissipated and the estate had fallen into disrepair.

In 1971 the abandoned property, now in ruins, was purchased by Joseph Alfano. Fortunately, Scenic Hudson was able to obtain the land in 2003 from the Alfano family and transferred ownership to the New York State Office of Parks, Recreation and Historic Preservation in 2006.

black railing might indicate that a structure of some kind must have once overlooked the river from here.

History: *Walkway over the Hudson*—After work was started in 1886, the 6,756-foot-long, double-track Poughkeepsie-Highland Railroad Bridge was completed in 1889. It has also been called High Bridge because of its staggering, 212-foot height. It has the distinction of being the first bridge ever built to cross the Hudson River between New York City and Albany.

The contract for bridge construction went to the Union Bridge Company after funding was organized by the Manhattan Bridge Building Company. When completed, the Poughkeepsie Railroad Bridge became the longest cantilevered & truss span bridge in the world. It contained two sets of tracks, allowing trains to pass from opposite directions until 1918, at which time the tracks were switched to gauntlet tracks (two tracks interlaced in such a way that they take up little more space than a single track). This was done so that the imposing weight of diesel locomotives could be managed.

The initial reason for the Poughkeepsie-Highland Railroad Bridge being built was for the transportation of coal and grain from the Midwest to New England. Later the bridge facilitated the transport of World War II troops. During its peak years, 3,500 railcars were crossing daily.

The Poughkeepsie-Highland Railroad Bridge operated until 1974 when 700 feet of its east end was consumed by fire produced, it is believed, by the brakes of the last train to cross the bridge. The bridge burned for three solid days, but remained standing. In 1979 it was placed on the National Register of Historic Places.

Beginning in the mid-1990s, the seemingly outrageous thought of turning an abandoned, derelict bridge into something greater than itself began to percolate in the community, spearheaded by Ray Costantino, John Canino and Everton Henriques—three active members of the Highland Rotary Club. Then, in 1998, after owners of the bridge failed to pay back taxes to both Dutchess and Ulster Counties, Vito Moreno (the owner of the bridge at that time) deeded the property to a not-for-profit volunteer organization called Walkway over the Hudson. Financial support for the bridge came from state grants and individual donors. Many others donated labor. Rehabilitating the bridge was a prodigious job. Repairs to the structural steel had to be made and concrete slabs for the Walkway laid. But somehow it was all accomplished without a single dollar of local taxes being spent on the project.

The Walkway over the Hudson opened to the public in October 2009 thanks to the efforts of the Walkway organization, the Dyson Foundation, and New York

3. WALKWAY OVER THE HUDSON & CEDAR GLEN RUINS

State. It was dedicated to Claire and Ray Costantino, whose vision and steadfast determination transformed an abandoned railroad bridge with structural problems into a magnificent pedestrian bridge.

In 2010 the Walkway over the Hudson became part of the Hudson Valley Rail Trail when the 2.5 miles of paved rail trail between Highland and Tony Williams Park, which had opened to the public in 1997, was extended eastward another 1.2 miles to connect with the Walkway over the Hudson.

2,600 people lined up on the bridge to do the hokey pokey, in June 2012, breaking the Guinness World Record.

In 2014 a 21-story-high, glass-enclosed riverfront elevator was erected to connect the Walkway with the Upper Landing Park and the Poughkeepsie riverfront. This was followed by the bridge being inducted into the Rail-Trail Hall of Fame in 2016.

The New York State Department of Parks (Taconic Region) presently manages and maintains the Walkway.

Hudson River—The Hudson River, at a length of 315 miles, is the longest river in New York State. Some have called it the "Rhine of America," both because of its incredible scenery, which includes the Palisades and Hudson Highlands, and because of its 400 years of recorded history, in addition to the unrecorded history of Native Americans who occupied the area for thousands of years previously. (How much more we would know if only Native Americans in New York had had a written language!)

The Hudson River rises in the High Peaks Region of the Adirondack Mountains from a pond source near the summit of Mt. Marcy (New York State's highest point) and from a stream source at Indian Pass; 315 miles later it pushes out into the Atlantic Ocean far beyond Staten Island. What makes the Hudson River unlike any other river in New York State is that it is tidal until north of Albany, rising and falling in lockstep with tides produced by the Atlantic Ocean. It's not until the Federal Dam in Troy is reached that this magical spell over the river is broken, and the Hudson flows just one way from the Adirondacks to the Federal Dam.

Because the river oscillated, its currents switching directions two times a day, Native Americans called it *Muhheakantuck*, or "the river that flows two ways." To them the Hudson was a supernatural river, inexplicably changing its course first one way, then the other. No other New York river did this, not even the mighty Mohawk River (New York's second-largest river and a tributary to the Hudson River).

This is the river that you will be crossing on the Walkway over the Hudson.

PART ONE • HUDSON RIVER VALLEY & CATSKILL REGIONS

The Johnson-Iorio Memorial Park—A memorial at the center of this tiny park commemorates all of the local men who died in the Vietnam War, including R.E. Johnson and L.R. Iorio.

From the Johnson-Iorio Memorial Park there are superb close-up views of the Mid-Hudson Bridge as well as the Hudson River and nearby Walkway over the Hudson. There are also more distant views along the east side of the river of the Mid-Hudson Children's Museum, Kaal Rock Park, Dooley Square (the center of Poughkeepsie's riverfront revitalization), and the 1918 Poughkeepsie Railroad Station.

The Johnson-Iorio Memorial Park is part of a huge rock-cut that was made in order to create Haviland Road. Until the mid-1970s, Haviland Road served as the western access to the Mid-Hudson Bridge. At that time Route 44/55 was rerouted and Haviland Avenue became a dead-end road.

The Johnson-Iorio Memorial Park also serves as the north entrance to Franny Reese State Park, requiring that you exit the park via a flight of steps down to the archway under the Mid-Hudson Bridge, where a carriage road begins.

Franny Reese State Park contains 251 acres with 2.5 miles of trails and provides scenic views of the Hudson River, Mid-Hudson Bridge, and the Walkway over the Hudson. The park's name comes from Frances "Franny" Reese (1917–2003), who was an environmentalist and a founder of Scenic Hudson, a conservation organization. From 1966 to 1984, Reese served as chair of the Scenic Hudson Board. Her motto was: "Care enough to take some action; do your research so you don't have to backtrack from a position; and don't give up!"

The park's main attraction, aside from its views of the Hudson River, is the partially intact ruins of the Cedar Glen estate. ■

Cedar Glen as it looked in the late nineteenth century.

4. VAL-KILL
Eleanor Roosevelt National Historic Site

Location: Hyde Park (Dutchess County)
NYS Atlas & Gazetteer, Tenth Edition, p. 103, B8; **Earlier Edition,** p. 37, BC4–5
GPS Parking: 41.761688, –73.900351
GPS Destinations: *Val-Kill Stone Cottage*—41.762721, –73.899400;
Top Cottage— 41.765147, –73.888871
Hours: *Grounds*—dawn to dusk; *Val-Kill*—check Web site for hours;
Top Cottage—reservations required
Fee: *Grounds*—none; *Val-Kill*—modest fee; *Top Cottage*—modest fee
Restrictions: no motorized vehicles, bikes, hunting, trapping, camping, fires, swimming, or removal of artifacts; carry in, carry out
Accessibility: *Top Cottage*—1.0-mile hike; Note: shuttle bus to cottage is part of the Home of Franklin D. Roosevelt National Historic Site tour; *Eleanor's Walk (loop)*— 0.8-mile hike
Degree of Difficulty: *Top Cottage*—moderate; *Eleanor's Walk*—easy
Additional Information: *Trail map*—hydeparkny.us

Directions: From Poughkeepsie where Route 9 goes under Route 44 at the east end of the Mid-Hudson Bridge, drive north on Route 9 for >4.0 miles. Turn right onto St. Andrews Road/Route 40A and head east for >1.1 miles. Bear left onto Violet Avenue/Route 9G and proceed north for 0.5 mile. When you come to the entrance to the Eleanor Roosevelt National Historic Site, turn right and drive east for 0.3 mile to the parking area.

Val-Kill stone cottage, a retreat for Eleanor Roosevelt and her two friends, Nancy Cook and Marion Dickerman.

PART ONE • HUDSON RIVER VALLEY & CATSKILL REGIONS

Description: Val-Kill is a former residence of Eleanor Roosevelt and the only National Historic Site dedicated to a First Lady. President Jimmy Carter signed the bill creating the Eleanor Roosevelt National Historic Site in 1977. Val-Kill became the getaway cottage of Eleanor during the presidency of her husband, Franklin Roosevelt. In her later years, after the president died, Val-Kill was Eleanor's main residence.

Eleanor named the spot "Val-Kill" because of the nearby stream, the Fall Kill, which encompasses 40 miles of brooks with a watershed of 12,476 acres. Val-Kill loosely translated means "waterfall stream"; *val* is Dutch for "falling," and *kill* is Dutch for "stream."

Val-Kill was not the only home where Eleanor Roosevelt resided, but it was the most personal and informal of her residences—and it is the only home that was designed and built specifically for her.

The Val-Kill property spans 181 acres. It includes three main buildings: Stone Cottage; Val-Kill Industries/residence; and Top Cottage (built in 1938 as a retreat for Franklin Roosevelt). Stone Cottage, constructed in 1925, was the original residence. The idea of a cottage in the woods near the Fall Kill stream grew out of a conversation during a picnic near the stream attended by Eleanor, Franklin, and two of Eleanor's friends, Nancy "Nan" Cook and Marion Dickerman. What may have started as fanciful musing later became a project that involved all four picnickers.

About a year after Stone Cottage was completed, Eleanor, Nan Cook, and Marion Dickerman decided to expand their furniture crafting endeavor and added a second building on the property for Val-Kill Industries. The three women plus a third partner, Caroline O'Day, founded Val-Kill Industries with the idea of providing local farmers with craft skills.

Highlights: Landscaped grounds of Val-Kill • Stone Cottage, including the pond, tennis courts, swimming pool, and dollhouse • Top Cottage • Val-Kill Industries • Woodland walking trails on former carriage roads

Hike: *To trailhead for Top Cottage Trail & Eleanor's Walk*—From the parking area follow the park road across a bridge with views of Val-Kill to your left. Continue following the road, veering steadily right, to reach the trailhead road for Top Cottage and Eleanor's Walk after 0.1 mile.

Follow the trailhead road (an old carriageway) southeast for several hundred feet. You will reach the point where the 1.0-mile-long Top Cottage Trail continues straight ahead and the 0.8-mile-long Eleanor's Walk Loop veers off to the right.

4. VAL-KILL

Top Cottage Hike—Head east, immediately crossing under power lines and then reaching the end of the carriage road in >0.05 mile. At this point the way ahead turns into a trail as you bear right and cross a footbridge, and then another footbridge immediately after. You will cross over two more footbridges as well as going through two stone walls along this portion of the hike, which consists of a meandering trail. After >0.5 mile the trail turns left and starts heading northeast. You will begin to see houses in the woods off to your left. Soon the trail widens and reverts back into a carriage road. After going downhill for the next >0.1 mile, heading toward a private homeowner's backyard, the trail sudden veers right and heads south, climbing steeply for the next >0.1 mile. You will emerge from the woods at Top Cottage, perched on top of a hill. The house faces west, providing excellent views of the valley in the distance.

Take time to walk around the cottage, but do not disturb the grounds or the house. There are guided tours of the cottage's interior at times, but you have to register for these in advance.

As you head back down, descending steeply, you will again reach the point where the trail does a U-turn and then gradually ascends for 0.1 mile. As soon as the carriage road levels off, you will come to a trail marker on your right indicating the way to Top Cottage and the way to Val-Kill. Note that it is at this point that Eleanor's original carriageway came uphill from the west. Over the intervening years the carriageway was truncated by a housing development, which is why a portion of the hike now consists of a trail.

Photograph of Eleanor Roosevelt, Marion Dickerman, and Nancy Cook.

PART ONE • HUDSON RIVER VALLEY & CATSKILL REGIONS

Eleanor's Walk—Eleanor's Walk is a loop trail, taking you on a carriage road that Franklin D. Roosevelt had specifically constructed for Eleanor. The walk takes you on an easy hike with minimal change in elevation past a ponded stream to your right, along rock walls, and twice under power lines. It is an opportunity to take a gentle hike while contemplating Eleanor Roosevelt and the time she spent at Val-Kill.

History: The idea for a cottage that would be a small retreat primarily for Eleanor's use grew out of a conversation in 1924 at an autumn picnic near the Fall Kill stream on the Franklin Delano Roosevelt (FDR) property. Eleanor, Franklin, two of their sons, and two close friends, Nancy "Nan" Cook and Marion Dickerman, were relaxing and chatting by the stream when Eleanor mentioned that it would be nice to have a cottage to go to in the winter once Springwood closed down after the summer season. (Springwood was the seasonal mansion of Sara Delano Roosevelt, Eleanor's mother-in-law; Springwood was closed in the cold weather, and Sara then stayed in her Manhattan apartment.)

Hiking along the Top Cottage Trail.

4. VAL-KILL

Eleanor's relationship with her two friends was based upon mutual admiration and political congruency. Nan was a suffragist, educator, businesswoman, and political organizer. Marion was also a suffragist and educator, and served as vice-principal of the Todhunter School, a private school for upper-class girls that had been founded by Winifred Todhunter. Nan and Marion cohabited as partners.

FDR immediately warmed to the idea of a country cottage. He personally owned the land they were picnicking on and said he would happily lease the land for life to the three women so that they could build a year-round cottage of their own as an informal place where Eleanor wouldn't be encumbered by the formalities and obligations of Sara's mansion.

FDR loved to design buildings. He engaged a local architect, Henry J. Toombs, to assist him in the design of what became a Dutch Colonial–style cottage. Toombs was also the architect for Franklin D. Roosevelt's residences at Hyde Park and at Warm Springs, Georgia (which became known as "the Little White House"). The Stone Cottage was completed, and a party of sorts to celebrate the opening was held on New Year's Day, 1926. Franklin liked to say it was for "my missus and some of her political friends."

Val-Kill was shared by all three women as equal partners. Nan and Marion lived there full-time, and Eleanor stayed there most of the time unless she was needed at the big house for official duties. There were only occasional visits to Val-Kill by FDR and the rest of the family. For the most part it remained a hideaway for Eleanor and her friends. Over the years the Val-Kill project expanded to include a building for Val-Kill Industries, a swimming pool, pond, tennis courts, dollhouse, walking paths, and carriage trails. Top Cottage was built for FDR in 1938.

Eleanor, Nan, and Marion were dedicated to political issues and were involved with the Women's Division of the New York Democratic Party. Eleanor also supported the Todhunter School, of which Marion took leadership. It was Nan who had promoted the idea of developing a furniture craft shop that would hire local people to build reproduction colonial wooden furniture and craft pewter implements. They successfully established a small company called Val-Kill Industries and hired local farmers and recent immigrants with craft skills. At one point Val-Kill Industries employed as many as twenty people. Eleanor was in charge of marketing, and hosted small exhibitions of finished pieces at her townhouse in Manhattan. FDR used Val-Kill Industries pieces to furnish the Little White House at Warm Springs.

Eventually, years later, Eleanor dissolved the housing partnership with Nan and Marion, perhaps spurred on by her friendship with the American journalist Lorena Hickok, but continued to maintain her own residence on the Val-Kill property.

Though Val-Kill became Eleanor's personal home, dignitaries were occasionally hosted there. One of the most famous events to take place on the estate was Eleanor Roosevelt's Royal Picnic in 1939.

Eleanor told King George VI and the future Queen Elizabeth that "you'll likely be surprised" at what she was planning. "Instead of giving you another formal state dinner, I want you to see how ordinary Americans enjoy a leisurely evening."

Top Cottage, built in 1938 as a retreat for Franklin D. Roosevelt.

Top Cottage—In 1938 FDR commissioned architect Henry Toombs to design his private retreat on the Val-Kill property. All aspects of this two-bedroom house accommodated his disability, from its single-floor layout to the height of the light switches. When FDR won an unprecedented third term in 1940, his retirement plans were shelved, but he continued to enjoy Top Cottage, often taking dignitaries there. Among those who enjoyed the commanding Hudson Valley views from its front porch were England's King George VI (who reigned from 1936 until his death in 1952) and his daughter Elizabeth (currently the reigning queen of the United Kingdom and fifteen other Commonwealth realms as of the first publication of this book in 2021).

Top Cottage is one of only two buildings designed by a sitting U.S. president (Thomas Jefferson's "Popular Forest" is the other). Today, Top Cottage contains a mix of period pieces and reproductions matching the furnishings that were in the house at the time of Roosevelt's death in 1945.

Neighbors and other area residents were invited to the affair, which was going to be strictly informal. The food was typically American, including baked ham, smoked turkey, and baked beans. But King George was puzzled by the frankfurters. "What is the name of this delicacy?" he inquired. "Hot dogs," Eleanor replied. "It's the only food I know how to cook!" (That was not strictly true. Eleanor could also cook scrambled eggs.)

Eleanor's picnic was a great success. When he left, King George VI remarked, "You have given us a delightful time. Until now, I had never tasted smoked turkey. I must also confess I shall never, never forget my first hot dog!"

The First Lady's charm and hospitality made an impression on the monarchs, strengthening the goodwill between the U.S. and the U.K. that grew even stronger when the United States entered World War II. ■

Val-Kill Industries.

PART ONE • HUDSON RIVER VALLEY & CATSKILL REGIONS

5. VANDERBILT MANSION & BARD ROCK
Vanderbilt Mansion National Historic Site

Location: Hyde Park (Dutchess County)
NYS Atlas & Gazetteer, Tenth Edition, p. 103, B7; **Earlier Edition,** p. 36, B4
GPS Parking: 41.798200, –73.940667
GPS Trailheads: *Upper—*41.791100, –73.943348; *Lower—*41.789772, –73.945097
GPS Destinations: *Vanderbilt Mansion—*41.796433, –73.942417; *Bard Rock (rock at end of peninsula)—*41.806634, –73.944640; *Bard Rock (glacially planed bedrock)—*41.805159, –73.944714; *Waterfall—*41.789271, –73.944732; *White Bridge—*41.794589, –73.939667; *Dam & downstream cascades—*41.793241, –73.939999; *Italian Gardens—*41.793576, –73.941869
Hours: *Grounds—*daily, hours vary seasonally; *Vanderbilt Mansion—*check Web site for hours
Fee: *Grounds—*none; *Mansion—*modest charge
Accessibility: *Vanderbilt Mansion—*0.1-mile walk; *Bard Rock—* ~1.7-mile hike
Degree of Difficulty: *Vanderbilt Mansion—*easy; *Bard Rock—*moderate

Directions: *Vanderbilt Mansion and Bard Rock—*From Poughkeepsie where Route 9 passes under Route 44/55, drive north on Route 9 for ~6.5 miles and turn left into the entrance for the Vanderbilt Mansion. Follow the park road through the grounds for 0.5 mile until you reach the main parking area just beyond the mansion.

The late-nineteenth-century Vanderbilt Mansion.

5. VANDERBILT MANSION & BARD ROCK

Description: The *Vanderbilt Mansion*, built by one of America's wealthiest families, is an impressive edifice that harkens back to the late-nineteenth-century "Gilded Age" of industry-generated wealth. The estate includes 211 acres of parkland.

Bard Rock is a 0.05-mile-long peninsula of rock that juts out into the Hudson River.

The Park's *waterfall* is located at the southwest corner of the estate on Crum Elbow Creek, a stream that was used by the Vanderbilts to generate hydroelectric power.

Highlights: Vanderbilt Mansion • Bard Rock • Hyde Park Trail • White Bridge • Main waterfall • Dam & cascades

Hike: *Hyde Park Trail to Bard Rock*—From the parking area walk southwest for <0.2 mile to the south end of the Vanderbilt Mansion. You will see a sign directing you to the "Italian Gardens." Consider this the beginning of the upper Hyde Park trailhead. Follow the path south, passing by the Italian Gardens to your left in 0.2 mile. From this point on you will see markers for the "Hyde Park Trail." The trail continues south along the edge of a towering slope to your right and then descends quickly, reaching a park road at a lower elevation in another 0.2 mile. Turn right onto the park road and walk downhill, heading southwest, for another <0.2 mile. Just before you reach the Lower (South) Gate and a private home, look for a sign on your right that reads "Hyde Park Trail." This is the lower trailhead.

Before starting on the Lower Hyde Park Trail, however, you may wish to visit a spectacular, dammed, 10-foot high waterfall on Crum Elbow Creek. From the trailhead walk slightly southeast across the park road and look for a short wide path that takes you to the top of a dammed waterfall. A "no swimming" sign is posted along the path to warn those who might not be aware that it is very dangerous to swim above the top of a waterfall.

Crum Elbow Creek is the name of the stream cutting through the southeast end of the Vanderbilt Estate. The name, of Dutch origin, originally appeared as *kromme hoek*, meaning "rounded corner." That later was changed to *krom elleboge*, or "crooked elbow," a reference to a significant bend in the creek. The Vanderbilts used Crum Elbow Creek to power a hydroelectric plant on their property and thus became the first in the town of Hyde Park to have electricity in their home.

After viewing the waterfall, return to the Hyde Park trailhead and start hiking north, paralleling the Hudson River to your left. There are a number of spots along the trail where you can scramble over for views of the Hudson River beyond the Amtrak railroad tracks that run next to the shoreline. After hiking 1.1 miles through woods that are primarily composed of deciduous trees with stands

PART ONE • HUDSON RIVER VALLEY & CATSKILL REGIONS

Crum Elbow Creek Falls.

of mature hemlocks, Bard Rock Road is reached. Turn left and follow the park road west for 0.1 mile as it takes you across the 1912 Bard Rock Bridge spanning the rail tracks. Once you reach Bard Rock, be sure to take a look at the bedrock planed by glaciers near the shoreline (an area that looks terraced) and walk to the northern tip of Bard Rock, where there is a very sizeable rock that we refer to as the "Bard Rock."

Glacially planed slabs of bedrock at Bard Rock.

5. VANDERBILT MANSION & BARD ROCK

Take in the views from the shoreline as well. Directly north is a large house on the opposite side of the cove. Slightly northeast, 1.1 miles upriver, is 0.4-mile-long Esopus Island, an uninhabited island that is part of Margaret Lewis Norrie State Park. Framing the distant northwest are the Shaupeneak Ridge and the Catskills. Just downriver and slightly southwest is West Park, home of the famous nineteenth-century nature writer John Burroughs (see following chapter, "Slabsides").

As you walk about you might notice two parallel rows of four red bricks and a tall pipe. This remnant of an earlier structure is next to what would be a good boat launching site, and we suspect that some kind of boathouse or bath house once stood here.

If you wish to turn the hike into a round trip, follow Bard Rock Road east, heading steadily uphill. Soon after crossing the bridge over the Amtrak rails, look for a small, elongated, 10-foot-high cascade 100 feet into the woods to your left on a tiny tributary of the Hudson River. When you come to an open field on your right, follow a grassy path next to the road for another 0.1 mile. The path now veers to the right, following along the edge of a copse of pines and then going through it briefly. After a total of 0.4 mile from Bard Rock, you will come to the barricaded end of the park road, nearly at the point where cars exit from the Vanderbilt estate onto Route 9. Walk south from here back to your car, either across the open field or along the park road.

Alternate route to Lower Hyde Park Trail—The reason for suggesting an alternate approach to the Lower Hyde Park trailhead is that it will afford you the opportunity to see different points of interest along the way. This would be especially worthwhile if you are hiking to Bard Rock a second time.

From the parking area walk south across the lawn in front of the Vanderbilt Mansion for >0.1 mile until you reach the barricade in front of the road going to the mansion. Walk across the main road and follow a gravel path southwest until you come to a concrete arch bridge, known as the White Bridge, which you initially crossed over on the drive in.

From the southwest end of the White Bridge, follow a park road downhill. In 0.1 mile you will reach a protrusion of land to your left where you can stand and get a good look back at the concrete arch bridge.

The *White Bridge*, erected in 1897, is one of the first Melan arch bridges to be built in the United States. It replaced an older frame bridge. This type of bridge design was named after Josef Melan, a Viennese engineer who came up with a way of making a reinforced concrete arch bridge by combining concrete with metal I-beams. The White Bridge makes for a great photo shoot thanks to its ornamented balustrade, graceful arch, pure white color, and placid reflection in a dam-created pool of water.

In another 100 feet you will reach a 10-foot-high stone dam. A series of small cascades on Crum Elbow Creek have formed below the dam. A path leads over to the top of the dam, and from there a fairly rough path leads down to near the cascades.

Continue southwest on the park road, heading steadily downhill. After <0.3 mile you will pass by the spot to your right where the Upper Hyde Park Trail comes in (you will see a trail sign), and then after another >0.1 mile you will reach the Lower Hyde Park trailhead to your right just before the Lower (South) Gate and private residence is reached.

Walk: *Vanderbilt Mansion*—From the parking area walk southwest for >0.1 mile to reach the front of the Vanderbilt Mansion. Take a moment to walk around the mansion and admire the views from the top of the towering slope. Charles Augustus Murray (son of the fifth Earl of Dunmore) wrote of the view from Hyde Park around 1834 while visiting the estate of Dr. David Hosack: "Below us flowed the Hudson, studded with white-sailed sloops as far as the eye could reach, even until they looked no larger than the edge of a seagull's wing; the opposite bank, which slopes gently from the river, is variegated with farms, villages, and woods, appearing as though they had been grouped by the hand of taste rather than by that of industry; while on the northwest side the prospect is bounded by the dark and lofty outline of the Catskill range."

The famous White Bridge, one of the first Melan arch bridges built in the United States.

5. VANDERBILT MANSION & BARD ROCK

We strongly recommend the guided tour through the Vanderbilt Mansion, a trip back in time to when wealthy people living ostentatiously lined the banks of the Hudson River, "America's Rhine."

History: *Vanderbilt Mansion*—In 1895 Frederick and Louise Vanderbilt purchased the property from the estate of Walter Langdon, Jr., and then added on more land along the east bank of the Hudson River to create a 600-acre "pleasure-ground." Realizing that the current Langdon mansion was structurally unsound, the Vanderbilts decided to raze that building and start anew. The result was a 54-room mansion whose exterior was designed by Charles F. McKim of McKim, Mead, and White—a firm that specialized in the American neoclassical revival style—and much of the interior was the work of Stanford White, a leading designer of the day.

Despite its impressive size, the mansion is the smallest of the ten homes that were owned by the Vanderbilts and served as just one of their vacation homes.

In 1938 Louise Vanderbilt's niece, Margaret "Daisy" Van Alen, inherited the estate upon Frederick's death. Margaret was encouraged by President Franklin D. Roosevelt, a neighbor, to donate a significant portion of the estate including the residence to the National Park Service, which she did in 1940. This transfer of property to the National Park Service however, didn't stop Roosevelt from using the basement and third floor of the mansion to house his Secret Service personnel from 1941–1943.

If we peel back enough layers of history, however, the story of Hyde Park begins in 1764 when Dr. John Bard, a noted physician and pioneer in hygiene, bought the 3,600-acre Fauconnier Grant (named for Peter Fauconnier, secretary to Edward Hyde, 3rd Earl of Clarendon) and built a house in 1772 opposite what is known today as the North Gate of the Vanderbilt estate. Bard called his new home "the Red House." He also built a secondary residence on the west side of the Albany Post Road (Route 9), and that one became known as "Bard Cottage."

In 1799 Bard gave 1,500 acres of his property to his son, Dr. Samuel Bard, who went on to build his own home, erected on what would become the site of the future Vanderbilt Mansion. Samuel Bard is noted for being the founder of the first medical school in New York City and as a personal physician to George Washington.

In 1828 Dr. David Hosack purchased 700 acres of land from William Bard, who had inherited the property from his father after Samuel's death in 1821. Hosack remodeled the house and enlarged it, turning the estate into a Hudson Valley showpiece. Its fame extended all the way to Europe.

Enter John Jacob Astor, real estate mogul. In 1840 Astor bought 108 acres of the south portion of the park, which included Hosack's mansion, for his daughter,

PART ONE • HUDSON RIVER VALLEY & CATSKILL REGIONS

Dorothea, and her husband, Walter S. Langdon. When fire destroyed the Hosack mansion, Langdon had it rebuilt. This was the second house to be erected on the site of the future Vanderbilt Mansion.

Meanwhile, the Hosack family sold 64 acres of the north portion of the park, including Bard Cottage and Bard Rock, to James Curtis. Curtis, in turn, built a large, Italian Villa–style mansion that he called "Torham." Gardens and farmlands were laid out on the lower tract down by the New York Central Railroad (today's Amtrak). In 1890 Curtis sold the property to Samuel Sexton and the property then became known as the Sexton Tract.

After Frederick and Louise Vanderbilt built their mansion in 1896–1899, they acquired the 64-acre tract of land that included Bard Rock in 1905 and removed all of the buildings on the Sextons' land except for a boathouse.

The shape of things to come—Although the Vanderbilt Mansion looks sturdy and likely to endure for many years to come, there remains one potential problem that could affect its longevity. The Vanderbilt Mansion (like the nearby Roosevelt mansion, "Springside") is built on the crest of the Crum Elbow Creek Delta—an elevated mass of land that slopes off dramatically into the Hudson River. The delta formed during the last ice age when enormous amounts of sediment from Crum Elbow Creek were deposited into Lake Albany (a glacial lake that extended 160 miles from Newburgh to Glens Falls). Geologists call this sloping mass of land a "hanging delta," a phenomenon that is fairly common in the Hudson Valley.

Bard Rock.

5. VANDERBILT MANSION & BARD ROCK

In *The Hudson Valley in the Ice Age*, Professor Robert Titus of Hartwick College writes, "Both the Vanderbilts and the Roosevelts chose to position their homes as close as practical to the edge of these slopes. They no doubt wanted to maximize the picturesque views of the Hudson Valley. The architects of the time apparently did not understand the ice age history of these properties, and they certainly did not recognize the scars left by a history of slumping. Both mansions have stood for a very long time, but we fear that both will not last; each will someday begin to tumble toward the river."

A tragic example of just how such a thing could happen occurred on January 19, 1996, when part of Hamilton Hill in Schenectady, built on a steeply sloping delta, collapsed onto Broadway, killing an Amsterdam man who was pumping gas at a convenience store below the hill.

Bard Rock—Bard Rock is named after the Bard family—John, Samuel, and William—and consists of a large area of exposed bedrock that extends northward into the Hudson River, forming a peninsula. At the very tip of this peninsula is a large rock that may very well have given the name to the peninsula.

The section of Bard Rock that is of particular interest to geologists is located near the Hudson River on the peninsula's west side. There, hikers will see flat slabs of inclined bedrock formed out of black shale and sandstone, rocks that came into existence ~340 million years ago, long before the present Hudson River existed. These flat slabs of bedrock were planed by glaciers during the last ice age and serve as a vivid reminder of just how influential glaciers were in shaping our present landscape.

In 1832 David Hosack commissioned an eighteen-year-old artist named Thomas Kelah Wharton to sketch the landscape from a viewpoint near Bard Rock. From Wharton's sketches we know that there used to be a domed, temple-like shelter at Bard Rock that very much resembled a Grecian pavilion.

A gravel ramp at the south end of Bard Rock provides day-use access via the Hudson River Greenway Trail. ■

PART ONE • HUDSON RIVER VALLEY & CATSKILL REGIONS

6. SLABSIDES
John Burroughs Nature Sanctuary

Location: West Park (Ulster County)
NYS Atlas & Gazetteer, Tenth Edition, p. 103, B7; **Earlier Edition,** p. 36, B4
GPS Parking: *Slabsides*—41.799587, –73.971795; *Pond House*—41.804723, –73.971427
GPS Destinations: *Slabsides*—41.798065, –73.973517;
Pond House—41.799097, –73.976455
Hours: Open dawn to dusk, daily
Fee: None
Accessibility: Mileage variable depending upon trails taken
Degree of Difficulty: Easy to moderate
Additional Information: Trail guide available at Slabsides or at research.amnh.org/burroughs/trail_work/slabsides. Contributions can be sent to the John Burroughs Association, Inc., American Museum of Natural History, 15 West 77th Street, New York, NY 10024.

Directions: From north of Highland (junction of Routes 299 West & 9W), drive north on Route 9W for ~3.6 miles.

From Esopus (junction of Routes 9W & 16), drive south on Route 9W for ~2.3 miles.

From either direction, turn onto Floyd Ackert Road and drive west for a total of <0.8 mile. Along the way you will cross over railroad tracks at ~0.2 mile.

→ *Slabsides*—Turn left onto Burroughs Drive and head south. At 0.1 mile you will drive past the north end of the East Overlook Trail (also called the William G. Fennell Memorial Trail) to your left, and then immediately past the North Pond Overlook Trail to your right. At 0.3 mile you will drive by the south end of the East Overlook Trail to your left and then come to parking for Slabsides on both sides of the road.
Walk past a chained barrier on the west side of the road and follow John Burroughs Drive (a gravel road) southwest for less than 0.1 mile. As soon as you pass by the trail to South Pond, on your right by an outhouse, you will reach a fork in the road. Bear left. The road to your right leads to land that is privately owned. In >100 feet you will come to Slabsides, just past a large rock outcrop. This is a magnificent spot with high rock walls towering above you to your left. Small-to-medium-sized blocks of talus litter the slopes.

→ *Pond Road*—From Burroughs Drive go northwest on Floyd Ackert Road for 0.1 mile. Turn left onto a dirt road where a sign states "To Pond and Trail," and then immediately turn left into a small parking area.

6. SLABSIDES

Description: The John Burroughs Nature Sanctuary is a 200-acre preserve that includes approximately 4.5 miles of trails. John Burroughs was a famous nineteenth-century writer and naturalist (1837–1921). The sanctuary includes land where Burroughs spent time observing the natural habitat and in 1895 built a cabin that he called "Slabsides." Slabsides and other features such as the stone staircase to Julian's Rock were built by Burroughs and his son Julian, and they remain intact.

Burroughs constructed Slabsides as a refuge where he wrote about the natural area in the vicinity as well as about other timely topics of interest until his death in 1921. While at Slabsides, he entertained many curious students of nature as well as famous luminaries of the day. Though the cabin is opened to visitors only a few times during the year, the premises around the cabin are open during regular park hours.

Highlights: Slabsides (rustic cabin) • Rock shelter • Interesting boulders and cliff walls • Julian's Rock • Glacial lakes/ponds

Hike: There are many hikes that can be taken via the multiple trails contained in the preserve, trails that were established for a better appreciation of the natural environment and that lead through scenic surroundings once enjoyed by the writer John Burroughs. Mixed deciduous trees and scattered stands of hemlock predominate in the sanctuary woods. The hike we suggest here puts together some of the best elements of the preserve, but it should be considered just one of many hiking possibilities.

From Slabsides cabin, follow the white-marked Ridge Trail south between towering rocky cliffs on your left that range in height from 40–100 feet and Celery Swamp to your right. The swamp is aptly named, for Burroughs cultivated nearly 30,000 celery plants there during his time in residence.

In 0.05 mile you will come to the south end of Celery Swamp, where the path continues to your right along a series of boardwalks across a marshland. To your left a steep flight of stone steps leads up to a mid-level plateau in the escarpment. Some of the steps look unreliable and caution should be exercised. The steps take you up to a rustic, abandoned, two-story cottage (which was not constructed by Burroughs). There are a number of medium-sized talus blocks next to the cottage. Do not enter the cottage for safety reasons. Instead, follow the plateau south as it narrows and becomes road-like. After a couple of hundred feet, just before posted signs are encountered, you will come to a large rock shelter on your left with a 10-foot overhang.

According to the sanctuary's trail map, the general area where the cottage and rock shelter are located is called Julian's Rock. Julian's Rock may be the name for the cottage, or the name for one of the larger blocks of talus lying about the plateau, or it could be the name for the rock shelter. It could even be the name for a rock formation farther up above on the cliff.

Julian's Rock is named for Julian Burroughs (1878–1954), the only son of John and Ursula Burroughs. Julian achieved a degree of fame on his own as a landscape painter, photographer, writer, farmer, and architect. He married in 1902 and had three children with his wife, Emily. During the early part of his married life, he lived in a house he had built on his father's property at Riverby.

Return to the Ridge Trail and walk across the series of boardwalks at the south end of Celery Swamp. Follow the trail south/southwest for ~1.0 mile. You will continue to have impressive views of the huge cliff to your left even when the trail heads up a ridge of its own. In fact, as you hike along the trail(s) at the John Burroughs Nature Sanctuary, you will be impressed by how many levels of terrain there are. It is as though huge ripples formed in the landscape. Just when you think you are on the bottommost level, you discover that you have not yet reached the lowest point.

Eventually a huge flight of stone steps takes you down to a lower level and then, in 0.1 mile farther, to a junction. By now you have gone >1.0 mile. The trail to the left is the "Ladder Trail to Chodikee Lake" (an oval-shaped, 63-acre body of water formed by Black Creek). The trail to the right is the 0.1-mile-long continuation of the Ridge Trail (a sign at the junction states that this part of the trail can be a little rough). Take the trail to the right.

In 0.1 mile you will reach a "T." Turn right onto the "Chodikee Trail to the Pond House." After a short distance you will come to another "T." Turning left, the trail leads in 0.05 mile to a small, beautiful pond. Back at the "T," turn right this time and follow the "Amasa Martin Trail." In >0.1 mile you will reach Pond Lane, a gravel road that comes in from Floyd Ackert Road.

Cross over the road and follow the "Peninsula Trail" as it leads east for over 0.1 mile, culminating with views from both sides of glacial South Pond. Because it is a Peninsula Trail, it dead-ends. Return to Pond Lane.

Walk northeast along the gravel road for 0.1 mile, passing by some truly enormous blocks of talus that have broken off from the bank of the peninsula cliff (41.801397, -73.973727). One piece is as large as a small house; two others are the size of automobiles or trucks.

(Note: if you walk in the opposite direction, northwest, along Pond Lane, you will reach the Pond House in 0.1 mile.)

As soon as you have crossed over the outlet stream from the pond and are at the north end of the pond, pick up the "North Pond Trail to Burroughs Drive" and proceed southeast for >0.1 mile. You will end up on Burroughs Drive. Turn right and walk uphill for 0.2 mile uphill to return to your car and starting point.

6. SLABSIDES

Massive blocks of talus litter Burroughs's pond.

Pond Road—Hike southwest along the dirt road. In 0.2 mile you will reach the north end of glacially created South Pond just past the "North Pond Trail to Burroughs Drive," which goes off to your left. From here the dirt road takes you along the west side of South Pond, past other trail crossings, and ultimately ends up at the Pond House (a private residence occupied by the John Burroughs Association Naturalist).

History: The John Burroughs Sanctuary is in the midst of a wild and scenic region of the Mid-Hudson Valley. From 1873 and for the rest of John Burroughs's life, this

Slabsides, John Burroughs's rustic cabin.

area supplied much of the nature lore and inspiration that the naturalist recorded in his essays.

In 1895 Burroughs built the rustic cabin he called "Slabsides" on what is now the sanctuary property. Slabsides is a small cabin made from branches and bark found in the nearby woods. Burroughs built it by hand with assistance from his young son, Julian. Today this cabin is still intact and furnished just as Burroughs left it. The retreat served the naturalist for the last twenty years of his life as a place where he could write, study nature, and entertain his friends. He also confided that it was a place where he could get away from his wife, who felt he spent too much time at his writing desk. At Slabsides, Burroughs wrote some of the essays that made him the foremost American nature writer of his time. This cabin is about a mile and a half from his home in West Park on the Hudson called "Riverby," which he shared with his wife and son Julian.

About spending time reflecting on nature, Burroughs said, "Let me say a word or two in favor of the habit of keeping a journal of one's thoughts and days. To a countryman, especially of a meditative turn, who likes to preserve the flavors of the passing moment ... it is a sort of deposit account where one saves up bits and fragments of his life that would otherwise be lost to him."

Burroughs's fame made Slabsides a Mecca for other nature lovers and writers. The Slabsides guest books contain the names of hundreds of Burroughs admirers who visited from 1896 to 1921. Some luminaries who visited include Theodore Roosevelt, Thomas Edison, and Henry Ford. Today, hundreds of visitors still come to the sanctuary each year.

One of the very first visitors to Slabsides was another famous naturalist—John Muir—whom Burroughs invited to visit in 1895. Muir rode the train from Manhattan to Hyde Park on the other side of the Hudson River. Burroughs and his son Julian rowed across the river and met Muir at the train depot. They then rowed back to Riverby on the west side of the river. From there they trekked two miles up the mountain to Slabsides, where they spent long hours talking, mostly about Ralph Waldo Emerson, who had been a hero to both men in their youth. The next day Burroughs took Muir to visit Black Creek Falls, a scenic area where Burroughs had taken Walt Whitman on an earlier visit.

As Burroughs's fame grew, he became a nationally known literary figure. As a result he was called upon to lecture and give presentations. One of the most interesting ventures he was invited to join was the Harriman Expedition to Alaska, mounted and sponsored by Edward H. Harriman in 1899. Burroughs was designated as "historian" for the expedition. Other noted members of the Expedition included Louis Agassiz Fuertes (bird artist), John Muir (naturalist), Edward Curtis

6. SLABSIDES

(photographer), Henry Gannett (geographer), Trevor Kincaid (biologist), Bernhard Fernow (forester), Robert Ridgway (ornithologist), as well as many, many other men at the top of their field.

After Burroughs's death in 1921, Slabsides with its surrounding nine acres was presented to the newly formed John Burroughs Association. In 1964, and again in 1965, the woodlands surrounding Slabsides were threatened by logging and land development operations. Contributions from hundreds of individuals and several foundations raised funds to purchase additional acreage surrounding the cabin that, together with the original tract, now comprise the 200-acre John Burroughs Sanctuary. While Burroughs was not a strict conservationist or an environmental activist, his message of land stewardship and his quiet warnings about the potential impact of unchecked development and resource consumption resonate today.

Designated a National Historic Landmark in 1968, Slabsides is preserved today much as Burroughs left it. Slabs of lumber with their bark cover the exterior walls, and the rustic red cedar posts that Burroughs helped set in place still hold up the porch. Inside the cabin, the furniture that Burroughs used—much of which he made—remains as it was when he resided there.

John Burroughs at Slabsides. Photograph, Library of Congress.

PART ONE • HUDSON RIVER VALLEY & CATSKILL REGIONS

Woodchuck Lodge—Following his death on March 29, 1921, Burroughs was buried on his eighty-fourth birthday in what is now Burroughs Memorial Field, a state historic site just up the road from Woodchuck Lodge and within a mile of the farmstead outside Roxbury, New York (Delaware County), where he was raised.

Woodchuck Lodge was built by Burroughs's brother on the east end of the family farm where Burroughs spent his childhood and where he chose to stay at the end of his life. Woodchuck Lodge is open for tours the first weekend of each month, May through October, from 11 AM to 3 PM.

Memorial Field, where an outdoor exhibit offers photos and information about the life and work of John Burroughs, is open to visitors daily during daylight hours.

Directions to Woodchuck Lodge—From Grand Gorge (junction of Route 23 & Route 30), drive southwest on Route 30 for ~5.8 miles. Turn right onto Hardscrabble Road/Burroughs Memorial Road and head west for 0.8 mile. When you come to Burroughs Memorial Road, turn left and proceed southwest for 1.1 miles. The historic house is at roadside to your right, at a GPS reading of 42.296409, –74.583582.

Riverby was the name of Burroughs's estate located above the west bank of the Hudson River in the town of West Park. It was in the study of this house that Burroughs wrote many of his most influential essays. The property was designated a National Historic Landmark in 1968. It is private property, still partially held by the Burroughs family, and is not open to the public. ■

7. DOVER STONE CHURCH CAVE

Location: Dover Plains (Dutchess County)
NYS Atlas & Gazetteer, Tenth Edition, p. 104, C1–2; **Earlier Edition,** p. 37, BC7
GPS Parking: 41.738907, –73.579584
GPS at trailhead: 41.739646, –73.581198
GPS Stone Church Cave: 41.738082, –73.588969
Hours: Dawn to dusk
Fee: None
Restrictions: Swimming, rock-climbing, firearms, and alcoholic beverages are not permitted; hikers are asked to stay on designated trails
Accessibility: 0.4-mile hike
Degree of Difficulty: Easy to moderate except for last 0.05 mile, which may require some rock hopping, particularly when the stream is running at full force
Additional Information: *Trail map*—nynjtc.org
Friends of the Dover Stone Church—(845) 832-6111
Dutchess Land Conservancy—(845) 677-3002

Directions: From north of Dover Plains (junction of Routes 22 & 343 West), drive southeast on Route 22 for ~0.4 mile into Dover Plains and turn left onto School Street. Immediately bear right into the parking area for Dover Elementary School.

From Wingdale (junction of Routes 22 & 55), drive north on Route 22 for <7.0 miles to Dover Plains. Turn right onto School Street and then immediately right into the parking area for Dover Elementary School.

From the school parking area walk northwest along Route 22 for ~250 feet. Cross over the street where you see a New York State historic sign for the Stone Cave. From there follow a gravel driveway uphill for 100 feet to the trailhead.

Although parking is seemingly available at the trailhead, it is actually reserved for homeowners next to the driveway. Do not park there.

Note: If school is in session, you will need to find alternate parking in the village.

Description: The Dover Stone Church Cave is an impressive 30-foot-high cavern that extends as far back as 50 feet to where a 20-foot-high waterfall cascades. A huge rock deep inside the cave reaches up almost halfway to the ceiling. Its resemblance to an old-fashioned New England church pulpit is undoubtedly part of what contributed to the cave's mystique.

PART ONE • HUDSON RIVER VALLEY & CATSKILL REGIONS

Highlights: Historic cave • The Pulpit (Rock) • Stone Church Brook • Scenic waterfall • Deep gorge • Multiple side trails

Hike: From the trailhead sign that states "Welcome to Dover Stone Church," follow a flight of railed stone steps down the side of a small hill to the valley floor. The path continues through a grove of recently planted maple trees in an open field and then through a grove of older trees in the woods. By the time you have gone >0.1 mile, Stone Church Brook will be to your left. Soon you will pass by the Stone Church Cave kiosk, which contains information relevant to the hike. Continue to follow the trail as it veers left and then takes you across Stone Church Brook via a footbridge.

Take note that three other trails begin near the footbridge, each leading away from the Stone Church Cave: the 1.0-mile-long, red-blazed Lower Loop Trail heads southeast; the 1.0-mile-long, yellow-blazed Upper Loop Trail heads south; and the 1.5-mile-long, blue-blazed Lookout Point Trail heads southwest.

For purposes of this hike, follow the Stone Church Cave Path along Stone Church Brook, to your right. Very quickly you will find yourself inside a deep gorge with walls rising up steeply above you. Cleverly positioned slabs of rock provide ample footing in the beginning, but the trek can become more challenging the farther upstream you go. The hike can be particularly difficult if Stone Church Brook is fully engorged. After another 0.1 mile you will reach the entrance to Stone Church Cave, which can be seen to resemble a gothic arch. (To our eyes it looked more like the entrance to a train tunnel.) If the stream is not running fast, there should be

The path to Stone Church Cave takes you through a grove of recently planted maple trees.

7. DOVER STONE CHURCH CAVE

Reaching the historic Dover Stone Church Cave.

sufficient rock slabs to enable you to rock-hop into the interior of the cave without getting too wet. You will hear the thundering sound of a waterfall emanating from the back of the cave, but it cannot be easily seen unless you maneuver around a huge rock boulder rising up nearly halfway to the ceiling. The great rock was given the name "The Pulpit" by Richard Francis Maher, town historian and author of the 1907 book *Historic Dover*.

On a sunny day under the right conditions, a shaft of sunlight enters into the cave from the back producing an effect as though the cave were illuminated through a stained-glass window.

In warmer months, the walls are sprinkled with white lichen and green moss.

History: The Dover Stone Church Cave is the creation of Stone Church Brook, a moderate-sized tributary of Ten Mile River. The cave was named for its church-like appearance.

According to legend, Sassacus, a Mashantucket Pequot chief, and a number of his warriors took refuge in the cave for a week in 1637 to avoid being captured by a party of pursuing Mohawk. Unfortunately, their respite was short-lived; after leaving the cave, they were seized by the Mohawk and summarily executed.

Starting in the 1830s and continuing into the early 1900s, Stone Church Cave was a major tourist attraction for thousands of visitors from New York City and adjacent states. The sudden influx of tourists was in part due to an article that appeared in *The Family Magazine*, which described the cave as a "singular and

PART ONE • HUDSON RIVER VALLEY & CATSKILL REGIONS

interesting curiosity." As tourists grew in number, the demand for lodging increased, resulting in the erection of the Dover Plains Hotel next to the railroad depot in 1848. As with Howe Caverns in Schoharie County, weddings were performed in the cave—perhaps another reason for its name.

Stone Church Cave became even more prominent after it was depicted by several Hudson River School painters, including Asher Brown Durand in 1847, and described extensively in a book by Benson J. Lossing that was entitled *Dover Stone Church and the History of Dutchess County.* Later, during the Great Depression, the cave was depicted in paintings by Arthur James Emery Powell and a number of other landscape artists under the Works Program Administration (WPA) established by President Franklin Delano Roosevelt.

The privately owned Stone Church Cave property became available for sale in 2002. The Town of Dover, Dutchess Land Conservancy, and Friends of Dover Stone Church worked together to secure funds to buy the land. In this endeavor, grants and matching funds were provided through the Dutchess County Open Space and Farmland Protection Program, the Berkshire Taconic Community Foundation, and the New York State Office of Parks, Recreation and Historic Preservation. These efforts came to fruition in 2004 when 58.5 acres of land around the cave were purchased. In 2009 adjacent landowners donated a 50-acre conservation easement next to the historic right-of-way. This was followed in 2010 by the generous donation of additional property along the southern border of the preserve. ∎

Stone Church Cave, looking out from inside.

8. ICE CAVES & SAM'S POINT
Minnewaska State Park Preserve: Sam's Point Area

Location: Cragsmoor (Ulster County)
NYS Atlas & Gazetteer, Tenth Edition, p. 102, C2; **Earlier Edition,** p. 36, C1
GPS Parking: 41.670033, −74.361667
GPS Destinations: *Sam's Point*—41.669882, −74.357462;
Lenape Steps—41.669996, −74.357457; *Ice Caves*—41.672617, −74.347133
Hours: Opens 9:00 AM; closing times vary seasonally
Fee: Modest charge per car
Restrictions: Dogs must be on a <6-foot leash
Accessibility: *Sam's Point*—0.6-mile hike; *Ice Caves*—1.3-mile hike;
Ice Caves loop trail— <0.5-mile hike
Degree of Difficulty: Moderate
Additional Information: Sam's Point Visitor Center, 400 Sam's Point Road, Cragsmoor, NY 12420, (845) 647-7989

Directions: From Ellenville (junction of Routes 209 & 52), take Route 52 southeast for ~4.8 miles and turn left onto Cragsmoor Road.

From Pine Bush (junction of Routes 55 & 302), drive northwest on Route 55 for ~7.5 miles and turn right onto Cragsmoor Road.

From either direction head northeast on Cragsmoor Road for ~1.5 miles. When you come to Sam's Point Road, turn right and proceed east for another 1.2 miles (or a total of >2.7 miles from Route 52) until you come to the parking area by the Conservation Center at Minnewaska State Park Preserve: Sam's Point Area.

Description: The ice caves, formerly known as Ice Caves Mountain, consist of a series of deep fissures and caves created by massive blocks of bedrock that have separated from the cliff face and are being inexorably pulled downslope by gravity. There are a number of rock shelters along the base of a long cliff face as well.

Sam's Point consists of a towering bluff of Shawangunk conglomerate that provides expansive views of the landscape to the southwest.

Highlights: Sam's Point Overlook • Ice Caves • Dwarf pine bush barren

Hike: From the Conservation Center bear right at a junction, following signs that point the way uphill to Sam's Point, 0.6 mile distant. The first road up to Sam's

PART ONE • HUDSON RIVER VALLEY & CATSKILL REGIONS

Point was constructed by Thomas Botsford in 1858 after he had purchased between 300–500 acres of land in the area.

Along the way up to Sam's Point, the carriageway does a couple of switchbacks, thus ensuring an easy grade for hikers. At ~0.5 mile you will pass by an area to your left where Thomas Botsford erected his short-lived Sam's Point Mountain House (hotel).

When you reach the top of the bluff, bear left and follow signs that lead you quickly to Sam's Point. On a clear day hikers can see as far distant as High Point in New Jersey.

Sam's Point Mountain House and the Lenape Steps—The 25-foot-wide, 92-foot-long, seasonal Sam's Point Mountain House was erected by Botsford in 1858. He anchored it directly into the side of the cliff wall so that the structure would resist being blown apart by strong winds. Conceptually, it was a unique hotel: the cliff served as the back wall for the hotel; fissures in the rock—instead of a conventional chimney—vented out smoke; and running water was continuously at hand, provided by a spring that ran through the main room of the hotel. Unfortunately the hotel lasted only until 1862, destroyed not by wind, but by fire.

Botsford also constructed a 75-step stone stairway in 1860–1861 through a fissure in the cliff that allowed hotel patrons to bypass part of the road and go directly to the top of Sam's Point. The passageway came to be known as "the Indian Steps." The stone stairway has deteriorated and is no longer in use today, and it also became obscured by foliage. However, staff and volunteers are presently at work reconstructing this iconic stairway, and the work is expected to be completed in 2021. The project is called "the Lenape Steps," after the Leni Lenape (or Lenni Lenape), Native Americans who lived in the lower Hudson Valley as well as in New Jersey, eastern Pennsylvania, Long Island, and New York City.

Lenape Steps. Postcard circa 1910.

8. ICE CAVES & SAM'S POINT

Take note of a 6-foot-high glacial erratic on top of the bluff. In 1871 this rock was temporarily encased by a 30-foot-high, 20-foot-square wooden observation tower. Strong winds, however, made quick work of the tower and it failed to survive through that winter. The rock, needless to say, remains firmly in place.

Return to the main carriageway and continue hiking northeast for another 0.3 mile through a forest of dwarf pitch pines. At a junction turn right and walk downhill along the carriageway. In another <0.4 mile you will reach the ice caves' former parking area from the time when it was a commercial attraction. The entrance to the ice caves is on your right near a kiosk.

From this point, you are on your own. As you enter the ice caves you will follow a white-marked trail that takes you down through a wide crevice and then through a

Samuel Gonzales—Sam's Point is named for Samuel Gonzales, a larger-than-life figure who according to folklore leaped from the bluff at Sam's Point in order to flee from a pursuing Lenape war party. The hemlocks partially broke his 40-foot fall, and Gonzales was able to make good his escape. Understandably, members of the war party were reluctant to follow.

Gonzales's famous leap, which is very reminiscent of Robert Rogers's leap at Rogers Rock in Lake George, was recorded in an epic poem written by Blanche Desmore Curtis in 1910 and titled "The Legend of Sam's Point." A diorama of Sam's leap is on display at the Ellenville Public Library & Museum on 40 Center Street in Ellenville.

Gazing across Cragsmoor from Sam's Point.

PART ONE • HUDSON RIVER VALLEY & CATSKILL REGIONS

series of fissures and chambers, along boardwalks, wooden steps and stairways. This becomes a self-guided tour here, so take time to explore all the nooks and crannies along the trail. Back in the days when Ice Caves Mountain was a commercial attraction, your attention would have been drawn to such formations as "Wall Street Canyon," "Rivers of Mystery," and "Cupid's Rock" (as has been done at such other New York commercial attractions as Ausable Chasm, Howe Caverns, and Secret Caverns). As far as we know, these monikers are not used today and were just part of the marketing of Ice Cave Mountain's attractions during its heyday.

Eventually, the one-way trip is completed after ~0.5 mile and you exit north of where you started, essentially completing a loop.

History: The ice caves are located at Sam's Point Dwarf Pine Ridge Preserve, a ~5,000-acre area encompassing over 8 square miles of highlands and a globally rare community of high-altitude pitch pine barrens. What's particularly interesting about pitch pines is that their cones are serotinous, meaning that they need fire in order to open up to release their seeds. The seeds then are able to germinate in a nutrient-rich bed of soil created by the fire. As to the pitch pine itself, although large branches may be consumed by the fire, the thick trunk will survive and will produce new branches. When you walk down to the ice caves, you will see a section of the dwarf pine pitch barren that was burned in 2016. Ultimately, 2,208 acres of land were consumed by fire.

Ice Caves Mountain during its commercial days. Photograph circa 1980.

8. ICE CAVES & SAM'S POINT

Beginning in 1967 the ice caves were part of a commercial attraction called Ice Caves Mountain, the work of Frederick Grau, a local resident who purchased a 30-year lease from Ellenville. Improvements were made on incoming roads, a parking area was established near the cave entrance, and stone stairways, walkways, colored lights, and railings were added to improve the caves' accessibility, illumination, and safety.

In 1972 the caves were designated a National Landmark by the federal government.

After the 30-year lease had expired, Ice Caves Mountain closed for good in 1996. Six years later the caves were reopened, this time under the auspices of The Nature Conservancy (a land preservation organization that started up in New York State in 1955) and became part of Sam's Point Dwarf Pine Ridge Preserve. The Nature Conservancy rehabilitated the caves by adding solar-powered motion-sensitive lamps to sections that were otherwise in darkness, as well as a number of other subtle improvements.

The Nature Conservancy sold the 1,063-acre Sam's Point Preserve to New York State, which added it to Minnewaska State Park Preserve in 2015.

Readers should take note that the ice caves near Sam's Point are not the same as the Ellenville Ice Caves (also known as the Greater Ice Caves). The Ellenville

Entering the Ice Caves.

Ice Caves are also near Sam's Point, and some claim that they represent the greatest open fault in the United States. The Ellenville Ice Caves, however, are accessible via permit only.

The roads that you see throughout the preserve were constructed as fire roads in the 1930s by the Civilian Conservation Corps (CCC). The road by Lake Maratanza led to a fire tower.

The Sam's Point Conservation Center opened in 2005 and includes educational facilities, exhibits, interactive displays, and a gift shop.

Geology: *Ice Caves*—The ice caves are the result of the bedrock at the top of the cliffs fracturing and being slowly, imperceptibly pulled downhill by gravity, forming huge blocks with widening gaps between them. Table Rock, in the northwestern part of Minnewaska State Park Preserve, is another excellent example of this process. Snow and ice tend to linger in the ice caves throughout most of the year, finally yielding to the sun's warmth in mid-summer. Thus the term "ice caves."

The Nature Conservancy once designated the ice caves as one of the "75 Great Places in the Western Hemisphere."

Sam's Point—Sam's Point (2,255 feet), at the southernmost part of Minnewaska State Park Preserve, constitutes the highest point in the Shawangunks—30 feet higher than even Castle Point, five miles north. The Sam's Point region is defined by rugged cliffs that form the perimeter of a massive, high, flat plateau. Huge blocks of talus have collected at the base of the plateau.

The Shawangunks, or "Gunks" as they are informally called, were formed between 417 and 440 million years ago. The primary rock found here is Shawangunk conglomerate—a light-to-dark-gray-colored sandstone ranging in texture from fine to very coarse. It is a highly erosion-resistant rock.

The Shawangunk Ridge geologically is the western border of the Great Appalachian Valley.

Additional attractions—Besides the ice caves and Sam's Point, there is much else to see in this section of the state park, including Indian Rock, 187-foot-high Verkeerderkill Falls (the highest waterfall in the Shawangunks), Ellenville Ice Caves (also called Shingle Gully Ice Caves; access by permit only), 2,245-foot-high Maratanza Lake (one of five glacially carved sky lakes in the Shawangunks), High Point, and the surviving ruins of seasonal camps lived in by itinerant blueberry pickers from the 1870s to the 1970s. ■

9. FALLING WATERS
Falling Waters Preserve

Location: Glasco (Ulster County)
NYS Atlas & Gazetteer, Tenth Edition, p. 98, D2; **Earlier Edition,** p. 52, D2
GPS Parking: 42.048732, –73.940690
GPS Destinations: *Father C. Jorn Trail Cascade*—42.048008, –73.939912; *Icehouse area*—42.047413, –73.939479; *Upland Trail Cascade*—42.058381, –73.940693
Hours: Open daily from sunrise to sunset
Fee: None
Restrictions: Hikers are asked to stay on marked trails and to respect the privacy of the Dominican Sisters; pets must be leashed; carry-in and carry-out
Accessibility: *Father C. Jorn Trail*— >0.5 mile-hike; *Upland Trail*—0.9-mile hike; *Riverside Trail*— <0.7-mile hike
Degree of Difficulty: Easy to moderate
Additional Information: Falling Waters, Dominican Lane, Saugerties, NY 12477
Trail map—esopuscreekconservancy.org

Directions: From the New York State Thruway take Exit 20 for Saugerties & Woodstock, then take Route 32 southeast into Saugerties. At the center of Saugerties (junction of Routes 9W North & 9W South/Route 32 South), proceed south on Routes 9W South/32 South for ~2.2 miles. At a fork go left and proceed southeast on Route 32 for 0.5 mile. Bear left onto Glasco Turnpike/County Route 32 and drive east for 0.4 mile, going through the village of Glasco in the process. When you come to York Street, go left and proceed north for 0.2 mile, passing by Market Street to your right. You will come to a sign directing you to Falling Waters. Turn right onto Dominican Lane and proceed northeast for <0.3 mile to the parking area, on your left, for the Falling Waters Preserve.

Description: Falling Waters Preserve features two cascades, views of the Hudson River from a lower trail, and the historic ruins of the Mulford Icehouse.

Falling Water's main attractions and namesakes are its two cascades located at opposite ends of the preserve. Both are formed on fairly small streams that tumble down the escarpment and flow into the Hudson River.

Highlights: Two waterfalls • Scenic views of the Hudson River • Mulford Icehouse ruins

PART ONE • HUDSON RIVER VALLEY & CATSKILL REGIONS

One of two cascades at Falling Waters.

Hike: From the kiosk next to the parking area, walk downhill along the red-blazed gravel road for 100 feet to reach the first junction. Here, the Father C. Jorn Trail goes off to your right.

Father C. Jorn Trail—The 0.5-mile-long, blue-blazed Father C. Jorn Trail is named for Farther Charles Jorn who served as chaplain at the Dominican Sisters' Sparkill Infirmary. For 39 consecutive years, Father Jorn would spend every day of his vacation except Sundays working on trails and clearing brush around the ice-house site.

Follow the blue-blazed trail downhill for 0.1 mile until you come to a 10-foot-high waterfall on your right with a wonderful viewing area that consists of rustic wooden benches and a wooden canopy reminiscent of the summerhouses at Mohonk Mountain House. After cascading over the waterfall, the stream, now diked, follows the road downhill to your right.

Continue walking downhill on the road for another 0.1 mile until you reach the Hudson River, where an 8-foot-long bench donated by the Tortuga Foundation faces the river. The stream producing the waterfall empties into the Hudson River to your right.

From here follow the blue-blazed road as it turns into a path and makes an elliptical loop around a huge area of unvaryingly flat terrain where the Mulford Icehouse once stood.

Follow the blue-blazed trail counterclockwise. As the trail swings to your right to head north, detour straight ahead to visit the southernmost ruins of the icehouse near the river shoreline, where you will see a cement abutment, bricks, and dock

9. FALLING WATERS

Brick fragments of the Mulford Ice House.

The Mulford Icehouse, owned and operated by Charles Mulford (1842–1920), in its day was one of the largest, if not *the* largest, of icehouses on the Hudson River. It consisted of a windowless well-insulated building capable of holding up to 10,000 blocks of ice. The icehouse burned down in 1915 when a night watchman's lantern ignited the sawdust that was used for insulating the main building. Charles Mulford had established the Mulford Fire Engine Company in Glasco to address just such an occasion, but help was not able to arrive in time to save the building. Sadly, destruction by fire proved to be the common fate for most Hudson River icehouses.

Sometimes freak accidents occur that can never be anticipated. In January 1903, Mulford and a friend, Oscar Osterhoudt, were walking on the frozen Hudson River when an ice boat manned by Clarence Low and Frank Briody went out of control. Pushed by a stiff wind, the ice boat raced directly toward the men. Mulford was just barely able to get out of the way in time, his boot leg grazed by a runner plank, but Osterhoudt suffered a number of broken bones as well as bruised legs and a lump on the back of his head. No doubt this was just one of numerous injuries sustained by men while ice-harvesting.

The old Mulford Homestead, completely remodeled by the Dominican Sisters of Sparkill in 1947, rests at the top of the escarpment on a small hill overlooking the former icehouse site.

pilings that become visible at low tide. Look straight across the river to the east shore and you will see <0.3-mile-long Magdalen Island (also known as Goat Island or Slipsteen Island), with Tivoli Bays directly behind it.

Return to the path and head north for >0.1 mile. Along the way you will come across numerous cement blocks, cemented chunks of bricks, and at one point wall supports for the shoreline. The immensity of the icehouse soon becomes apparent as you make your way through the area.

The trail takes you to the north end of the loop where you reach a "T" junction. The path to the right leads in 100 feet to a 20-foot-by-20-foot wooden building about 10 feet high. It resembles the weathered structure near the parking area, both in terms of construction and age. This short detour quickly ends at the river's edge where there is a picnic table and wooden bench for hikers to relax and enjoy the river view.

Return to the "T" and continue counterclockwise, now heading south, on the blue-blazed trail for ~0.1 mile, completing the loop. You will see more remnants of the icehouse as well as a fair amount of blowdown. A 25–30-foot-high bluff hugs the side of the escarpment to your right. Near the end of the loop, look up to your right to see the cascade that you passed by earlier, as well as a brick wall support that was erected years ago to buttress the descending road.

From the end of the loop, follow the road north, back uphill, for 0.2 mile to reach the junction with the red-blazed Upland Trail.

Old pilings at low tide.

9. FALLING WATERS

Upland Trail—The 0.9-mile-long, red-blazed Upland Trail is a gravel road that passes by working hayfields and pastures, eventually reaching the preserve's north waterfall. In its last <0.1 mile the road turns into a path as it follows along the crest of a deeply cut gorge and down to the Hudson River. The last part of the trail is every bit as scenic as the preserve's two waterfalls.

Starting at the junction with the Father C. Jorn Trail, follow the red-blazed gravel road north. In <0.1 mile you will pass the white-blazed Riverside Trail as it comes in to your right. If you choose to do a loop by returning on the Riverside Trail instead of the Upland Trail, this will be your point of exit. From the junction with the Riverside Trail, the Upland Trail heads uphill, leveling off after 0.1 mile as it begins to parallel farmland and open pastures to your left. A rustic chair awaits those who wish to enjoy sitting for a moment to gaze at the fields.

At the end of the fields, the road enters the woods and then, after 0.1 mile, begins to descend, passing by facilities in the distance to your left that are part of the Dominican Sister's Villa St. Joseph. Soon the road comes to a barrier at the end of an old bridge spanning a medium-sized stream. This is as far north as you can go, for the land beyond is privately owned by the Dominican Sisters. The estate that lies beyond the north end of the bridge is the rehabilitated Spaulding home, whose name, "Falling Waters," gave rise to the preserve's name. A white statue on a pedestal, presumably of St. Joseph, stands next to the bridge. Veer right here, continuing on the red-blazed road heading downhill, now paralleling the stream. In >50 feet, take a short side path to your left that leads in a couple of hundred feet to a scenic viewing area, complete with rustic wooden benches and wooden canopy. The view overlooks a fairly flattened, 15-foot-high cascade that ends in a waterslide.

Return to the red-blazed trail and continue your descent, paralleling the stream. You will soon reach a junction where the red-blazed trail veers left and the white-blazed Riverside Trail begins and proceeds straight ahead. For the moment continue on the red-blazed trail, which leaves the road and turns into a path as it follows along a spiny ridge that gradually narrows. The ridge is defined by the deep-cut gully of the waterfall-bearing stream to your left and the Hudson River escarpment to your right. The path steadily leads downhill to the level of the Hudson River, where the stream disgorges its waters. This is a very wild, scenic area, and one not to be missed.

Return to the junction of the red-blazed Upland Trail and white-blazed Riverside Trail.

Riverside Trail—The 0.7-mile-long white-blazed Riverside Trail is named for its dramatic views of the Hudson River. It is much closer to the river than the Upland

Trail, and because it is a meandering, up and down trail, it is more strenuous and difficult to traverse, but should be within the abilities of most hikers.

From the junction with the red-blazed Upland Trail, follow the white-blazed Riverside Trail downhill as it leads to the shore of the Hudson River. At the very last moment, turn right and follow the white-blazed trail as it turns into a path that heads south, next to the Hudson River, and traverses a sloping escarpment with little ravines. Excellent views of the Hudson River are continuously provided. Be prepared for some loose rock here and there, but the hike is really not all that demanding. Midway a rustic wooden bench provides views and a respite for those who wish to take a breather or just admire the scene.

The white-blazed trail eventually becomes more road-like near its end, and then intersects the red-blazed Upland Trail. Return to your car via the Upland Trail.

History: The 149-acre preserve was created through a partnership between the Dominican Sisters of Sparkill (who provided an easement), the Esopus Creek Conservancy, and Scenic Hudson.

The name of the preserve comes from an eighteenth-century farmhouse at the end of Spaulding Road that Gilbert Spaulding, a veterinarian, and his wife remodeled and dubbed "Falling Waters." They had chosen that name because of the cascades located south and southeast of their house. The Spauldings had purchased the farmland from a minister named Peter Overbaugh, who lies buried in a tiny cemetery on the property. Prior to that, the Spaulding property was owned by the Van Leuven family, who had received it as part of a grant from George Meals and Richard Havers in 1731 and 1747.

Dominican Sisters of Sparkill—After the icehouse property was abandoned following the heyday of ice-harvesting in the Mid-Hudson Valley, the Dominican Sisters of Sparkill purchased the Mulford property in 1931 and then the Spaulding property in 1932. The Mulford property today is known as Corazon Center Villa St. Dominic, a 17-room retreat; the Spaulding property today is called Falling Waters' Villa St. Joseph and serves as a 43-room retreat and public conference center.

The Dominican Sisters of Sparkill, also known as the Dominican Congregation of Our Lady of the Rosary, was founded as an order in 1876 to care for indigent women. Since then the order has become heavily involved in education.

Ice-Harvesting Industry—The naturalist John Burroughs wonderfully described the parallels between ice-harvesting and crop-harvesting:

9. FALLING WATERS

No man sows, yet many men reap a harvest from the Hudson. Not the least is the ice harvest, which is eagerly looked for and counted upon by hundreds, yes thousands, of laboring-men along its course. … It is a crop that takes two or three weeks of rugged weather to grow, and, if the water is very roily or brackish, even longer. It is seldom worked till it presents seven or eight inches of clear-water ice. Men go out from time to time and examine it, as the farmer goes out and examines his grain or grass, to see when it will do to cut … It is a crop quite as uncertain as any other. A good yield every two or three years, as they say of wheat out West, is about all that can be counted upon. When there is an abundant harvest, after the ice-houses are filled, they stack great quantities of it, as the farmer stacks his surplus hay. … The best crop of ice is an early crop. Late in the season, or after January, the ice is apt to get "sun-struck," when it becomes "shaky," like a piece of poor timber. The sun, when he sets about destroying the ice, does not simply melt it from the surface—that were a slow process; but he sends his shafts into it and separates it into spikes and needles—in short, makes kindling-wood of it, so as to consume it the quicker.

Burroughs also recounted what it looked like to watch the ice-harvesters from his home at West Park: "Sometimes nearly two hundred men and boys, with numerous horses, are at work at once, marking, plowing, planing, scraping, sawing, hauling, chiseling; some floating down the pond on great square islands towed by a horse or their fellow workmen; others upon the bridges, separating the blocks with their chisel-bars; others feeding the elevators; while knots and straggling lines of idlers here and there look on in cold discontent, unable to get a job."

Interestingly, although the hamlet of Glasco is best remembered for its role in the ice-harvesting industry, its name actually comes from a glass-making company whose Hudson River warehouse was painted with the large letters GLASCO, for "glass company." It didn't take long before boaters, always seeing that name in big letters, began to call the landing "Glasco." ■

PART ONE • HUDSON RIVER VALLEY & CATSKILL REGIONS

10. DIBBLE'S QUARRY

Location: Platte Clove (Greene County)
NYS Atlas & Gazetteer, Tenth Edition, p. 97, C10; **Earlier Edition,** p. 52, CD1
GPS Parking: *Seasonal*—42.151068, –74.130997; *Winter*—42.149770, –74.126188
GPS Dibble's Quarry: 42.139127, –74.133017
Hours: Dawn to dusk
Fee: None
Accessibility: <1.0-mile hike; 400-foot gain in elevation
Degree of Difficulty: Moderate

Directions: From the traffic light at the center of Tannersville (junction of Route 23A & Railroad Avenue), turn south onto Railroad Avenue and drive southeast for 0.2 mile. When you come to a stop sign, bear right and head southwest on Railroad Avenue/Spruce Street as it soon turns into Platte Clove Road/Route 16. After ~1.1 miles from the stop sign, Bloomer Road is passed to your right, followed by Elka Park Road, also to your right, at ~1.5 miles. From Elka Park Road, continue southeast on Platte Clove Road/Route 16 for another 2.7 miles (or a total of ~4.4 miles from when you left Route 23A). When you come to Dale Lane, turn right.

From West Saugerties, follow Platte Clove Road (Route 16) northwest through Platte Clove (this is a seasonal road). At ~2.0 miles you will cross over a stone bridge spanning Hell's Hole Creek. Using the bridge as a starting point, continue northwest on Platte Clove Road for another ~2.0 miles, then turn left onto Dale Lane.

From either direction, drive southwest on Dale Lane for 0.5 mile. At a fork bear right onto Roaring Kill Road and proceed northwest for another 0.6 mile (the last 0.2 mile being seasonal, with no maintenance from November 15–April 15), then turn left into the parking area.

Description: Dibble's Quarry is a sizeable, multi-leveled, bluestone quarry. It lies along a trail that eventually leads up to Pecoy Notch and, from there, to Twin Mountain and Sugarloaf Mountain. There is a remote feel to the quarry, with nothing else close by. The most remarkable features of Dibble's Quarry are its pieces of "Catskill Furniture" that hikers have fashioned out of slabs of rock over the years.

Highlights: Bluestone quarry • Catskill "stone furniture" • Overview of nearby mountains • 10-foot-high cascade on nearby stream

10. DIBBLE'S QUARRY

The main section of Dibble's Quarry.

Hike: From the south side of the parking area, follow the yellow-blazed Roaring Brook Trail southwest for 0.3 mile. (Note: If you do this hike off-season, be prepared to add on another 0.2 mile from the winter parking area). At a trail junction turn left and follow the blue-blazed Pecoy Notch Trail south as the blue-blazed Mink Hollow Trail goes right. The Pecoy Notch Trail quickly ascends to one shelf, and then to a second, at which point the trail essentially levels out and remains flat until you reach Dibble's Quarry.

On the way up from the junction, you will pass by an interesting balanced rock to your left where one large rock is precariously perched on a second one of equal size that rests on a steeply inclined slope. After ~0.3 mile from the junction, a medium-sized quarry is encountered to your right; the *Guide to Catskill Trails 8* refers to this as Mudd Quarry. We suspect that this quarry may predate the main quarry farther up the trail. As you walk past Mudd Quarry, look for three stone-slab chairs and a small stone-slab bench along the trail—harbinger of things to come.

At ~0.9 mile you will enter a hemlock forest and, within 200 feet, come to the edge of an escarpment. Follow the trail as it takes you down a 25-foot-high ledge. As soon as you reach the bottom and turn right, you will emerge onto an immense talus slope, the beginning of Dibble's Quarry. Follow the path up the talus slope and then onto steps that lead into a low-walled room made of bluestone slabs. The room contains three large stone chairs as well as an even larger chair that looks like a king's throne. The "king's throne" affords expansive views of Platte Clove, the mountains to the north of Platte Clove (Round Top and Kaaterskill High Peak), as well as Twin Mountain. The low-walled room also contains a fire pit made of slabs as well as a square-shaped, 8-foot-high obelisk. In *Catskill Mountain Guide*, Peter Kick writes, "Hikers have assembled a variety of stone art here in fascinating druidic configurations, including a pair of comfortable seats surrounding an arch Druid's throne." Carol and David White, in *Catskill Day Hikes for all Seasons*, assert, "Across from the amazingly comfortable seats are a stone fireplace with overhanging stone wood box and slab benches. A child's rock seat is left of the triangular throne. Other fire pits are in this area."

From the room, gaze down at the sloping talus field below you. You will see a series of low, parallel rock walls that partition off one level from another. A few more, but minor, rock creations are visible downslope. Below the lower walls the talus field extends downward at an even steeper angle (making it impossibly dangerous to descend) until it reaches the tree line, some 50 feet below. Listen quietly and you will hear the roaring sound of a stream below in the distance, a tributary to Schoharie Creek.

After taking in the magnificent views of the valley and mountains, leave the room from the opposite entrance and walk around to a quarry behind the room. At the far right corner of this quarry, next to a 15-foot-high excavated wall, is an 8-foot-by-8-foot room delineated by a 2-foot-high rock-slab wall.

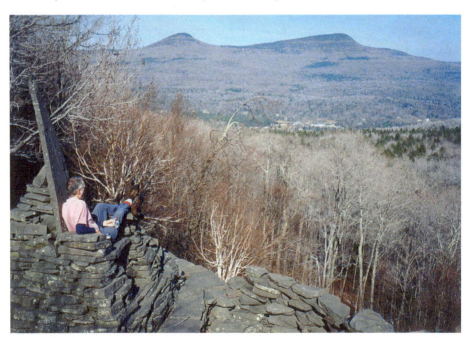

Joe Zoske looks out across Platte Clove to the northern mountains.

10. DIBBLE'S QUARRY

Return to the blue-blazed trail and continue south for several hundred feet, passing by another quarry to your right and then hiking between huge piles of talus that lie along both sides of the trail.

At the end of the quarry, look for a white-colored slab lying on the trail with the faded letters GEORGE CERTLE LEC chiseled into it. So far, we have not been able to find out who George Certle was. From the end of the quarry, continue walking south on the trail for another 100 feet to reach a small stream. If you enjoy waterfalls, cross over the stream and then bushwhack down along the east bank for 50 feet to obtain views of a hidden 10-foot-high cascade that is probably best seen in the early spring when the stream is fully engorged. This creek is part of the stream that you heard below you back at the quarry.

Turn around and return to Dibble's Quarry, and you will quickly discover that a significant part of the quarry lies hidden from view at a slightly higher elevation. Look for a path to your left between the first and second quarries and follow it uphill. When you reach the top, bear left and find your way over to the beginning of the upper quarry. (Note: This path from the lower quarry might provide an alternate, gentler approach for those who are wary about scampering down the initial 25-foot-high ledge.) Once you reach the upper quarry, look for a large, three-person stone chair that faces a one-person stone chair, the two being separated by five feet of earth that is often pooled with water. Eight feet above the chairs is a low-walled room with a stone chair in its center. From this room you can look down into the lower quarry and see the blue-blazed trail as it wends its way through the rock piles (take note, however, that the upper room that you are standing in is not visible from below).

Just beyond this room is a slightly higher, three-foot-diameter, low-walled room with a small stone chair in the center. We call it "the Turret Room" because of its shape. If there were a "command center" in this quarry, this room would be it.

Just up from the Turret Room is a half-enclosed low-walled room with a stone-slab fire pit.

With this, we have covered the main points of interest, but one big question remains—how did the quarrymen access the quarry? Consider this: although the trail coming up from Roaring Brook Road is an old tote road that was used by the quarrymen, it seems to terminate at the edge of an escarpment ledge after >0.9 mile. There is no way that wagons loaded with bluestone could have made their way up or down this 25-foot-high ledge. We think that wagons and machinery entered the upper quarry somewhere to the right of the ledge, which means that where you first entered the quarry was not its entrance, but rather its back side, where the quarry dead-ended.

PART ONE • HUDSON RIVER VALLEY & CATSKILL REGIONS

After exploring Dibble's Quarry, you may wish to continue south for another 0.7 mile to Pecoy Notch where, at a "T" junction, you can either head left up to 3,632-foot-high Twin Mountain or right up to 3,806-foot-high Sugarloaf Mountain, both of which are part of the high-elevation Devil's Path.

History: The stone walls and the pieces of Catskill furniture shaped into thrones, tables, obelisks, spiral staircases, benches, fire pits, and so on are made out of bluestone, which is a form of sandstone. At Dibble's Quarry a particularly large number of these unique pieces of outdoor furniture can be found.

According to Robert Titus, retired professor of geology at Hartwick College in Oneonta, bluestone quarries are generally located at an elevation of around 1,500–2,800 feet. Dibble's Quarry falls right into this range at an elevation of 2,600 feet. The largest bluestone quarry in New York State was located at West Hurley in nearby Ulster County.

Although most of the rock that was harvested at Dibble's Quarry has a somewhat bluish hue to it, the term "bluestone" is also applied to a variety of red, green, brown, and purple sandstones and limestones. Bluestone formed during the Devo-

Passageway through mounds of bluestone debris.

10. DIBBLE'S QUARRY

nian Era some 400 million years ago. The world's most famous bluestones are found at Stonehenge in England, where 42 of Stonehenge's smaller stones were transported by ancient people across the countryside from the Preseli Hills in Pembrokeshire.

Limestone is a very durable rock, which is what gives it such value. The Great Pyramids were made out of limestone and have stood for 4,500 years.

The Catskill bluestone industry began not far from Dibble's Quarry near Overlook Mountain, where a number of quarries are located along the old Overlook Mountain Road, which is now a hiking trail between Platte Clove and Overlook Mountain. Stone slabs from these quarries were once a principal source for the sidewalks of New York City as well as for many other towns and cities. Bluestone has one property that made it highly desirable for sidewalks—it is impervious to water, which means that chemical weathering that could otherwise break the rock down cannot take place.

Bluestone quarries began to decline starting in the mid-1910s. Three reasons have generally been cited. First, bluestone began to be replaced by cement; cement was more versatile and less expensive. Secondly, a new Worker's Compensation Law was enacted to protect workers engaged in hazardous employment. And thirdly, the rural labor force, which had been plentiful during the nineteenth century, began to taper off as workers left upstate New York for urban regions.

Dibble's Quarry operated until the late nineteenth century. The stone furniture and walls were made after quarry operations ceased, but no one knows when, nor who the creators were. What we do know is that the work was labor-intensive and probably took place over a period of many years as one creation came into existence followed by another. Perhaps the process is still ongoing as new, motivated hikers try their hand at arranging pieces of bluestone.

Professor Titus, for one, believes that the stone furniture may not be very old. His conjecture is based on the fact that not much lichen has accumulated on the rocks; if a great many decades had passed since the furniture was created, the rocks would be covered with much more lichen.

The quarry may have been named for Edward Dibble who, along with Collins Hyser, constructed the carriage road from Palenville to the Hotel Kaaterskill. Perhaps Dibble used bluestone from the nearby quarry for his road.

In the *Early Settlement of the Town of Hunter*, J.B. Beers and Company in 1884 wrote about Dibble's achievement as an engineer:

> In this park, leading to and around the house [the Hotel Kaaterskill], there are now completed, or in the course of construction, 20 miles of the most perfect roads extant in the Catskill region, the principal one of which being

PART ONE • HUDSON RIVER VALLEY & CATSKILL REGIONS

the Mountain Turnpike leading from Palenville. In the location of this road the skill and experience of some of the most noted railroad engineers of the country were called into requisition to supply plans for its construction; but they were all found either impracticable or to [sic] costly, and the plan of one of Hunter's sons, Edward Dibble, "a native mountain engineer," was finally adopted. A little anecdote will explain his method of working. Instead of running trial lines, they went to the mountain, which directly faced the park, and standing there, with the thermometer at zero and with snow drifting over their paths, with glass in hand, surveyed with their eyes the route they wished to take, and returning, they staked almost the identical line they had "surveyed." The choice could not have been a better one, as the result proves; from among the most famous of the mountain roads of Switzerland, including few with more seemingly dangerous precipices. The park comprises within its bounds nearly 21 square miles, over which Mr. Dibble has acted as chief engineer.

Dibble's Quarry is not the only site in the Catskills where Catskill furniture can be found. Some of the quarries along the Old Mountain Road between Platte Clove and Overlook Mountain contain interesting arrangements of stone slabs. One of the best examples is at the Palenville Overlook, where a three-person throne overlooking Kaaterskill Clove was created from the stone slab foundation of Elizabeth Adkins and Thomas Dodd's Palenville Mountain House.

For those interested in seeing a more artistic version of Catskill furniture as well as learning more about quarrying in general, a trip to Opus 40 and the Quarryman's Museum in High Woods, Saugerties, is well worth the effort. Opus 40 is the work of one man, Harvey Fite, who converted an abandoned bluestone quarry into an enormous outdoor work of art. Its centerpiece is a 9-ton monolith. What's even more impressive is that Fite did all the work using the tradition tools of quarrymen—hammers, chisels, drills, blasting powder, and a large hand-powered boom with a flat wooden tray for moving rocks. All of these implements are exhibited in the Quarryman's Museum. ■

11. OLD STAGE ROAD TO CATSKILL MOUNTAIN HOUSE SITE

Location: Palenville (Greene County)
NYS Atlas & Gazetteer, Tenth Edition, p. 98, B1; **Earlier Edition,** p. 52, C1
Parking GPS Coordinates: 42.212433, −74.007572
Destination GPS Coordinates: *Black Snake Bridge*—42.214333, −74.016100; *Rip Van Winkle House site*—42.215333, −74.024650; *Rip's Rock*—42.215190, −74.024925; *Little Pine Orchard*—42.207333, −74.021867; *Junction with Palenville Overlook Trail*—42.198617, −74.030000; *North Lake*—42.197317, −74.034517; *Otis Elevating Railway Summit Station site*—42.196550, −74.035338; *Catskill Mountain House site*—42.194797, −74.034682
Hours: Daily, dawn to dusk
Fee: None
Accessibility: *Black Snake Bridge*—0.5-mile hike; *Rip Van Winkle House*—1.0-mile hike; *Little Pine Orchard*—1.5-mile hike; *North/South Lake area*—3.2-mile hike; *Catskill Mountain House site*—3.5-mile hike
Elevation gain from trailhead to Catskill Mountain House site: 1,470 feet
Degree of Difficulty: Moderate to difficult

Directions: *Catskill Approach*—Driving south on the New York State Thruway (I-87), take Exit 21 for Catskill & Cairo. Turn left onto Route 23B and head south for ~0.3 mile, then bear right onto Route 23 and proceed northwest for ~6.5 miles to Cairo. When you come to Route 32, turn left and proceed south for ~5.4 miles. Turn right onto Game Farm Road. After heading west for <0.2 mile, bear left onto Bogart Road. Proceed southwest for ~1.2 miles and then turn right onto Mountain House Road.

Saugerties Approach—Driving north on the New York State Thruway (I-87), take Exit 20 for Saugerties. Turn left onto Route 32/212 and head west for 0.2 mile, going under the New York State Thruway in the process. As Route 212 continues straight ahead, turn right onto Route 32 and proceed north for >6.0 miles. When you come to Route 32A, turn left and drive northwest for 1.9 miles to Palenville. At a traffic light, bear left onto Route 23A and head west for <0.2 mile. Turn right onto Bogart Road, proceed northeast for ~2.6 miles, and then left onto Mountain House Road.

From either direction drive northwest on Mountain House Road for 0.7 mile. Park to your right along the wide shoulder before the old barn, several hundred feet from the barrier where the Old Mountain Turnpike begins.

PART ONE • HUDSON RIVER VALLEY & CATSKILL REGIONS

The old Saxe Farm tollgate. Postcard circa 1900.

Description: The Old Mountain Turnpike takes you through Sleepy Hollow, a deep clove cut by Stony Brook, past waterfalls, the site of the Rip Van Winkle House and Rip's Rock, and eventually up to North-South Lake and to the site of the historic Catskill Mountain House.

Highlights: Waterfalls • Black Snake Bridge • Site of Rip Van Winkle House • Rip's Rock • North Lake • North-South Lake Campground • Otis Elevating Railway bed • Catskill Mountain House site

Hike: The hike up the Old Mountain Turnpike, also known as the Sleepy Hollow Horse Trail and the Old Stage Road, begins at the end of the drivable portion of Mountain House Road, a historic road that leads up to the North-South Lake area and the site of the famous Catskill Mountain House. The old road is marked by red blazes for snowmobiles and yellow blazes for horses. The road was built in the early nineteenth century and preceded an earlier version of Route 23A, "the Rip Van Winkle Trail," which snakes its way up into the mountains through Kaaterskill Clove.

    The Old Mountain Turnpike will forever be associated with Washington Irving's legendary character Rip Van Winkle. The turnpike wends its way through Sleepy Hollow, where Rip Van Winkle Brook, the Rip Van Winkle House, and

11. OLD STAGE ROAD TO CATSKILL MOUNTAIN HOUSE SITE

Rip's Rock are located and where local lore would have us believe that Rip Van Winkle took his long nap and woke up in an America no longer under British rule. (Note: This is not the Sleepy Hollow of Irving's "Legend of Sleepy Hollow," a story that was set by the Poconos River at Headless Horseman Bridge in Westchester County.)

Although there is no charge for you to walk this historic road today, that wasn't the case in the 1800s. A farmer named Frederick Saxe owned the right-of-way across his farmland and charged a toll for travelers making their way up the mountain through Sleepy Hollow. His farm was known as Saxe's Farm; it has also been called Mt. View Farm.

For the first mile of the hike, which continuously leads uphill on the carriage road, you will be accompanied by the sound of Stony Brook (also called Rip Van Winkle Brook and Sleepy Hollow Brook) as it flows through a deep gorge on your left. Stony Brook rises on the eastern shoulder of North Mountain. After flowing through Sleepy Hollow, it becomes a tributary of Kaaterskill Creek. A number of pleasing waterfalls can be heard, particularly a 15-foot-high waterfall that is encountered at the very beginning of the hollow. The fall can be viewed from an overlook next to the trail. (For further details regarding Sleepy Hollow's waterfalls, consult Russell Dunn's *Catskill Region Waterfall Guide*, published by Black Dome Press).

After 0.5 mile you will come to Black Snake Bridge, a wooden bridge that crosses a tiny tributary of Stony Brook at an elevation of ~960 feet.

Along the way, take note of sandstone ledges that appear at intervals along the upper slopes. At first they are high above you, out of reach, but gradually come down to the level of the carriageway as the road continues its ascent. What you are observing are the sandy deposits from old sea beds that hardened into sandstone under enormous pressure.

Charles Rockwell describes the first part of this hike in *The Catskill Mountains and the Region Around*, published in 1867. He writes how the road follows along

> … the margin of a deep, dark glen, through which flows a clear mountain stream, seldom seen by the traveler, but heard continually for nearly a mile, as in swift rapids or in little cascades it hurries to the plain below. The road is winding, and in its ascent along the side of the glen, or, more properly, magnificent gorge, it is so enclosed by the towering heights on one side, and the lofty trees that shoot up on the other, that little can be seen beyond a few rods except the sky above or glimpses of some distant summit, until the pleasant nook in the mountain is reached wherein the Rip Van Winkle cabin is nestled.

PART ONE • HUDSON RIVER VALLEY & CATSKILL REGIONS

At ~1.0 mile you will reach the point where the road abruptly veers left, crossing over Stony Brook. You have reached the site of the old Rip Van Winkle House (a former boardinghouse, the "cabin" mentioned by Rockwell) and the boulder where Rip Van Winkle allegedly napped for twenty years. Foundation ruins are visible on both sides of the stream.

The Rip Van Winkle House in its prime. Postcard circa 1910.

Rip Van Winkle House—Most of our source material here comes from the *Catskill Mountaineer* (CatskillMountaineer.com). The first version of the Rip Van Winkle House, essentially a shanty, was built in 1845 at an elevation of 1,260 feet. There may have been an even earlier version, for in Roland Van Zandt's book, *The Catskill Mountain House*, mention is made of a rude structure called Rip Van Winkle's shanty that dates back to 1828.

The spot chosen was ideal, for a fairly wide space existed for erecting a small structure, and there was a constant source of fresh water for drinking and bathing. It was also the perfect place for horses to take a breather before facing the more demanding "Dead Ox Hill" and "Featherbed Hill" stretches of the upper roadway.

11. OLD STAGE ROAD TO CATSKILL MOUNTAIN HOUSE SITE

Ira Saxe, who owned the shanty in 1867, hired William Comfort to build a boardinghouse, which became a three-story hotel with an upper and lower front porch. Although Comfort alleged that the famous Hudson River School artist Thomas Cole had painted the boardinghouse sign, that claim is highly dubious, as Raymond Beecher points out in his book *Kaaterskill Clove: Where Nature Met Art*, because Thomas Cole died nearly two decades earlier, in 1848.

In 1880 Saxe sold the property to Gilbert and Elizabeth Lusk, who managed the boardinghouse. After Gilbert died in 1885, Elizabeth continued running the business, but the actual day-to-day management was taken over by H.A. Schuff and J.M. Miller.

The Rip Van Winkle House did a fairly brisk business, but it was obviously highly dependent on the draw of the Catskill Mountain House—the destination for most of the folks journeying up into the mountains along the turnpike. Travelers could receive refreshments at the Rip Van Winkle House, and the horses could be fed and watered. Some travelers even made the boardinghouse their destination.

Although the trip up to the Catskill Mountain House was a long and arduous one (particularly for the horses who struggled to pull the stagecoaches up the mountainside), it was one that many tourists made. But then, all at once, the Rip Van Winkle House saw its brisk business plummet dramatically. The reason for the sudden decline was the opening of the Otis Elevating Railway in 1892. This inclined railway was only one mile south of the Rip Van Winkle House, and its narrow-gauge rail line now offered travelers an alternate, and much quicker, mode of transportation. In less than 20 minutes the railway could take travelers and their luggage up to the top of the Wall of Manitou by North Lake, and it could do it both expediently and comfortably. The grueling trek up the Old Mountain Turnpike was no longer necessary to get to the mountain house.

The handwriting was on the wall, and Elizabeth Lusk sold the property to Sarah Emory, who within three years sold the property to Robert M. Mabie. The property immediately proved to be a poor investment for Mabie, who lost interest and failed to maintain the business. By 1902 the boardinghouse was abandoned, and it ultimately burned down around 1917 or 1918.

PART ONE • HUDSON RIVER VALLEY & CATSKILL REGIONS

Rip Van Winkle resting on Rip's Rock. Postcard circa 1910.

Rip's Rock—There really is no such thing as a Rip's Rock, of course. It was merely a contrivance created by the proprietors of the Rip Van Winkle House to make their waypoint more of an attractive stopping point for travelers going up the mountain.

Rip Van Winkle was not a real person. He was a fictional character created by Washington Irving in *The Sketch Book*, his 1819–1820 collection of essays and stories. Irving's Rip Van Winkle was an amiable Dutch farmer who ventured into the mountains and came upon a group of mysterious dwarfish Dutchmen playing ninepins who then proceeded to get Rip rip-roaring drunk. Rip went into a deep, prolonged slumber and woke up 20 years later to a post–Revolutionary War America.

The rock close to the site of the Rip Van Winkle House that has long been designated as Rip's Rock rests at an elevation of 1,290 feet. Postcards depicted this rock, and one of those is included in this chapter. Rip's Rock is not impressively large, but it is still an interesting destination for those who like to seek out historical curiosities. Robert Gildersleeve in his book *Catskill Mountain House Trail Guide* writes, "Stand at the center of the bridge and face the southwest corner. Straight ahead and a little uphill is a stone retaining wall with a flat area at its top. Rip's Rock is along the same line and partway up the hill beyond the flat area. It rests alone on the side of a hill below a rock ledge. Some weathering has occurred, but it closely matches the nineteenth-century photos. Initials carved in the top further support the idea that it was an important local landmark."

There is another Rip's Rock, which is also known as Rip's Ledge. It is an overlook 600 feet above the site of the Rip Van Winkle House and is accessible via the Winter Clove trail system from Round Top.

11. OLD STAGE ROAD TO CATSKILL MOUNTAIN HOUSE SITE

From the site of the Rip Van Winkle House, cross over the little bridge spanning Stony Brook and continue around the bend. From here the road becomes increasingly steeper. You will climb a section known as "Dead Ox Hill," probably because an overburdened ox died right on the spot. Then, at 1.5 miles, a 50-foot-long spur path leads left to Little Pine Orchard (which takes its name from the Pine Orchard—the site of the former Catskill Mountain House—located at a higher elevation on the mountain). Little Pine Orchard is a small area of cleared land that contains a hitching post for horses. It also offers a grand overlook, with views of the Hudson Valley to the east.

In another 0.2 mile the trail takes you to a hairpin turn known as "Cape Horn." Perhaps the name arose from stagecoaches having to struggle around the sharp turn, much like ships that had to go around the treacherous southern tip of South America's Cape Horn.

From here the road moderates for a while, gaining little elevation, and is known as "the Short Level."

At ~2.0 miles another switchback is encountered, leading up to "Featherbed Hill," an odd name for a section of steady ascent. At the end of the climb, the road moderates again and is known as "the Long Level."

At 2.9 miles the junction with the Palenville Overlook Trail is reached. Continue straight ahead as the Palenville Overlook Trail goes off acutely to your left, descending to a lower level. In another 0.2 mile you will come to where the road bears right, heading up to the top of the escarpment. It was in this general area that nineteenth-century travelers could look up to see the Catskill Mountain House looming above them, beckoning weary passengers onward and upward. Thomas Cole's painting *View of the Catskill Mountain House, New York* depicts this very scene. According to Robert Gildersleeve in *Catskill Mountain House Trail Guide*, this glorious vista vanished in 1892 when the Otis Elevating Railway was constructed, forcing the Old Mountain Turnpike to be rerouted slightly north and farther away from the mountain house.

In 0.1 mile you will reach the top of the high escarpment, known as the Catskill Front and the Great Wall of Manitou (so-called by the Algonquian natives, with "Manitou" meaning something akin to "great spirit," a fundamental life force). This truly is a "great wall," extending south to north for ten miles and unbroken except for two magnificent mountain passes, or canyons—Kaaterskill Clove and Platte Clove.

In front of you is the North-South Lake Public Campground & Day Use Area. North Lake lies directly to your west, South Lake to your southwest. Legend has it that the lakes are the eyes of the reclining giant Onteora, a monster that was turned

PART ONE • HUDSON RIVER VALLEY & CATSKILL REGIONS

into the Catskill Mountains by the Great Spirit Manitou. You may wonder why two enjoined lakes have separate names. At one time they were separated by a causeway over which a rail line took passengers from the Otis Elevating Railway toward Haines Falls and Tannersville. At that time South Lake was privately owned. As the North Lake Campground, which started in 1929, continued to grow through a series of expansions in the 1930s, 1960s, and 1970s, South Lake was acquired, incorporated into the campgrounds, and the causeway was removed, returning the two lakes to one body of water.

Walk south from the picnic area along the blue-blazed Escarpment Trail for 0.05 mile and you will arrive at where the Otis Elevating Railway came up onto a relatively flat stretch of land saddled between North Mountain and South Mountain. The Otis Elevating Railway was responsible not only for the ultimate demise of the Rip Van Winkle House, but also for increasing the numbers of tourists coming up into the Catskill Mountains.

From where the Otis Summit Station once stood along this area of flat land, continue following the blue-blazed Escarpment Trail south for >0.2 mile as it

Thomas Cole (American, born England, 1801–1848). A View of the Two Lakes and Mountain House, Catskill Mountains, Morning, 1844. *Oil on canvas, 35 13/16 × 53 7/8 in. (91 × 136.9 cm). Brooklyn Museum, Dick S. Ramsay Fund, 52.16.*

11. OLD STAGE ROAD TO CATSKILL MOUNTAIN HOUSE SITE

takes you diagonally up the side of a hill. When you get to the top, the trail veers left, passes between the original 4-foot-high stone pillars marking the entrance to the famous hotel, and then finally brings you to the site of the Catskill Mountain House. The site consists of an enormous area of exposed bedrock where a large kiosk and a New York State historic marker deliver the history of the mountain house. The view from the edge of the escarpment overlooking the Hudson Valley is stunning and a well-deserved payoff for the challenging climb up the Old Mountain Turnpike.

The Otis Elevating Railway, from the bottom looking up. Postcard circa 1910.

77

PART ONE • HUDSON RIVER VALLEY & CATSKILL REGIONS

History: The *Otis Elevating Railway* was a funicular railway, not a traditional train, meaning that as one car went up, a second one came down, each counterbalancing the other. A passing track in the middle of the run allowed the cars to pass each other and then return to the single track both cars shared.

The railway was created by the Otis Elevator Company, headed by Charles Owen Otis. The Otis Elevator Company later went on to construct a similar rail system at Beacon Mountain in Dutchess County and at Prospect Mountain in Warren County. The company was hired by Charles L. Beach, owner of the Catskill Mountain House, who was facing increased competition from the nearby Hotel Kaaterskill, which was well served by the Kaaterskill Railroad line.

The elevating railway was designed by Thomas E. Brown, Jr., who was the chief engineer for Otis. Brown had impressive credentials; he had designed the elevators for the Eiffel Tower in Paris in 1879.

Construction of the railway began in 1892 and was completed the same year. The railway, going up the mountainside at an average gradient of 12 percent, was 7,000 feet long (over a mile in length!), rising up a total of 1,630 feet in elevation gain.

The two cars, named Rickerson and Van Santvoord (the latter perhaps named after Alfred Van Santvoord, the director of the Catskill Mountain Railroad), could

The Catskill Mountain House. Postcard circa 1910.

11. OLD STAGE ROAD TO CATSKILL MOUNTAIN HOUSE SITE

each hold up to 75 passengers. They were built by the Jackson & Sharp Co., an American railroad car manufacturer.

The cable cars were powered by two Hamilton Corliss steam engines located at the Otis Elevating Railway Summit Station, which drove a set of cogs that pulled the cables.

The railway ran until 1918, at which time it was permanently shut down. You can still view the bed of this former rail line from the saddle between North and South Mountains. The rail bed forms a distinctive scar on the mountainside that will probably take another century or more to heal.

The Catskill Mountain House has been forever memorialized in Roland Van Zandt's book of the same name published by Black Dome Press. The hotel has been gone for more than half a century, but you can see a wooden model of it on exhibit at the Bronck House Museum and Vedder Research Library of the Greene County Historical Society on Route 9W in Coxsackie (42.344926, -73.846416).

The Catskill Mountain House was essentially created by Erastus Beach, a stagecoach operator who helped form the Catskill Mountain Association in 1823. By 1824 a primitive hotel with ten rooms was erected on Pine Orchard. It included a ballroom and male and female dormitory bunk beds.

Despite the rather primitive conditions, the hotel proved to be an immediate success. Charles Beach, Erastus Beach's son, leased the hotel in 1839 and later bought it. Charles improved the Old Mountain Turnpike up from Saxe's farm and began to expand the hotel to accommodate a growing number of tourists. In 1845 he increased the size to 50 rooms. Then he added on two large wings to the main structure, which increased the capacity to 300 rooms.

It was patchwork architecture, at best, for what had started off as a Federalist-style hotel quickly blossomed into a Greek Revival structure when thirteen Corinthian columns were added onto a 140-foot-long colonnade around 1845. Thousands of guests over the years would get up early in the morning to sit on the porch at the front of the hotel among the columns to watch the sun rise in the east. It was a glorious sight, as attested to by innumerable persons both famous and not famous who stayed at the hotel.

Not only did the hotel grow in size, but its control over the surrounding area grew as well, eventually increasing to 3,000 acres of land including both North and South Lakes.

The hotel was a Victorian hiker's dream, with numerous destinations to stroll or hike to such as Kaaterskill Falls, The Boulder, Druid Rock, the Palenville

PART ONE • HUDSON RIVER VALLEY & CATSKILL REGIONS

Overlook, Alligator Rock, Fat Man's Misery, Inspiration Point, Newman's Ledge, and many more.

For most of its existence the hotel was overseen by the Beach family. They did run into difficulties, however, when the "Fried Chicken War" erupted in 1880 (see *Trails with Tales* for details), resulting in strong competition from the much larger and even grander Hotel Kaaterskill built on top of nearby South Mountain.

When Charles Beach died in 1902, his sons Charles and George H. became the new owners. Their involvement was relatively short-lived. Charles died in 1913 and George H. in 1918. John Van Wagonen took over management of the hotel, which was now approaching the century mark. Even before the Great Depression of the 1930s, business at the hotel was beginning to wane, accelerated in its decline by the automobile, which gave families newfound freedom to go wherever they wanted and to stay for briefer lengths of time.

In 1930 Van Wagonen sold over 2,000 acres of mountain house land to New York State. This parcel, with the help of the Civilian Conservation Corps (CCC), became the nucleus for North-South Lake Campground.

Ownership of the hotel changed again, and Claude Moseman and Clyde Gardiner took charge for a brief period of time. Then, around 1933 the hotel was leased to Jacob, Eli, and David Andron, who ran the hotel as a kosher resort and changed the hotel's name to Andron's Mountain House. With the outbreak of World War II and the economic struggles that ensued, the Androns chose not to renew their lease.

View of the Hudson Valley from the Catskill Mountain House. Postcard circa 1910.

11. OLD STAGE ROAD TO CATSKILL MOUNTAIN HOUSE SITE

As a result, by 1942 the hotel was abandoned. No attempt was made to save the once magnificent hotel, and it fell into increasing disrepair. Fortunately, Roland Van Zandt took a great number of black and white photographs of the hotel before it was destroyed, and a number of those images can be seen in his book *The Catskill Mountain House*.

As time went on the ruins became ever more unstable. Park rangers, fearful that people exploring the ruins would come to harm, torched the great hotel on January 25, 1963. It is said that the fire was so large that the flames could be seen clearly from Albany.

All that remains of the hotel today are memories and photographs. It was built on top of bedrock, so there are not even basement ruins.

Note: For those who just wish to see the Catskill Mountain House site and enjoy the magnificent view, the site is also accessible by way of the North-South Lake public campground. ■

View of the Otis Elevating Railway rail bed from the top of the escarpment.

PART ONE • HUDSON RIVER VALLEY & CATSKILL REGIONS

12. HIGH FALLS
High Falls Conservation Area

Location: Philmont (Columbia County)
NYS Atlas & Gazetteer, Tenth Edition, p. 99, AB6; **Earlier Edition**, p. 53, BC4
GPS Parking: *High Falls Conservation Area*—42.247233, –73.657648; *Summit Lake*—42.246766, –73.648083; *Canal Street (off of Elm Street)*—42.247095, –73.651088
GPS Destinations: *High Falls*—42.245760, –73.650185; *Agawamuck Falls*—42.246121, –73.651492; *Summit Knitting Mill*—42.246689, –73.648500; *Aken Knitting Mill*—42.247027, –73.651413
Hours: Daily, dawn to dusk
Fee: None
Restriction: Pets must be leashed
Accessibility: *Waterfall*—0.4-mile hike; *Waterfall & Blue Trail*—0.7-mile hike; *Green Trail*—0.5-mile long; *Red Trail*—0.5-mile long; *Blue Trail*—0.2-mile long
Degree of Difficulty: Easy to moderate
Additional Information: Trail map—philmont.org

Directions: From the Taconic Parkway take Exit 91 for Harlemville, Philmont, & Route 217. Bear left onto Route 217 and head southwest for 2.5 miles to Roxbury Road. Turn left onto Roxbury Road, go south 0.1 mile, and then turn left into the parking area for the High Falls Conservation Area.

Along the way, to your left, you will pass by Summit Street at 1.9 miles and Elm Street at 2.0 miles. Both lead to some of Philmont's old industrial ruins.

Description: High Falls is a 150-foot-high waterfall, the highest waterfall in Columbia County and the highest single-drop waterfall in the entire Hudson Valley.

Highlights: High Falls • Agawamuck Falls • Agawamuck Creek • Summit Reservoir • Industrial ruins

Hike: *High Falls Conservation Area*—From the parking area follow the Green Trail southeast. It leads downhill, paralleling a small stream that flows through a fairly deep ravine to your right. The stream originates from 2-acre Moore Pond, east of Oak Hill Road. The trail quickly crosses over the stream via a footbridge. On the right side of the ravine, look for a low stone wall that parallels the ravine and testifies to past days of farming.

12. HIGH FALLS

At 150 feet, High Falls is the tallest single-plunge waterfall in the Hudson Valley.

A hundred feet past the footbridge, the junction with the Lower Blue Trail is reached, to your left. The Lower Blue Trail leads north immediately down to Agawamuck Creek. From there you can go either upstream (east) or downstream (west) for short distances. Look for water emerging from a 3-foot-diameter drainpipe at one point, 15 feet above the level of the stream.

Back at the junction, continue southeast on the Green Trail for another 0.05 mile. When you come to the 0.4-mile-long Red Trail on your right, bear left, staying on the Green Trail, and proceed southeast for 0.1 mile.

At the junction with the Upper Blue Trail, turn sharply left (west) onto the Upper Blue Trail and gradually descend to the level of the streambed. Upon reaching the bottom of the gorge by Agawamuck Creek, take note that the trail extends in two directions. For the moment continue left (west), following the trail until it

PART ONE • HUDSON RIVER VALLEY & CATSKILL REGIONS

dead-ends by the edge of the river. If you look closely you will see that the road/trail at one time continued directly across the river and up the other side of the gorge. With a little imagination you can picture how this area was once a hub of activity.

Retrace your steps back to where the trail divided. This time head east on the Blue Trail, following along Agawamuck Creek, now to your left. In 0.1 mile you will reach Agawamuck Falls—a 75-foot-high cascade that tumbles down the sloping north wall of the gorge. A bench has been placed by the stream to allow hikers to sit and enjoy the view of the waterfall.

Agawamuck Falls—This artificial waterfall, also called Sluiceway Falls, came into existence at the time Agawamuck Creek was dammed above the top of High Falls. Water was diverted through a sluiceway to power a waterwheel, and a small holding pond was created (you can see the stone wall reinforcement of this pond if you park at the end of Canal Street and walk uphill for a hundred feet or so). Water then tumbled downhill from the pond, creating the waterfall that you see today.

Agawamuck Falls—an artificially created waterfall.

12. HIGH FALLS

Some people hiking in to see High Falls from the level of the river may stop at this point, believing that they have reached High Falls. They haven't. High Falls is farther east.

Walk back northwest along the river for 0.1 mile, turn left, and follow the Blue Trail as it ascends the side of the gorge and joins again with the Green Trail.

From here proceed southeast on the Green Trail. In 0.05 mile the Red Trail enters on your right. After this junction the Green Trail turns into a short loop, leading you immediately to the High Falls overlook.

From the overlook High Falls looms directly in front of you in the distance, framed by nearby trees as though seen through a picture window. The full height of High Falls is now visible, including a dam at its top.

To ruins downstream from fall—Once you turn onto Roxbury Road from Route 217, you will cross over a bridge spanning Agawamuck Creek. Take note of this. After parking in the High Falls Conservation Area parking lot, walk back to this point and look upstream. If the trees are leafless, you can see a 12-foot-high dam made partly of stone slabs and partly of cement located where the river falls impressively and where there appears to have been a natural cascade at one time. Huge ruins are visible on the north bank next to the dam. Ruins are also clearly visible where the river turns abruptly right just before passing under Roxbury Road.

Village Walk: *Site #1*—From Route 217 turn onto Summit Street and drive south for <0.2 mile. Park to your left in a small area just before crossing over a bridge that spans Agawamuck Creek in front of the Summit Lake dam.

There is little walking required here, for everything is close by. Next to the parking area is a 7-foot-square, stone-slab furnace that stands ~9 feet high.

Just beyond the abandoned furnace is the Summit Street Bridge, from where there are excellent views of the dam to your left (east) and Agawamuck Creek Gorge to your right (west). The gorge extends for <0.1 mile before the creek running through it plunges over the top of High Falls.

The 25-foot-high Summit Lake dam was constructed by George P. Philip to create a 48-acre reservoir for his mill. He also excavated a power channel with five different mill privileges. Summit Lake, also called The Reservoir, not only served as a mill pond but later was repurposed as a source of ready-made ice during the days of ice harvesting in the Hudson Valley.

The enormous three-story-high brick building next to the gorge, with its five-story-high centerpiece, is the abandoned Summit Knitting Mill. The south side of the factory is pressed directly against the side wall of the gorge and in some places even seems to be part of it. Behind the southwest corner of the factory is a section

PART ONE • HUDSON RIVER VALLEY & CATSKILL REGIONS

The Summit Knitting Mill.

made out of piled shale that looks entirely different from the brick structure and looks to be a different age.

Site #2—From Route 217 turn onto Elm Street, drive south for 200 feet, and then turn right onto Canal Street. After 250 feet park near the end of the street.

Straight ahead at the end of the street is a medium-sized, abandoned red-brick building. At the southwest corner a two-story green barn can be seen. Next to it is a

> **The Summit Knitting Mill** occupies the site of a former textile mill built by George W. Philip in the late eighteenth century. The mill became a satinet factory in 1820 and then was converted into the Ockawamick Hosiery Mills in the 1860s to supply shirts and drawers to the Union Army during the Civil War. The mill continued to operate as a knit hosiery until management was forced to declare bankruptcy in the early twentieth century. At that time the mill then became part of the High Rock Knitting Company, serving as a storage unit. In 1963 the Summit Knitting Mill building was purchased by Preferred Print Solutions. The building currently appears to be abandoned.

large red-brick building—a surviving structure from the Aken Knitting Mill—that has been taken over by Vita Nova Woodworking for furniture-making.

The Aken Knitting Mill dates back to ~1878. In its heyday the mill employed 250 workers, mostly women, who finished the knit goods that were produced nearby on Main Street. The mill is named for Nelson P. Aken, who was born in Claverack in 1839 and moved to Philmont in 1862.

Along the east side of the parking area is a stone wall. If you walk up the slope in front of the red-brick building, you will immediately come to a mill pond. Look across the pond and you will observe a cement gate where water from Agawamuck Creek was diverted into the pond. From the pond the water continues to flow down a sluiceway that at one time powered the red-brick building at the end of the parking area. This sluiceway, in turn, has created Agawamuck Falls, which you can see from the High Falls Conservation Area Blue Trail and which has only come into existence within the last two centuries following the sluiceway's construction.

History: *High Falls Conservation Area*—The 150-foot-tall High Falls is the centerpiece of a 47-acre conservation area owned and managed by the Columbia Land Conservancy from land donated by the Meltz and Schnackenberg families.

High Falls is formed on Agawamuck Creek (sometimes called Ockawamick Creek)—a medium-sized stream that rises from branches north and east of Harlemville and flows into Claverack Creek (a tributary of the Hudson River) east of Mellenville. *Agawamuck* is a Native American word that translates as "creek of many fish," a description that was no doubt valid prior to European settlement of the area.

Looking upstream from the back wall of the Summit Knitting Mill.

PART ONE • HUDSON RIVER VALLEY & CATSKILL REGIONS

The forest in the conservation area was selectively cut years ago. As a result you will see large decaying stumps along various sections of the trail. The sloping southern ravine of the creek is composed of hemlock trees that have endured well in the acidic, shallow soil.

The dam near the top of High Falls was built in 1845 to provide waterpower through a series of aqueducts and diverter dams to a number of mills that flourished in the gorge directly above the falls. The top of the dam is visible from the High Falls overlook (but is hidden from sight when viewed from below the fall).

Philmont was known as Factory Hill during the nineteenth century, a nod to the numerous woolen mills that populated the village. By the late 1950s virtually all of the seventeen mills in Philmont had closed, the inevitable victims of the rise of new technologies and the migration of industries to cheaper labor markets.

High Falls dressed in the multicolors of autumn.

We end our visit with a poem about High Falls written by the Columbia Land Conservancy around 2005. It is a naturalist's journey through the High Falls Conservation Area.

High Falls

At the arbor made of cedar wood is where you start
On your quest to see what lies at Philmont's heart
Lifelong residents tell of stories, childhood memories and lore
Both cultural and natural history on this hike you will explore
Down the path and on the green trail is the plan
Stonework steps lead you to cross the wide span
This perennial stream flows down from Moore Pond
To the Agawamuck Creek, the Hudson River and beyond
Welcome to an Eastern hemlock covered "cool ravine"
Uncommon plants make up this unique habitat scene

12. HIGH FALLS

You might find walking fern or purple cliffbrake
Bloodroot, red trillium, and trout lily in spring's wake
Red trillium's flower is beautiful and catches the eye
But it smells like dead meat to attract the carrion fly
Dark blood red color and putrid odor its adaptation
"Stinking Benjamin" lures the flies in for pollination
If you see these plants look close, take a sniff and inspect
However, on this site and our others please don't ever collect
On your left will be the blue trail to the Agawamuck Creek
Remain on the green trail to find that which you ardently seek
This land was once hardscrabble farmed and used as woodlots
Rocks break through the shallow and acidic soil in spots
Signs remain of stone walls and fences of barbed wire
Farther up the trail is a wooden bench to rest if you tire
Walk through woodlands of sugar maples and oaks of red
Thick tree branches form a leafy canopy above your head
A fine hunting ground for hawks or a barred owl
Perhaps a coyote or red fox on a quiet night's prowl
An understory of witch-hazel, striped maple and black birch
You can see them all close to the bench on which you perch
Black birch is used in birch beer and smells of wintergreen
And striped maple is by far the moose's favorite cuisine
Witch-hazel is discussed in the Round Ball Mountain quest
Yellow leaves in the fall—do that quest to find out the rest
Time to keep moving, gather your things and head up the hill
That's where you'll see the power that supplied seventeen mills
Soon you should hear the sound of the waterfall's torrent
Its closeness will make you pick up your pace we warrant
There is a large clearing as the trail comes up and curves around
Turn to the north, prepare to be transfixed and spellbound
From Philmont Reservoir and Summit Lake the water drops down loudly
The tallest waterfall in Columbia County we can report quite proudly
One hundred fifty feet from the dam at the top to the plunge pool at the bottom
The water rushes and gushes over the rocks in a magnificent column
In 1847, High Rock Mill was constructed for making fine woolen goods
Followed by a feed mill and paper mills using lumber from nearby woods
After a century of industry by waterpower the mills all began to close
But over High Falls and into the Agawamuck Creek the water still flows ■

PART ONE • HUDSON RIVER VALLEY & CATSKILL REGIONS

13. HUDSON RIVER SKYWALK:
THOMAS COLE HOUSE TO OLANA & MAWIGNACK PRESERVE

Location: Catskill & Hudson (Greene County & Columbia County)
NYS Atlas & Gazetteer, Tenth Edition, p. 98, B3–4; **Earlier Edition,** p. 52, C3
GPS Parking: *Thomas Cole National Historic Site*—42.226204, –73.860765;
East end of Rip Van Winkle Bridge—42.219683, –73.832121;
Olana State Historic Site—42.218150, –73.828975
GPS Destinations: *Thomas Cole House*—42.225745, –73.861504;
Rip Van Winkle Bridge—42.223447, –73.850565; *Olana*—42.217121, –73.829297
Hours: *Thomas Cole House*—grounds open daily; *Olana*—grounds open daily
Fee: Grounds—none; admissions charged to enter interior of historic homes
Accessibility: ~3.0-mile trek from Thomas Cole House to Olana; *From Cole House to bridge toll booths*— <0.3 mile; *from toll booths to east end of bridge*—1.0 mile; *from east end of bridge to Hudson River Skywalk parking*—0.3 mile; *from Hudson River Skywalk parking to North Road Trail*—0.5 mile; *from North Road trailhead to Olana*— ~1.0 mile
Degree of Difficulty: Moderate
Additional Information: *Thomas Cole House*—218 Spring Street, Catskill, NY 12414, (518) 943-7465; *Olana*—5720 State Route 9G, Hudson, NY 12534, (518) 828-1872

Directions: *Thomas Cole House*—From the New York State Thruway take Exit 21. Turn left onto Route 23B and head south for 0.5 mile, then turn left onto Route 23 and proceed southeast for >1.5 miles. At the junction with Route 385, turn right onto Route 385/Spring Street, drive south for 0.1 mile and turn left into the parking area for the Thomas Cole National Historic Site.

→ *Olana*—From the east end of the Rip Van Winkle Bridge south of Hudson (junction of Routes 9G & 23), drive south on Route 9G for ~0.8 mile and turn left onto the entrance road for Olana. Follow the road uphill for 0.9 mile to the main parking area for Olana. (There is another parking area lower down, near Cosy Cottage.)

→ *Midway parking area*—This parking area is favored by many visitors since it lies midway between the Thomas Cole House and Olana. It is located near the east end of the Rip Van Winkle Bridge at the junction of Routes 23 West and 9G.

Description: This walk takes you from Cedar Grove, the home of Thomas Cole, to Olana, the home of Frederic Church. Cole and Church were contemporaries and both were renowned nineteenth-century painters. Their homes have been beautifully main-

13. HUDSON RIVER SKYWALK

Hudson River Skywalk. Image courtesy of the Thomas Cole National Historic Site and the Olana Partnership.

tained and are open to the public. To venture from the Cole House to Olana, you will cross the Hudson River on a walkway over the Rip Van Winkle Bridge that provides you with views up and down the Hudson. The walk is a scenic adventure through areas that were often the subjects of the two artists' paintings. They were aptly called artists of the "Hudson River School."

Highlights:
Cedar Grove, the Thomas Cole House • Olana, the estate and home of Frederic Church • Rip Van Winkle Bridge • Rogers Island

Hike: We will start the hike from the Thomas Cole House, where historically the Hudson River School of painting began, and finish at Olana. Naturally, the hike can be done in reverse, from Olana to the Cole House, or it can be a one-way walk with a second car stationed at the opposite end.

From the parking area at the Thomas Cole House, walk east, following a walkway as it parallels Route 23 to your left. In >0.2 mile you will pass by the toll plaza where a bronze dedication tablet provided by George W. Williams (a state engineer) can be seen on a boulder that was taken from the excavation site. At 0.4 mile you will reach the west end of the Rip Van Winkle Bridge and begin to head over the river.

PART ONE • HUDSON RIVER VALLEY & CATSKILL REGIONS

Follow the new pedestrian walkway, completed in 2018, toward the east side of the bridge. Excellent views of the Hudson River begin to emerge. To your right, 0.9 mile in the distance, is Dutchman's Landing, an outthrust of land created by the confluence of the Hudson River and Catskill Creek. It was in this general area, originally called Hop-O-Nose, that a Native American village once flourished. The land was purchased from the Native Americans in 1682 under what became known as the Loveridge Patent, named for William Loveridge, who owned land south of Catskill.

As you traverse the walkway, you may observe a vessel or two plying the waters below, or even a barge heading upriver to the Port of Albany. In another 0.4 mile

The 5,040-foot-long Rip Van Winkle Bridge, constructed in 1935, connects the village of Catskill and the city of Hudson. Postcard circa 1940.

The Rip Van Winkle Bridge is named after a character of the same name in an 1819 short story by Washington Irving. Irving's Rip Van Winkle was a loyal subject of King George who fell asleep in the Catskill Mountains and woke up twenty years later in what was now the United States, independent from Great Britain.

The Rip Van Winkle Bridge was built in 1935 by the Frederick Share Corporation of New York. It is 5,041 feet long—nearly a mile in length—and at its highest point provides a clearance of 145 feet for vessels making their way along the Hudson River.

Prior to this bridge being built, a ferry operated between Catskill and Greendale (a tiny hamlet across from Catskill Creek) for about 200 years, finally ending services in 1937.

13. HUDSON RIVER SKYWALK

you will see land below you. You have not yet reached the opposite shore, however. What you are looking at is the south end of Rogers Island.

In another 0.2 mile the land below you vanishes momentarily as you pass over a channel that bisects the south end of Rogers Island. Land returns again for the next 0.1 mile before you cross over the southeast corner of Rogers Island and then Hallenbeck Creek.

Along the way take note of the tall hill northeast of Olana. This is 502-foot-high Mount Merino, one of the first places in the United States to graze Merino sheep, which were prized for their extremely fine wool.

Once you reach the east shore you will pass over Amtrak (the passenger train service) and come to the midway Skywalk parking area in 0.3 mile.

From the Skywalk parking area walk northeast along a paved sidewalk to the right of the guardrail for 0.5 mile. When you come to a gated carriage road, bear right and go around a barrier at the end of the road. Look for a plaque that provides information about Olana. The carriage road (the old North Road to Olana) is not only part of Hudson River Skywalk, but also part of the Empire State Trail, a 750-mile route from New York City to Canada and from Buffalo to Albany.

The hike follows a graded dirt road that winds its way up the hill through woods for <1.0 mile. You will come out near the north side of Olana where the parking area is located.

Rogers Island, also known as Vastrick Island, is a low-lying, 1.2-mile-long, 0.4-mile-wide body of land that is separated from the east shore by diked Hallenbeck Creek.

In 1628 the island was the site of an epic battle between the Mohicans and Mohawks. The two tribes had been fighting each other for control of the Hudson River and thus control of the beaver trade with the Dutch in what became known as the Beaver War. The final battle started on the mainland, where the Mohicans initially gained the upper hand. The Mohawks retreated to Rogers Island and camped for the night. Pursuing the Mohawks stealthily, the Mohicans waited until dark and then attacked. The Mohawks, however, had anticipated the raid and were able to outflank the Mohicans, defeating them soundly. The surviving Mohicans retreated back to the mainland and then into Connecticut, and the war came to an end. No trace of this battle remains on the island. Any surviving artifacts and relics were picked over a century or two ago by souvenir-hunters.

PART ONE • HUDSON RIVER VALLEY & CATSKILL REGIONS

Hiking along the old road to Olana, now a foot trail.

History: *Thomas Cole and Cedar Grove*: Thomas Cole traveled to Europe and throughout the American Northeast, but he came to live in the village of Catskill by the Hudson River and is credited with being the founder of the Hudson River School of landscape painting. In addition to his beautiful paintings featuring Hudson Valley scenes, he painted the rocky coast and turbulent ocean along the coast of Maine as well as breathtaking scenes of Europe, especially the Italian countryside.

The Cedar Grove property, former home of Thomas Cole, has a long history that began with a 1684 land grant followed by a land subdivision in 1773. John A. Thomson and his family developed adjoining lots beginning in 1797. Then, in 1815, they built the Federal-style main house that stands today, and quickly compiled a substantial farm property of about 110 acres. Despite fronting on the Hudson River, the Cedar Grove house and infrastructure were built along a local turnpike road—today's Spring Street—that crossed through the western portion of the property where the land sloped away toward the river.

In 1825 Thomas Cole ventured from New York City to Catskill. He was fascinated by the scenery and eventually came to board in the summers with John Thomson at his Cedar Grove estate. From there Cole could explore the area and

13. HUDSON RIVER SKYWALK

sketch and paint the mountain scenery. Maria Bartow, John Thomson's orphaned niece, lived at Cedar Grove. On November 22, 1836, Cole and Maria Bartow were married at Cedar Grove, which then became the Coles' home. The couple was given a suite of rooms on the second floor of the house. Cedar Grove enjoys an orientation toward the west with views of the Catskill Mountains, the source of Thomas Cole's artistic inspiration.

In addition to the main house, Cedar Grove included a cluster of outbuildings. Several of these are significant for their use as studios during distinct periods of Thomas Cole's career. Earliest was a farmhouse, often called "the cottage," which was used until 1839 when a separate storehouse/studio was built. Many of the great painters and literary figures of the day began to visit the Coles at their Catskill home. Among the calling cards in the Cole papers of the Albany Institute of History and Art is that of James Fenimore Cooper.

On January 1, 1838, the Cole's first child, Theodore Alexander Cole, was born.

1846 was a red-letter year for Thomas Cole. In 1846 Cole designed a freestanding studio—called the New Studio—south of his home at Cedar Grove. The New Studio was demolished in more recent times, but has now been reconstructed on its original footprint. Also in 1846, John Thomson died, and Thomas Cole wrote of "new duties and cares," lamenting the loss of Cedar Grove's "master's hand." But it was also in 1846 that Cole agreed to take on and mentor Frederic Church as a student, a decision of profound consequence. The two artists became friends and each admired the other's talent. After Thomas Cole's death in February 1848, Church stayed close to the Cole family. Eventually, after Church built his home, Olana, on the east side of the Hudson River across from Cedar Grove, he hired Theodore Cole, Thomas's son, to help manage the estate's farm.

Cole is buried near Cedar Grove in the Thomson family vault overlooking his beloved Catskills. Cole had mused that this location held one of his favorite views.

After Thomas Cole's death, his wife and children remained at Cedar Grove. In the late 1850s, Cole's oldest son, Theodore Cole, became active in managing the Cole farm, a role he continued into the twentieth century. In these decades there were few alterations to the house grounds or farm. Then, beginning in 1901, numerous subdivisions reduced the estate lands. In the 1930s the construction of the Rip Van Winkle Bridge approach cut diagonally through the historic Cedar Grove estate, obliterating what was left of its farmland.

Thomas Cole's grandchildren struggled to preserve his legacy at Cedar Grove, but eventually, in 1979, the property was sold out of the family. In the late 1980s the National Park Service recognized the significance of Thomas Cole and his life at Catskill, and Cedar Grove was declared a National Historic Site in 1999. But in the

PART ONE • HUDSON RIVER VALLEY & CATSKILL REGIONS

Thomas Cole House. Photo by Zio & Sons, courtesy of Thomas Cole National Historic Site and the Olana Partnership.

1980s and 1990s, funds to acquire the site were not forthcoming until the Greene County Historical Society purchased the property in 1998. Restoration of the main house followed and, in 2001, Thomas Cole's 200th birthday, Cedar Grove opened to the public.

Today the picturesque residential grounds reflect Thomas Cole's era, when the landscape was described by fellow artist Jasper Cropsey as "not to give off an atmosphere of luxury and wealth." Importantly, the panoramic views to the Catskill Mountains and their great "Wall of Manitou" (the 10-mile-long Catskill escarpment) experienced daily by Cole can still be enjoyed from the property. The entry driveway from Spring Street can still be traced, and the adjacent flower garden blooms each summer with renewed care. Close by is the Federal-style privy, built to complement the house, and Thomas Cole's studio at the old storehouse. These outbuildings have now been fully restored. Beyond is the grove of old trees, the woodlot mentioned in Thomas Cole's writings. A stand of cedar trees in the grove no doubt inspired the name of the estate, and it is possible that Cole himself selected the name before 1830.

With its scenic attributes and authentic rural amenities, the Thomas Cole National Historic Site is a living memorial to the art of its famous resident and the Romantic era in the Hudson River Valley.

13. HUDSON RIVER SKYWALK

The colorful 21-foot-high Pollinator Pavilion, a creation of Mark Dion and Dana Sherwood, was installed in 2020. It is a fantastic open-air piece—a lavender-painted work of art that pays homage to the ruby-throated hummingbird, the only hummingbird that is native to this region. It is well worth a stop while touring the Cole House, the Cole studios, and the Cole exhibition room.

Frederic Church and Olana: Frederic Church was a nineteenth-century painter and student of Thomas Cole. He traveled widely throughout the world, illustrating its features in his paintings. While studying under Cole, Church painted many Catskill region landscapes, emulating the style of his mentor, and eventually became the most successful of the Hudson River School artists.

Olana, the former home of Frederic Church, is a lavish, fanciful, Moorish-style mansion located on the east side of the Hudson River. Church designed it after his travels to the Middle East where he was captivated by Moorish architecture. Olana is almost directly opposite Cedar Grove, Cole's more modest estate. These two properties are now easily connected by the Rip Van Winkle Bridge across the Hudson River. The walk as described in this chapter is a fitting tribute to both artists, who were friends and colleagues during their lifetimes. Cole, the senior of the two artists, instructed Church for several years. After Cole's death in 1848, Church remained close to the Cole family for the duration of his life. He and his wife, Isabel, lived with the Coles while their first home, Cosy Cottage, was being built. Later, after the Churches built Olana, Frederic hired Theodore Cole to manage the Olana estate farm.

Frederic Church's extensive body of paintings includes scenes from across continents. Many are beautiful landscapes with dramatic skies. Some favorites include scenes of Niagara Falls, Mount Katahdin, and the Andes, as well as numerous Catskill Mountain scenes.

The Olana estate is extensive, providing five miles of hiking trails. In this chapter we will highlight some important features along the trails and roads at Olana, but for more extensive detail we refer you to one of our earlier books, *Trails with Tales: History Hikes through the Capital Region, Saratoga, Berkshires, Catskills & Hudson Valley*, published by Black Dome Press in 2006.

Olana Mansion—This Moorish-style castle is the centerpiece of the Olana estate. The mansion was basically complete in 1872, but Church continued to develop it for many years thereafter. It is a beautiful, enduring work of art.

The Greenhouse site and the site of Church's studio—These buildings were near the mansion at Olana but are now dismantled, and the sites are marked by interpretive signs.

PART ONE • HUDSON RIVER VALLEY & CATSKILL REGIONS

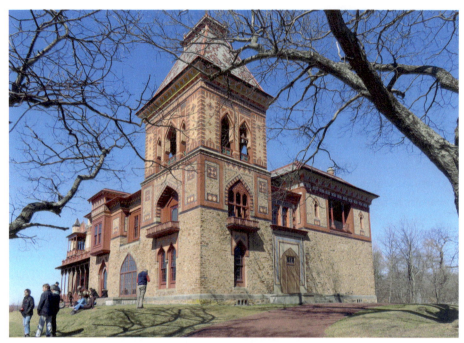

Olana—the Persian-style home of Frederic Edwin Church.

The Lake—This beautifully landscaped manmade body of water is bordered by trees and shrubs selected by Church, who designed the view from the top of the hill where the mansion is sited. He used the variety of trees much as a painter would choose dabs of paint from his palette.

Cosy Cottage—This was the first home built on the property. It was designed by Richard Morris Hunt and built in 1861 for the newlywed Churches. Cosy Cottage served as the Churches' residence until the artfully designed mansion was ready for occupancy.

The Barnyard and Kitchen Garden—These features are located near the lower parking area and served a functional purpose during Olana's period as a working farm. They are hidden from the main home and its landscaped views. ■

13. Hudson River Skywalk

MAWIGNACK PRESERVE

Location: Catskill (Greene County)
NYS Atlas & Gazetteer, Tenth Edition, p. 98, B3; **Earlier Edition**, p. 52, C2–3
GPS Parking: *Thomas Cole State Historic Site*—42.226204, –73.860765; *Mawignack Preserve*—42.227733, –73.883254
Hours: Dawn to dusk
Fee: None
Accessibility: 1.0-mile hike along loop trail
Degree of Difficulty: Easy to moderate
Additional Information: Mawignack Preserve, 52 Snake Road, Catskill, NY 12414

Directions: *Mawignack Preserve*—From the Thomas Cole National Historic Site, drive south on Spring Street for >0.1 mile. Turn right onto High Street and drive west for >0.2 mile. When you come to North Street, turn right and head north for 150 feet, then turn left onto Grand Street and continue west for 0.1 mile. Turn right onto Main Street and head northwest toward Jefferson Heights for <0.4 mile. Bear left onto Snake Road and drive northwest for 0.6 mile. Turn right into the trailhead parking area.

Van Vechten House—The Van Vechten House is near the terminus of Snake Road. The house is a privately owned residence. Enjoy a view of the house from the road and do not trespass.

Description: The trail in the Mawignack Preserve takes you through an area that Thomas Cole once hiked and that appears in several of his paintings.

A section of the trail takes you along the bed of the old Catskill Mountain Railway; another section leads along the bank of Catskill Creek.

Highlights: Open floodplain meadow & floodplain forest • Upland forest • Van Vechten House • Close-up views of Catskill Creek • Rail bed of the former Catskill Mountain Railway

Hike: The hike takes you through an area once frequented and depicted in paintings by Thomas Cole. From the parking area walk west to reach the loop portion of the trail. The trail takes you northwest and then does a mini-loop by Catskill Creek before returning southeast, following along near Catskill Creek for some of the distance.

Catskill Creek is a 46-mile-long stream that rises from the Franklinton Vlaie Wildlife Management Area in Schoharie County and flows into the Hudson River

PART ONE • HUDSON RIVER VALLEY & CATSKILL REGIONS

at Dutchman's Landing in Catskill. It is far from the largest tributary to the Hudson River, but it is a sizeable one.

Sticklers for correct grammar like to point out that Catskill Creek is tautological—"creek" is actually repeated twice because "kill" is the Dutch word for "creek." Thus, Catskill Creek is "Cats Creek Creek." The same holds true for a number of other streams with Dutch names, including nearby Kaaterskill Creek.

Take note that at the beginning of the hike you will be walking for a short distance along the rail bed of the Catskill Mountain Railway. The Catskill Mountain Railway was a narrow-gauge short line built by Charles L. Beach in 1882. The rail line originated at Catskill Landing and went through Austin Glen, a wild and impressive gorge just northwest of the Mawignack Preserve, then continued to Palenville. From Palenville, travelers, most of whom had debarked from Hudson River steamboats at Catskill Landing, would continue by coach up to Beach's Catskill Mountain House, which sat on top of the Wall of Manitou overlooking the Hudson Valley. Later, visitors to the Catskill Mountain House could continue by rail up the Wall of Manitou via the Otis Elevating Railway.

The Catskill Mountain Railway didn't have a long life, however, being abandoned in 1918 and ultimately sold for scrap metal.

History: *Mawignack Preserve*—The 144-acre preserve opened in 2018, the creation of the Greene Land Trust. It is owned by Scenic Hudson and managed by the Land Trust. The preserve includes part of the north shore of Catskill Creek, upland forests, a floodplain meadow, and a section of the rail bed of the former Catskill Mountain Railway.

A Mohican chief sold the property to a Dutch settler in 1649. *Mawignack* is a Native American word that means "the place where two rivers meet," in this case the confluence of Catskill Creek and Kaaterskill Creek. It was also the name of a seventeenth-century Algonquian village on the flats along Catskill Creek.

It was while hiking these lands that the famous Hudson River School landscape painters Thomas Cole and Frederic Church were inspired to paint some of their nineteenth-century masterpieces of the Catskill region.

Van Vechten House—Dirk Teunisse Van Vechten (1633–1702), who came to New York from the Netherlands in 1638, built a farmhouse that still stands just south of the Preserve property. The house is considered to be one of the earliest surviving examples in the Hudson Valley of a pre–Revolutionary War Dutch home. ∎

14. R. & W. SCOTT ICEHOUSE RUINS
HUDSON RIVER NATIONAL ESTUARINE RESEARCH RESERVE: NUTTEN HOOK RESERVE

Location: Nutten Hook (Columbia County)
NYS Atlas & Gazetteer, Tenth Edition, p. 82, E4; **Earlier Edition,** p. 52, B3
GPS Parking: 42.358331, –73.787375
GPS Destination: *Icehouse Ruins*—42.357665, –73.789050; *Farmhouse*—42.358790, –73.785732
Hours: Dawn to dusk
Fee: None
Special Restrictions: Removal of artifacts is prohibited
Accessibility: 0.5-mile hike along loop trail
Degree of Difficulty: Easy to moderate
Additional Information: Preserve contains a seasonal porta-potty and a pavilion

Directions: From Castleton (junction of Routes 9J/Main Street/River Road & 150/Scott Avenue), drive south on Route 9J for ~12.4 miles until you see a sign for "Nutten Hook Reserve. Part of the Hudson River National Estuarine Research Reserve" on your right.

From north of Stockport (junction of Routes 9J & 9), drive northwest on Route 9J for ~2.7 miles until you see the sign for "Nutten Hook Reserve" on your left.

From either direction, turn onto Ice House Road and head west for 0.3 mile. Be careful as you cross the Amtrak railroad tracks; the train swoops through on a regular basis, achieving speeds as great as 80 MPH. Park in the large parking area at the end of the graveled, drivable part of the road, by the kiosk.

The powerhouse ruins as seen from the Hudson River.

PART ONE • HUDSON RIVER VALLEY & CATSKILL REGIONS

Description: The R. & W. Scott Icehouse ruins represent a glimpse into part of New York State's industrial past when harvesting ice from the Hudson River was a big business. 135 icehouses populated the shoreline between Poughkeepsie and Albany.

The icehouse ruins are located at Nutten Hook, an outcrop of bedrock on the Hudson River.

Highlights: R. & W. Scott Icehouse ruins • Intact Powerhouse ruins • View of the Hudson River

Hike: From the yellow barrier at the kiosk, follow the gravel road west for 0.05 mile. Along the way take note of a gravel road to your right that leads to the shoreline in <100 feet for car-top boat launches, and also a trail opposite the road, coming in on your left. You will be returning on that trail later.

At the end of the gravel road are picnic tables, and to the left of the picnic tables is a long, 3-foot-high stone wall that faces a series of trapezoidal-shaped wedge-like blocks.

From the end of the gravel road, follow a path to the left that heads south. You will immediately pass by the surprisingly well-preserved exterior walls and stack of the powerhouse. You can walk around most of the building, if you wish, peering in through grated windows, but there is not much to see inside. Weeds and grass have essentially reclaimed the floor.

Continue south on the trail from the powerhouse ruins taking note, to your left, of the continuing foundation walls of the actual icehouse, roughly 20 feet away from the trail. The trail leads along next to the Hudson River, which is barely 20 feet away. When you come to the corner of the icehouse foundation, look for a 2-foot-by-2-foot cement block that says, "1885"—the date when the icehouse was constructed. At this point you will also have excellent views of Coxsackie across the Hudson River slightly to the south.

The icehouse's 1885 cornerstone block.

14. R. & W. SCOTT ICEHOUSE RUINS

The trail now begins to climb and does so for more than the next >0.1 mile. You are still close to the edge of the escarpment, but now the river is 50 feet below. This is an area of woods, with many chestnut trees.

At some point you will see a relatively flat area of land to your left. We wondered if this area of flatness near the top of the nubble (a small knob of land) was where a dance hall was reputed to have been located. We scoured the woods, but couldn't find any trace of a former structure.

When you come to the top of the nubble, the trail bears left and then proceeds steadily downhill. This part of the trail is wide and road-like, and was probably the road people used to drive up to the dance hall or whatever the structure was on top of the hill.

At the bottom of the nubble, you will come to a "T." Bear right and proceed south for 0.05 mile to reach Ferry Road, named for the ferry that once operated at its west end. On this short road is the circa-1900, two-story-high James Lynch house, which was placed on the National Register of Historic Places in 2009, and the circa-1881 Lynch Hotel (a single-family residence now since 1935), which was also placed on the National Register of Historic Places, in 2005. Near the end of the road is an informal public launch site where the ferry once operated.

Back at the "T," head north this time. The trail initially takes you past wetlands, to your right, and then up into a more wooded area; then the trail takes you back down into an area of thick brush and vine-strangled trees. This path is historically known as the Federal Footpath and was used by workers to go back and forth from the ferry to the icehouse.

Just before you reach the end of the trail, which enters the gravel road that you walked down to reach the icehouse, you will pass the ruins of a large building on your left. There are still a number of tall cement walls standing, as well as rusted artifacts.

As of the writing of this book, there are plans to reroute the trail.

History: The 117-acre Nutten Hook Unique Area is listed on the National Register of Historic Places and the New York State Register of Historic Places. Access to the area from Route 9J is protected by a conservation easement held by the Scenic Hudson Land Trust. It is classified as a "unique area" by the Department of Environmental Conservation because of its "special natural beauty, wilderness character, or for its geological, ecological or historical significance …" The "unique area" serves as a spawning and nursery habitat for such migratory fish as American shad, striped bass, American eel, blueback herring, short-nosed sturgeon, and alewife, and as a freshwater, tidal wetland for bald eagle and migratory waterfowl and marsh birds.

PART ONE • HUDSON RIVER VALLEY & CATSKILL REGIONS

Parts of ancillary structures can be seen near the icehouse ruins.

The name Nutten Hook is of Dutch origin, originally being *Nutten Hock* or *Newton Hock*, which means "nut-tree point." A ferry once crossed the Hudson River at this location, and a small hamlet grew up here, bolstered by the ice-harvesting and brick-making industries.

Ice harvesting as a commercial enterprise began in Boston in 1805 and rapidly spread throughout New England. In New York State the industry started in the region below Poughkeepsie and utilized a myriad of lakes and ponds. The Hudson River, being tidal, was not exploited in the beginning because it drew salt water up from the Atlantic Ocean to as far as Poughkeepsie, making the ice too brackish for use. It was also cheaper, at least initially, for the ice industry to use sources of water close to New York City.

All of this changed, however, in a matter of decades as the demand for ice for refrigeration exceeded supply. Between 1855 and the 1880s, harvested ice sold annually in New York City increased from 75,000 tons to 1.5 million tons. As the demand grew, ice harvesting expanded to include the Hudson River above Poughkeepsie.

The first really large icehouses on the Hudson River were at Castleton-on-Hudson. The industry continued to grow rapidly, and by the 1880s a total of 135 icehouses were exploiting the Hudson River for the ice it could yield. Many of these icehouses—usually painted white or off-white to deflect the sun's rays—were as large as six-story-high buildings. They were also well insulated, with the exterior walls containing a double layer.

14. R. & W. SCOTT ICEHOUSE RUINS

Ice was cut into large blocks on the river and taken to the shoreline by plow horses; from there the ice blocks were hoisted up to the icehouses by inclined conveyers or elevators powered by steam engines located in adjacent powerhouses. The ice was packed with sawdust, wood shavings, or hay in layers inside the icehouse, with each block helping to insulate the one next to it. The R. & W. Scott Icehouse could hold up to 51,000 tons of ice.

When spring arrived the ice would be transferred onto ice barges and taken downriver to service the greater metropolitan area.

The R. & W. Scott Ice Company was owned by Robert and William Scott. Their first, smaller icehouse on Nutten Hook rapidly proved insufficient in holding capacity. They then built a much larger icehouse that operated from 1885 to 1923. This icehouse was 300 feet long and 200 feet wide. Its massive size is attested to by the ruins of the foundation walls at Nutten Hook today. Fortunately, the fairly intact brick walls of the powerhouse and stack still remain standing, and it is that which first catches the eye and one's imagination.

Next to the historic ruins are two interpretive panels that provide insight into what this area once looked like. One of the panels, called "Harvesters of Winter Cold," reveals what life was like for the 100+ workers who toiled away at Nutten Hook. The other panel, entitled "Natural Ice's Rise and Fall," provides information about the icehouse itself, and ultimately its fate.

View of Coxsackie from the Nutten Hook nubble.

PART ONE • HUDSON RIVER VALLEY & CATSKILL REGIONS

In 1900 the Scotts sold their business to the Merchant Ice Company, which in 1922 sold it to the Knickerbocker Ice Company of New York. The business failed to prosper, and the property was soon abandoned. Later, the icehouse was sold to the Knaust brothers, who used the large, windowless building to grow mushrooms. The former icehouse burned down in 1934, which seemed to be the fate of most of the icehouses. It remains a study in irony—buildings purposed for ice destroyed by fire.

Since 1991 volunteers assisted by state and federal resources have worked to stabilize the powerhouse, shoreline, icehouse perimeter, and the barn. The work continues unabated, for weeds always grow back and shorelines erode.

On the dirt road leading to the Nutten Hook Preserve, you passed a yellow house with white trim on your right. Now the operational center for the Nutten Hook Preserve, it originally was a farmhouse. Next to it is a two-story barn that once housed 20 draft horses whose job was to pull the ice blocks up from the river.

The demise of the ice-harvesting industry—Why did the ice-harvesting industry decline by the early 1900s? The primary reason was modern refrigeration, of course, which began in the early 1900s and culminated in 1927 with General Electric producing and widely distributing a version of the kind of refrigerator that we are familiar with today. Refrigerators also became considerably safer around that time because methyl formate and sulfur dioxide, both deadly gases formerly used as coolants, were replaced by freon (which, to be sure, ultimately led to its own set of problems).

But a secondary factor was pollution. Thousands of factories operating on hundreds of tributaries to the Hudson River were discharging wastes into the river, making the water—and therefore the ice—increasingly toxic.

Looking back now, even if modern refrigeration had not been invented, the ice-harvesting industry in the Hudson Valley was ultimately doomed because of changes that have occurred to our climate. ■

15. JORALEMON MEMORIAL PARK

Location: Ravena (Albany County)
NYS Atlas & Gazetteer, Tenth Edition, p. 82, D3; **Earlier Edition,** p. 52, A3
GPS Parking: 42.471664, –73.863016
GPS Destinations: *Joralemon Cave*—42.471517, –73.862249; *Joralemon's Back Door Cave*—42.472146, –73.861833; *Lime kiln*—42.472120, –73.861422; *Hannacroix Maze*—42.478692, –73.862156; *Merritt's Cave*—42.475499, –73.864334; *The Fortress*—42.474625, –73.863144; *Joralemon Rock*—42.483235, –73.866292
Hours: Dawn to dusk
Fee: None
Restrictions: Normal park regulations including no hunting, littering, or damaging plants, and no open fires except in cooking areas
Accessibility: 1.0-mile hike
Degree of Difficulty: Easy if you stay on the trail; moderate for off-trail bushwhacks
Additional Information: Watch out for ticks and mosquitoes. This is an area of swamps and slow drainage.

Directions: From Ravena (junction of Route 143/Martins Hill Road & Route 9W), head west onto Route 143/Martins Hill Road and continue west for ~2.4 miles. When you come to Starr Road/Route 102, turn right.

→ *Joralemon Park*—Head northwest for 0.5 mile. You will pass by the Ravena Fish & Game Club at 0.4 mile. When you reach 0.5 mile, turn left into a large pull-off along the side of the road opposite the Blue Loop entrance. The Blue Loop entrance is just one of several entrances into the park. Additional entrances can be found along Starr Road at 0.6 mile, opposite the recreational entrance to Joralemon Memorial Park, and at 0.9 mile, diagonally opposite the tennis courts.

→ *Joralemon Rock*—Drive northwest on Starr Road for a total of 1.4 miles (or just past the junction of Starr Road and Route 106). Look for a large roadside rock (not part of the park) directly to your left. Turn around and park off-road just south of the rock.

Description: Joralemon Memorial Park is a unique 160-acre park that contains two solutional cave systems, a pre–Civil War kiln, bogs and swamps, and hundreds of moss-covered rocks and castle-like hills.

Highlights: Bogs & swamps • A nineteenth-century kiln that dates prior to the Civil War • Huge expanses of karst • Gigantic moss-covered limestone rocks • Caves • Unusual varieties of ferns • 38-hole disc-golf course • Joralemon Rock

Hike: Hikers should be prepared for a maze of trails, most of them unmarked. In places, red blazes can still be seen marking off the main road that leads through the park, but these blazes are slowly fading. Perhaps in the future new markers will be installed. In 2006 Kevin Rounds and Greg Kurtz created a wonderful disc-golf course, but an unintended consequence is that this has obfuscated the trails even further. Fortunately, the disc-golf course provides excellent points of reference, and we have used them whenever possible.

Before heading into the woods from the "Blue Loop" entrance sign, walk southeast along Starr Road for <100 feet. At the side of the embankment is a faint path on your left that leads up to a small cave approximately twenty-five feet from roadside. The cave is roughly 4–5 feet high and enterable for forty feet, although we recommend that you merely peer inside and then proceed on to the other surface features contained within the park.

Joralemon Cave is essentially dry year-round, making it geologically "dead" (meaning that it can no longer use water to produce new speleo-formations). It is thought to be the remnant of a pre-glacial master cave system, with Joralemon's Back Door Cave having been a part of it at one time.

Joralemon Cave.

15. JORALEMON MEMORIAL PARK

At one point within the last two decades, part of the interior of the cave was cordoned while an archaeological dig was undertaken.

Take note of a path to the right of the cave opening that heads slightly uphill. It quickly takes you to the top of the escarpment, or if you veer slightly to the right you will come to the top of a large stone wall foundation of an old house that once stood near the cave.

Blue Loop Trail—Begin the hike at the Blue Loop trailhead. You will immediately notice enormous blocks of limestone to your right. These are the first of many large rocks that you will see as you hike through Joralemon Memorial Park.

Following the old road into the woods, you will pass by disc-golf hole #19 in 200 feet. After another 100 feet, turn right and walk over to disc-golf basket #18, which overlooks a swamp. Facing the basket, bear right and walk between two, 8–10-foot-high rocks that are close by. Continue straight ahead, walking near the base of a ridge to your right that slowly increases in height. In 200 feet you will see Joralemon's Back Door Cave, slightly uphill. Geologists believe that this tiny cave at one time was connected to Joralemon's Cave. The opening permits a small crawl, but the cave really doesn't go any distance into the bedrock.

In another 100 feet you will reach the limestone kiln, located at the top of the small escarpment. As a point of orientation, disc-golf hole #11 is close by.

The remains of a pre–Civil War kiln.

> **Limestone Kiln**—The kiln is one of more than fifty that operated in the Clarksville-Coeymans area. Measuring approximately 8 feet by 8 feet, the kiln is set into the face of the escarpment. The roots of a tree that has taken hold at the top of the kiln have infiltrated the structure, breaking the middle section of the wall apart (yet now, ironically, holding what remains of the structure together). Keep in mind that you are looking at the foundation ruins of a kiln that dates back to the mid-1800s.
>
> Onondaga limestone, which constitutes most of the bedrock throughout the park, had many uses—as a building material, for the production of paper, and as a fertilizer by farmers eking out a marginal living in the local area. By the 1860s the lime kiln industry had hit its zenith and began its inevitable downslide.
>
> An 1865 map of the area shows that T. H. Martin was residing in the vicinity of the kiln, but whether he was associated with the kiln is not known. Perhaps the old ruins near Joralemon Cave are what remain of his house.

Continue following the escarpment wall southeast for another 100 feet or so to reach an old stone wall. This stone wall is just one of several that you will encounter in Joralemon Memorial Park, a reminder of days when the land was farmed or opened up to grazing animals. Twenty-five feet beyond the stone wall is a deteriorating stone foundation—the remnants of a small structure that at one time was probably associated with the kiln.

Return to disc-golf basket #18 and, from there, back to the main road, turning right. You will soon pass by disc-golf basket #19, to your left, and then come to a continuation of the swamp, on your right.

The swampy bog provides an opportunity to observe a variety of wetland inhabitants. Take note that the park is home to over 25 species of fern, making it one of the premier fern grottos in New York State. Depending upon the season, you will also encounter a wide variety of flowers that flourish on the limestone bedding—trilliums, wild geranium, Dutchman's breeches, violets, columbine, bishop's cap, Solomon's seal, may apple, anemones, squirrel corn, and jack-in-the-pulpit.

As you continue past the swamp you will see disc-golf basket #21, fifty feet off in the woods to your right. That will tell you that you are heading in the right direction.

Shortly after, you will walk past disc-golf hole #22, also to your right. The main road now starts to go uphill, and despite some minor variations continues to do so for another 0.2 mile. If you look very closely, you may notice one or two red blazes

15. JORALEMON MEMORIAL PARK

Christy Butler is dwarfed by one of the many large rocks in Joralemon Memorial Park.

on the trees along the way. When the road passes through an opening in an old stone wall, look to your right to see disc-golf hole #26, thirty feet into the woods at the edge of a small escarpment.

From here the road soon comes to a "T." Even when the trees are leaf-bearing, you should be able to see the Hannacroix Swamp straight ahead. Either bushwhack

Hannacroix Maze contains 2,000 feet of cave passageways, but all of these channels are contained within an area 200 feet by 200 feet. What this means, then, is that the cave is truly a maze, with passages endlessly crisscrossing but never leading very far in any one direction.

The Maze serves as a slow drain, siphoning off water from the swamp. The passageways are typically wet, slimy, and filled with leaches, which is generally unpleasant enough to discourage all but die-hard cavers from exploring its interior. Until the mid-1970s there were thought to be two separate caves here, named "Sleeping Alligator" and "Choice," but then two additional small caves were discovered and all four were subsequently linked together to form one huge complex.

Geologists believe that both Hannacroix Maze and Merritt's Cave (coming up next on our hike) were formed after the last glaciation.

over to it, walking straight ahead, or find a faint path from the road. You will end up on a plateau of fissured bedrock at the edge of the swamp close to disc-golf hole #27. If you find yourself at disc-golf basket #26, which overlooks the swamp from a rocky mound, then you have gone too far east.

Be careful of the footing in this area. It is easy to misstep and twist an ankle.

You are now standing on top of Hannacroix Maze, where the outlet stream from the swamp enters. Listen carefully and you will hear water draining out through the underground cave system.

If you walk around the fissured bluff overlooking the swamp, you will notice a 15-foot-wide dam between blocks of limestone that beavers have engineered to keep water from draining out too quickly from the swamp. Beavers have not only changed the topography of the land, but have substantially slowed down the rate by which Hannacroix Maze, a solutional cave, is developing.

The swamp next to Hannacroix Maze has an eerie look to it, with hundreds of dead trees jutting up from the still waters like skeletal toothpicks. A beaver lodge close to the shore provides a spark of life to what otherwise would be a dank and dreary place.

From the swamp, walk back to the "T" intersection.

Facing away from the swamp, turn right and follow the old road east. In a

Looking out across Hannacroix Swamp from a limestone bluff.

15. JORALEMON MEMORIAL PARK

moment the road heads steeply downhill and then veers left, going through an opening in a stone wall. After the stone wall, the road begins to pull away from the ridge. Instead of staying on the road, bushwhack to your left along the base of the ridge for 200 feet. It should be an easy bushwhack since you are following the bottom of a ridge line. After ~200 feet look to your left to see disc-golf basket #27, slightly uphill. This will reassure you that you are heading in the right direction. From here continue along the base of the ridge for another <100 feet as it becomes more cliff-like. When you reach a pile of massive rocks strewn across the side of the slope, you have reached Merritt's Cave.

Merritt's Cave—The huge blocks of talus belie the fact that there is a cave inside the hill, and one that is very maze-like, containing 900 feet of passageways. In this respect it is similar to Hannacroix Maze. As with the Maze, Merritt's Cave should not be entered except by experienced hardcore cavers who don't mind a little hardship. For most people it should be considered a surface feature to enjoy rather than a cave to explore. Hannacroix Maze and Merritt's Cave are connected, with water from the Hannacroix Maze flowing through Merritt's Cave, but it is doubtful that any caver has found a space large enough to crawl through in order to get from one to the other.

From the jumble of boulders, head south for 100 feet following what looks like a dry streambed. Turn left and head up a path along the side of the escarpment until you come to the top of Merritt's Cave and disc-golf hole #28. From here follow a path north for 50 feet to a nearby disc-golf basket that was unnumbered when we last visited.

From this point the goal is to follow the crest of the ridge for as far south as you can, negotiating a series of small rocky hills and rock-strewn dips in between. Starting off, you will descend to disc-golf hole #24 within a minute or two, and from there you follow a worn path that leads to disc-golf basket #23. This part of the hike can feel very adventurous as you make your way through a variety of rock formations.

The last hillock that you ascend to is what we are calling "The Fortress." It contains a rocky dome that has been fractured into large block-like pieces containing short passageways between them. It is the highest point along the ridge line.

Scamper down the west side of The Fortress to reach disc-golf hole #6. Follow the ridge line to disc-golf basket #20, and from there take a path that leads through a field of medium-sized rocks. Once through the rock field, veer left, bushwhack a short distance to the swamp you passed at the beginning of the hike, and follow the main road, to your right, out to the Blue Loop entrance.

History: *Joralemon Memorial Park*—The land encompassing Joralemon Memorial Park was purchased from the Joralemon estate in 1975 by the Town of Coeymans.

PART ONE • HUDSON RIVER VALLEY & CATSKILL REGIONS

In the early 1920s it was owned by Frank Joralemon, for whom the park is named, according to research by David Ross, vice president of the Ravena-Coeymans Historical Society.

Joralemon Park encompasses 160 acres of interesting and unique landscape in addition to its pavilion, tennis courts, playground, and ball field. This park truly has something for everyone. Perhaps the park's most readily distinguishable feature is its huge number of large rocks, some the size of cars or garages. It was after visiting this park that author Russell Dunn was prompted to write a regional guidebook about mammoth glacial erratics and rock formations, *Rambles to Remarkable Rocks: An Explorer's Hiking Guide to Amazing Boulders and Rock Formations of the Greater Capital Region, Catskills & Shawangunks.*

Joralemon Rock—The most amazing rock in the area, however, is not found in Joralemon Park, but nearby. "Joralemon Rock" (a name we have given it) is nearly 15 feet high and 15 feet long. It is an erosional remnant, meaning that all of the surrounding bedrock has been eroded away, leaving this rock standing on its own. The rock's most distinguishing feature is its incredibly long north side overhang that has produced a 10-foot-long shelter cave. There is enough space that you can almost stand up inside of it.

There is a second sizeable rock near Joralemon Rock, less than 30 feet away but mostly hidden by the trees. ■

Joralemon Rock with its astonishing ten-foot overhang.

PART TWO
CAPITAL REGION

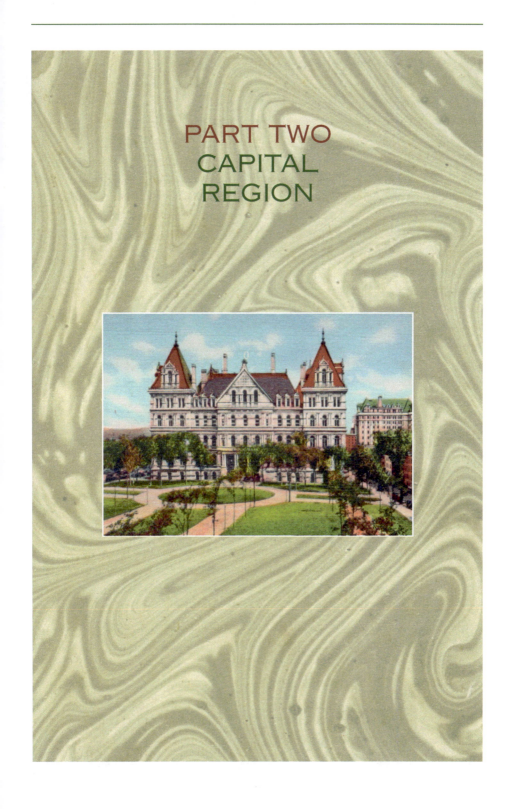

PART TWO • CAPITAL REGION

16. WASHINGTON PARK

Location: Albany (Albany County)
NYS Atlas & Gazetteer, Tenth Edition, p. 82, B4; **Earlier Edition,** p. 66, CD3–4
GPS Parking: 42.659147, –73.776087
GPS Destinations: *Rustic Pedestrian Bridge*—42.658058, –73.773513; *Lake House*—42.656250, –73.771943; *King Memorial Fountain*—42.655014, –73.770083; *Henry Johnson Memorial*—42.653818, –73.768969; *Robert Burns Statue*—42.655087, –73.767980; *Soldiers & Sailors Monument*—42.656688, –73.766783; *Willett Rock*—42.656522, –73.765629; *James H. Armsby M. D. Memorial*—42.656851, –73.768403; *Peninsula Rock*—42.655960, –73.772587
Hours: Daily, dawn to dusk
Fee: None
Restrictions: Dogs must be leashed.
Accessibility: 1.8-mile stroll
Degree of Difficulty: Easy
Additional Information: The Washington Park Conservancy (washingtonparkconservancy.org), founded in 1985, is a not-for-profit all-volunteer organization created to preserve, protect, and promote Washington Park.

Description: Washington Park is an urban park central to the city of Albany, the capital of New York State. The park was established in 1873 by the Albany Common Council. It is beautifully landscaped in the tradition of (but not by) Frederic Law Olmsted. Its central features are a manmade lake spanned by a decorative curved bridge with wrought-iron railings, a boathouse with an amphitheater, lovely gardens that surround a prominent fountain featuring Moses, and roads and paths designed to wend through a green landscape with carefully selected trees and shrubbery, some dating back to the earliest days of the park. Over the course of the park's history, a variety of monuments have been erected and are described in this chapter's history section.

Directions: From Albany (junction of Route 20/Madison Avenue & Route 443/Lark Street), drive northwest on Route 20/Madison Avenue for 0.6 mile. Turn right onto South Lake Avenue and drive northeast for 0.1 mile, parking on either side of the road near the traffic light at the end of Hudson Avenue (a one-way street).

A Stroll through Washington Park: From the traffic light at the end of Hudson Avenue, walk east down a paved walkway that leads to the northwest end of Washington Park Lake. You will come to a railed, square-shaped cement platform with

16. WASHINGTON PARK

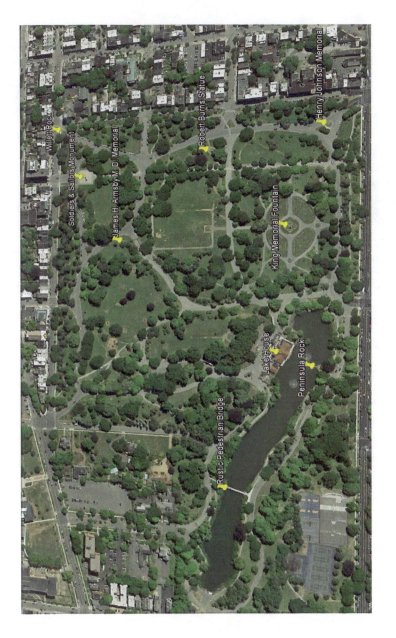

benches overlooking the lake where the underground inlet stream enters. This part of Washington Park Lake is much reedier than its main section, farther east.

Follow an earthen path clockwise around the north side of the lake. In >0.1 mile, you will reach a rustic pedestrian footbridge. The major features and attractions of the park, such as this bridge, have been added to the terrain piecemeal over the years.

PART TWO • CAPITAL REGION

Original Lake House. Postcard circa 1900.

The ***Rustic Pedestrian Footbridge*** was constructed in 1875. The elegant curved span of the bridge with its decorative wrought-iron handrails and lampposts spans the lake in an east/west direction. From the middle of the bridge, the views feature the lake fountains and the ornate Lake House.

From the north end of the footbridge, continue along the lakeshore path for another >0.1 mile, going around the Lake House and over to the southeast end of the lake. Take note of the Park Playhouse as you pass by the rear of the Lake House. The playhouse has been providing summer theater in Albany since 1989. The amphitheater opposite the playhouse stage can seat up to 1,500 patrons.

The original ***Lake House*** was constructed in 1875, the same year as the footbridge. During that period, the lake, the footbridge, and the Lake House were the central attractions in the park. Visitors loved the lake, which was stocked with several varieties of fish. Swans, as well as "Swan Boats" for hire, floated on the lake. In winter, after the lake froze solid, skaters glided on its surface.

By the 1920s the old Lake House was showing significant signs of deterioration and was torn down, replaced in 1929 by a Spanish Revival–style building created by J. Russell White.

Walk across an interior park road and then follow a brick-covered path that leads east for 250 feet to the King Memorial Fountain, also known as the Moses Fountain. As you walk along, pay particular attention to the variety of trees that you see on this stroll.

16. WASHINGTON PARK

The King Memorial Fountain. Postcard circa 1910.

The *King Memorial Fountain*, sculpted by J. Massey Rhind, a Scottish-American sculptor, was erected in 1893. The fountain's focal point is a bronze statue of Moses smiting the rock for water on Mount Horeb (the mountain upon which the Bible says Moses received the Ten Commandments from Yahweh). The four figures at the base of the mountain represent the four stages of life—infancy, youth, adulthood, and old age. The fountain is named for Rufus H. King and was presented as a gift to the people of Albany by his son, Henry Laverly King.

The fountain is located in the center of a formal garden laid out by William S. Egerton, who was superintendent of the park grounds for 38 years.

Such outdoor memorials, however, suffer from wear and tear. In 1988 the statue of Moses was thoroughly cleaned and wax-coated to protect it from further weathering. An arm was also reattached to one of the four statues on the base of the fountain.

From the King Memorial Fountain, walk south for >50 feet to a historic marker that provides background information about the origin of the Albany Tulip Festival. Take note that in May, generally coinciding with Mother's Day, this whole section surrounding the King Memorial Fountain is one huge display of multicolored tulips.

The *Albany Tulip Festival* began on May 14, 1949, and has been an Albany tradition ever since. It started in 1948 when Mayor Erastus Corning II passed a city ordinance declaring the tulip as Albany's official flower. But there were many kinds of tulips to choose from. Which one would be the official tulip for Albany? To have

PART TWO • CAPITAL REGION

this question answered by the country where Albany's Dutch heritage originated, Mayor Corning sent a request to Queen Wilhelmina of the Netherlands (the land of tulips) asking her to designate one specific variety of tulip for Albany. She did so, and the "Orange Wonder"—an 18-inch-tall tulip that is orange in color and scarlet toward its center—became Albany's official tulip. The "Orange Wonder" is a relatively rare flower, which increased its appeal as an Albany symbol. We should also note here that Albany was originally called Fort Orange when it was part of the Dutch colony of New Amsterdam.

The Pinksterfest, which can be traced back to Dutch tradition, has been incorporated into the festival, as well as Mother's Day, which includes the "Mother of the Year Award." Annually, a Tulip Queen is chosen. Every year without fail, approximately 90,000 tulip bulbs are planted in the fall around the King Memorial Fountain, timed to erupt into a magnificent display of color the following spring.

From the Tulip Festival sign, head east for >250 feet to reach the west end of the historic Promenade. Along the way look straight ahead and you will see in the distance the top of the 589-foot-high Corning Tower located in the Empire State Plaza.

The Promenade, which during the nineteenth century was referred to as "The Mall," is a wide pedestrian road lined with park benches that spans the park from Madison Avenue on the southern end to the Soldiers and Sailors Memorial on the

The Mall. Postcard circa 1910.

16. WASHINGTON PARK

northern end. It provides ample space for walkers in both directions, and the benches are generously distanced for maximum privacy and to provide a pleasant place to rest and contemplate your surroundings. Today we associate the word "mall" with a series of connected buildings typically containing retail stores and restaurants. In past centuries, however, the word "mall" meant something else. It referred to a promenade or sheltered walk, or a street that had been closed off to vehicular traffic.

Before you start walking along the Promenade, head east for another 150 feet to the Henry Johnson Monument. Be mindful of the traffic as you make your way across a fairly well-used street to reach the traffic island.

The *Henry Johnson Monument* memorializes (William) Henry Johnson, who was born in North Carolina in 1892, moved to Albany while in his teens, and died in 1929. Johnson was in the first African-American unit in the U.S. Army to see combat in World War I. In 1918 while on sentry duty in the Argonne Forest, he engaged a German raiding party in hand-to-hand combat, killing a number of German soldiers, rescuing a fellow American soldier, and receiving 21 wounds in the process. He received the *Croix de Guerre* from the French government for his heroism, but was not recognized by America until 1996, when President Bill Clinton posthumously awarded Johnson a Purple Heart. Then, in 2002, he was awarded the Distinguished Service Cross. Finally, after a staffer for Senator Charles Schumer discovered a letter from General John J. Pershing praising Johnson's actions, President Barack Obama added Johnson to the list of Medal of Honor winners in 2015. Nearly a century later, Johnson had finally received the recognition he deserved.

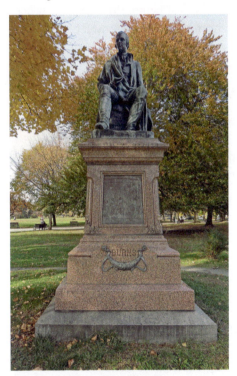

The Robert Burns statue framed by the colors of autumn.

The Henry Johnson Monument, which was erected in 2015—the same year that Johnson was awarded the Medal of Honor—lies on a tiny, triangular-shaped traffic island. Johnson was further memorialized with Henry Johnson Boulevard, which enters the northeast side of the park.

PART TWO • CAPITAL REGION

Return to the Promenade and walk northeast for 0.1 mile, imagining how it must have been in pre-automobile days when the walkway was filled with Victorian strollers and vintage bicycles. As soon as you cross over a wide road that is a pedestrian continuation of Hudson Avenue, follow a path to your right that quickly leads to and circles around the Robert Burns statue. The circular pathway encourages you to view the statue and its four copper panels from all angles.

Robert Burns, the Ploughman Poet and the National Bard of Scotland, lived from 1759 to 1796. He is perhaps best remembered for writing the lyrics to "Auld Lang Syne," the traditional New Year's Eve anthem. *Auld Lang Syne* translated means "old long since," or "long, long ago."

The bronze statue of Burns, sculpted by Albany-born Charles Calverley, was erected in 1888. The four panels around the base, each containing one of Burns's poems, were carved by George H. Boughton, a well-known illustrator, writer, and genre painter, and installed three years later. The Saint Andrew's Society, named in honor of Scotland's patron saint, raised the money in 1978 to ensure the statue's continued preservation.

Back on the Promenade, continue northeast. Just before the next wide pedestrian road crossing, follow a path to your right that leads to Lancaster Street. Look for a historic marker next to the street; you are standing by what were the Park's original tropical gardens.

The historic marker reads:

A Tropical Oasis: Originally part of the 1806 Middle Square, this was the first area of the Park to be reopened as Washington Park in 1871. It was not until 1878 that 25 thousand plants were brought here to create a large "tropical garden." In the late 1950s, the garden's 35-foot-diameter, central flowerbed was removed and the area cut in half when Lancaster Street was extended into the Park. Since then the gardens have dwindled. The paths and the outline of some beds can be seen north of Lancaster, but where you stand virtually no evidence remains.

Return to the Promenade and continue northeast for 0.1 mile to reach the imposing Soldiers and Sailors Monument, by far the largest monument in the park. Fittingly, it lies near the terminus of Henry Johnson Boulevard, named after an American World War I hero.

The *Soldiers and Sailors Monument* is made of Tennessee marble and sits on top of a Stony Creek granite base. A bronze statue holding the palms of victory represents our nation. It was sculpted in 1911 by Hermon A. MacNeil and erected in 1912 by the Grand Army of the Republic (a fraternal organization composed of Civil War veterans of the Union Army, Union Navy, Marines, and the U.S. Revenue Cutter Service). The monument contains the legend, "The Nation at Peace won through Victorious War."

In 1986 the monument underwent restoration and was renamed the *Albany Veterans Memorial Monument*. The same woman who had unveiled the original monument as a 12-year-old girl unveiled the restored monument as an 85-year-old woman. It is a massive piece of marble and granite, dwarfing any of the other monuments in the park. It stands at a height of 22 feet, is 21 feet long, and over 5 feet wide. The platform that it rests on is 70 feet long and 64 feet deep.

From the Soldiers and Sailors Monument, walk north to State Street. Turn right and head east on State Street for 250 feet to reach the historic Willett Rock at the junction of State Street and Willett Avenue. As you stroll along the sidewalk, take a moment to look at some of the old historic residences that face Washington Park.

Willett Memorial Rock is a 16-ton glacial erratic that was brought to Washington Park in 1907. A plaque was affixed to it commemorating Colonel Marinus Willett for his service during the French and Indian War and the American Revolution. It reads:

> In grateful memory of Colonel Marinus Willett 1740–1830. For his gallant and patriotic services in defense of Albany and the people of the Mohawk Valley against Tory and Indian foes during the years of the war for independence. This stone brought from the scenes of conflict and typical of his rugged character has been placed here under the auspices of the Sons of the Revolution in the State of New York by the Philip Livingston chapter of Albany. 1907.

Interestingly, the boulder was not originally placed where you see it today. Its back faced Henry Johnson Boulevard (in earlier days known as Northern Boulevard) but became a traffic hazard because of a sharp curve in the road in front of the rock. For this reason the boulder was moved to its present location in 2006, approximately 180 feet from its original position.

Return to the Soldiers & Sailors Monument and walk diagonally west across a grassy field for 0.1 mile to the James H. Armsby Memorial, which is next to an interior traffic road.

The *James H. Armsby Memorial* consists of an elevated bust of James H. Armsby who, along with Alden March, cofounded Albany Medical College in 1839. Dr.

Armsby was also instrumental in the creation of the Dudley Observatory, which remains the oldest non-academic institution of astronomical research in America. The bust of Armsby was erected in 1879 and has the distinction of being the first memorial in the park.

From the Armsby Memorial follow a pedestrian park road on your left north for 0.1 mile. At a "T" bear left and continue following the road back to the southeast end of Washington Park Lake. The serpentine-shaped lake, an impoundment of Beaver Creek, covers 5.2 acres and averages less than 7 feet deep. You won't see a stream issuing from the lake because, just like the inlet, all water is conducted underground, having been integrated into the Albany sewer system.

From here take a path along the south side of the lake past a tiny peninsula with a large rock at its end until you come to a historic marker titled "Boats & Music." This marker provides information about the original boathouse. The Lake House that appears in these images is very different from the building that stands in front of you today. The existing Lake House, designed by Albany's J. Russell White, was built of brick and terra cotta in 1929. It replaced the original 1875 wood structure attributed to Frederick Brown, who also designed the similarly featured row houses behind you on Madison Avenue.

Although different in style, both buildings were intended to facilitate lake-related pastimes such as boating, fishing, and ice skating. The original structure housed a

Washington Park Lake. Postcard circa 1900.

16. WASHINGTON PARK

bandstand in its open central tower; today's tile-vaulted bandstand is located on the north side of the structure, facing a terraced hillside.

From the historic marker continue on the lakeshore for 0.2 mile, passing by the rustic pedestrian footbridge after 0.1 to reach the northwest end of the lake and your starting point.

History: Step into any corner or byway of the park and you are walking through layers of Albany's and New York State's history. The approximately 90 acres that are now Washington Park have been walked by Native Americans, early Dutch settlers, and generations of immigrants and their descendants from the seventeenth century to today.

At one time the land that would become the park was on the outskirts of the city proper; hence, sections of it were used for various other purposes throughout Albany's rich history. In eighteenth-century colonial times, what came to be park land was a burial site for Native Americans and African slaves. By the early nineteenth century the land above Willett Street was the site of the old State Street burial grounds, possibly used for residential landowners; however, many of those graves were transferred to Albany Rural Cemetery by the late nineteenth century.

At one time the park area near the southern border was the location of a munitions powder house, but the fear of explosion of the ammunition stores was a constant worry. In 1786 the Albany Common Council issued an ordinance "for the better securing of Albany from the danger of gunpowder." The powder house was moved uptown to what is appropriately named Magazine Street. When Albany's Fort Frederick was dismantled, some of its stone as well as the enormous lock and key to its ammunition stores went to the new powder house. The historic old lock and key now repose at Albany Institute of History and Art (AIHA).

Washington Square was the remaining parcel of land on the southern border; it had long been used for military drills and as a parade ground.

In 1868 the concept of "a beautiful park"—the at-that-time somewhat startling proposal for a municipal park—was proposed to the Common Council by the Albany Institute. The idea was not so widely accepted in 1868 as it would become in the ensuing decade. Once the populace realized it was getting 90 acres of gracious space elegantly landscaped with flowerbeds, 1,000 trees, monuments, and a good-sized lake, it warmly embraced Washington Park. In 1871 the park was opened to the public, though it was not completed at that time. Important park features continued to be constructed through the 1870s. ■

PART TWO • CAPITAL REGION

17. HOLLYHOCK HOLLOW SANCTUARY

Location: South of Feura Bush (Albany County)
NYS Atlas & Gazetteer, Tenth Edition, p. 82, C3; **Earlier Edition,** p. 66, D2
GPS Parking: 42.540360, –73.870760
GPS Destinations: *Trailside Quarry*—42.541302, –73.869433; *Big Quarry*—42.544323, –73.869298; *Sinkhole*—42.547376, –73.870482; *The Cone*—42.542637, –73.873152; *O'Neil House*—42.541374, –73.871610; *Onesquethaw Rocks*—42.542240, –73.874833; *Second Sinkhole*—42.540886, –73.871049
Hours: Daily, dawn to dusk
Fee: None
Restrictions: No motorized vehicles, camping, or fires permitted; observe "carry in, carry out"; hikers asked to remain on trails
Accessibility: *White Trail*—1.5-mile hike (estimated); *Creek Trail*— ~0.4-mile hike
Degree of Difficulty: *White Trail*—Moderate; *Creek Trail*—Easy to moderate
Additional Information: Trail map available at kiosk shelter at start of hike or online at news10.com/off-the-beaten-path

Directions: From south Albany (junction of Route 9W & I–787) drive southwest on Route 9W for ~1.4 miles. Turn right onto Route 32 at a fork and continue southwest for ~6.3 miles. When you reach Feura Bush, turn left onto Old Quarry Road/Route 102 and drive south for 3.0 miles. Bear right onto Rarick Road, head northwest for 0.2 mile, and then left into the parking area for the Hollyhock Hollow Sanctuary.

Description: Hollyhock Hollow Sanctuary is a 138-acre preserve that contains nearly 3.5 miles of trails. The preserve offers hikes to interesting and unusual sites including several old limestone quarries, a large sinkhole, a dissected streambed, and giant boulders along Onesquethaw Creek. The preserve also features a wide assortment of songbirds, butterflies, hummingbirds, and wildflowers.

Highlights:
Several abandoned quarries varying in size from small to large • Huge limestone rocks along Onesquethaw Creek • Areas of karst with ledges, depressions, and fissures • Large trailside sinkhole • Site of an eighteenth-century farmhouse • Songbirds and flowers

Hike: *White Trail*—From the parking area, walk across Rarick Road to the kiosk shelter, where a map of the sanctuary can be reviewed. This hike follows

17. HOLLYHOCK HOLLOW SANCTUARY

One of a number of quarries that populate the landscape.

the White Trail for its entire distance, taking you around the perimeter of the preserve.

Head northeast on the White Trail for 50 feet and then veer right, following the White Trail as it wends its way southeast past a number of limestone ledges, depressions, fissures, and stony outcroppings. If you are doing this hike in the early spring or late fall when all the deciduous trees are leafless, it will be as though you possess x-ray vision and are able to see all of the landforms around you that otherwise would be obscured by foliage. Until the 1940s all the lands around you were open fields with just a smattering of old trees. What you see today is a second-growth forest of hickories, white pines, shagbark, hop hornbeams, and red maples.

Within 0.1 mile you will start to see old quarries on both sides of the trail. One quarry in particular, with 8-foot-high walls, is noticeable to your right.

Soon the path does a U-turn and quickly comes around to a *Trailside Quarry* on your right, where a 10-foot-high, 20-foot-long jumble of rocks and stone slabs is piled on the opposite side of the trail. The rocks in this heap were quarried and then discarded, perhaps because of imperfections that made them commercially unsuitable. A tiny, 15-foot-long spur path can be followed into the quarry for those who wish to take a closer look at the surrounding rock walls.

During the time that the sanctuary property was owned by the Audubon Society of New York, a reddish-colored sign with white lettering could be seen in front of the quarry. It read: "Stone Quarry. It is said that stones from the quarry are part of the Brooklyn Bridge."

The limestone at Hollyhock Hollow Sanctuary was formed by sand silts and fragments of animal and plant matter that settled to the bottom of an ancient sea 395 million years ago. Look carefully at the limestone blocks littering the landscape around you and you will see fossils and small shells embedded in the rock. Limestone proved to be a particularly good rock for quarrying because of its tendency to fracture in straight vertical and horizontal lines when struck.

Continue north on the White Trail for another 0.3 mile. As soon as you begin to see houses off in the distance to your right, look for a large quarry, also on your right, only 10 feet from the trail. We have named it the ***Big Quarry***. It's possible that this quarry or one close by is the quarry mentioned by John Johnsen in his report on limestones of Albany County, issued nearly half a century ago. Johnsen refers to a Quarry #2 on land owned by Robert Rienow and describes it as being 85 feet long, 65 feet wide, and 15 feet deep.

During the years that Quarry #2 operated, over 83,000 cubic feet of rock were removed, weighing in total an estimated 6,972 tons. The quarry began operating around 1870 and was overseen by a man named Jagger. The limestone extracted

The sanctuary's most curious feature is its large sinkhole.

17. HOLLYHOCK HOLLOW SANCTUARY

from Quarry #2 was used for railroad bedding. In the early 1900s the quarry was taken over by Callanan Industries and then permanently shut down in the 1930s.

As you continue your hike, take note of how the land around you exhibits increasingly more karst topography over the next 0.1 mile. In places you will be walking across bedrock loaded with fissures and open cracks.

At the junction with the Red Trail, bear right and head north. Up until recently a sign at this junction pointed out that the stone walls visible throughout the sanctuary are a reminder that this land, however rocky, was once farmed.

In another 0.05 mile you will pass through an opening in an old stone wall. Immediately after the stone wall, begin looking to your left for what initially looks like a fort on top of a small hill. Appearances can be deceiving, however, for what appears to be a fort turns out in the end to be just a hill with a stone wall at its top.

The trail takes you up to the top of this hill as it swings left and begins heading northwest. In <0.1 mile, you will come to the northernmost part of the preserve. Just as you turn away from posted land and open fields, a sinkhole comes into view on your left.

This *sinkhole*, virtually next to the trail, is one of the main attractions and landforms in the sanctuary. In the past, unsightly orange-colored plastic webbing encircled the sinkhole to safeguard the unwary from stumbling into the pit. Today an unobtrusive cord seems to suffice. Hikers, however, are asked to stay clear of the

The Cone is one of a number of strangely shaped rock formations.

sinkhole. You will see warning signs posted. What makes the sinkhole dangerous is not only its depth, but that the earth and rock overhanging the pit could break loose. Parents should keep a sharp eye on children here.

The sinkhole is around 30 feet long and 15 feet wide. We estimate its depth to be 20–30 feet.

There is a *second sinkhole* at the Hollyhock Hollow Sanctuary. It lies 40 feet north of Rarick Road, diagonally across from where the Rienow Memorial Building once stood. Although the sinkhole looks very small and barely enterable, it is covered with a locked grill that we are assuming cavers installed to keep the curious out. In spring an overflow of water gushes *out* from the sinkhole and is channeled underground through a pipe down to Rienow's pond.

From the large sinkhole continue west and then down two small ledges that are separated by 200 feet. You will begin to notice just how terraced and varied the landscape is.

Soon you will pass by the Green Trail, coming in on your left, and in another 0.2 mile you will enter a forest of evergreens. When you come to a large circular depression amidst the pines, take note of the rock formations near the center of the depression. We have named one *The Cone* because of its inverted cone shape. This rock formation is nearly 5 feet high and is fairly prominent, as it is located near the trail.

Leaving the evergreen forest behind, you will pass by the Orange Trail junction and then, after another 100 feet, come to where the Gree*n* T*r*ail enters on your left. Bear right here, following a sign that indicates the way to the parking area. In a moment the back of the O'Neil House, to your right, is passed (a spur path leads down to the house and Rarick Road). When you come to the junction with the Red Trail, in <0.1 mile, turn right and follow the White Trail back to the kiosk shelter in 100 feet.

These directions may sound complicated, but in reality all you need to do is stay on the White Trail from start to finish and you will automatically return to your starting point.

Creek Trail—Follow the blue-marked Creek Trail downhill from the rear of the parking area to Onesquethaw Creek, where 70-foot-high eroded bluffs loom above the stream, visual proof that erosion continues to shape the landscape before you.

Onesquethaw Creek is a small stream that rises in the hills south of John Boyd Thacher State Park and flows into Coeymans Creek southwest of Feura Bush. The name *Onesquethaw* is Mohawk for "place where the corn grows." What's interesting about Onesquethaw Creek is that the stream periodically vanishes underground, only to reappear at some point farther downstream. The reason for this disappearing

17. HOLLYHOCK HOLLOW SANCTUARY

act is the solubility of the limestone bedrock over which Onesquethaw Creek flows. This porous limestone has created a myriad of caves and underground passageways in both Albany and Schoharie counties. When you are walking on a dry section of Onesquethaw Creek, the river may actually be flowing silently and invisibly under your feet.

The Creek Trail leads up from the stream along a spine of land, then past a small pond and into more open ground. The seemingly insignificant pond that you passed by on your right was once the handmade swimming pool of Robert & Leona Train Rienow, who owned the land until the late 1980s. Water was brought up from Onesquethaw Creek to the pool through a filtration system, and then returned to the creek again.

The path that leads down to the pond from Rarick Road, directly across from the O'Neil House, was how the Raricks walked back and forth to their little Shangri-La area.

Although the buildings no longer exist, at one time there were several small cabins on the grounds that swimmers could use as changing facilities. Electric lights were also strung around the pool to provide illumination at night, and parties were frequently held here. A square-shaped cement block on the lawn near the pool is all that remains from those days.

Until recently a plaque displayed in the open area read, "England is a garden, and gardens are not made, By saying oh how beautiful, And sitting in the shade." What remains today are two hefty rocks in the center of the clearing.

At the edge of the open ground is a small pavilion called the "Water Watch," which overlooks Onesquethaw Creek. It is a nice place to linger while observing the scenery and natural fauna. Recently a bench has been added in memory of Margaret K. Parker.

Continue on the blue-marked trail as it parallels Onesquethaw Creek. Within 150 feet you will see on the opposite bank of the stream a curious stone wall 10 feet up the embankment. It goes nowhere and seems to serve no obvious purpose. Was it the side wall of a mill? A bridge abutment? For the life of us, we couldn't come up with an explanation for its existence. We later talked with Ron Dodson, a retired wildlife biologist and educator who worked for some time for the Audubon Society of New York State at the Hollyhock Hollow Sanctuary. He had no explanation for the stone wall either, but remembered that a gristmill once operated in the general area.

Within 0.1 mile from the parking area, the trail emerges onto Rarick Road. The views from the road are intriguing, for this small section of Onesquethaw Creek is strewn with enormous limestone boulders, a few of them nearly the size of automobiles.

Robert & Leona Rienow at work.

Stay alert for passing cars as you walk along this short stretch of the road.

After 200 feet the trail picks up again to your left and reenters the woods, where there are more large and varied boulders to view.

Follow the Creek Trail as it takes you around a bend in the stream where the west bank again towers above the water. Within a moment or two you will come to the part of the creek that excited us the most. Look for several enormous rocks in the streambed, and scamper down to the level of the creek. You will be rewarded with views not only of these rocks but also of where the rock-solid bank of the stream is breaking apart into huge blocks of limestone.

Scamper back up to the top of the stream bank and follow the Creek Trail straight out to Rarick Road. At this point you have gone >0.2 mile from the parking area.

The trail doesn't end at Rarick Road, however. Cross over Rarick Road and pick up the Creek Trail next to what looks like the walls of an old roadside quarry. Follow the blue-blazed Creek Trail into the woods for another 0.1 mile. When you

17. HOLLYHOCK HOLLOW SANCTUARY

come to the White Trail, next to where The Cone formation is located, turn right and proceed southeast. In 0.05 mile bear right onto the Orange Trail and follow it southeast for 200 feet. You will exit from the woods by the Rienow Memorial brass plaque, cemented into a large oblong rock. The plaque is located at the far western corner of where the Rienow house stood before it burned down. Look around and you will eventually find an old hand pump about 15 feet from the road, not far from the Rienow Memorial plaque.

The house that you see nearby was earlier called the Mary E. O'Neil Educational Center. It was named for a good friend and admirer of Dr. Rienow who bequeathed a substantial sum of money to the Audubon Society upon her death. O'Neil had no direct involvement with the Hollyhock Hollow Sanctuary, but the Audubon Society dedicated the building to her in recognition of her bequest and her association with Dr. Rienow.

When both of the Rienows were still alive, a woman caretaker by the name of Gertrude "Gerdy" Frasier lived in an upstairs apartment in the O'Neil house at a time when the lower part served as a garage. Leona Rienow was so captivated by Gerdy's personality that she wrote a book about her in 1987 entitled *Unbottled Scotch*.

It's hard to imagine today how the property along Rarick Road once looked. A number of the buildings no longer exist. You would never know, for instance, that near the O'Neil House was a large barn for 150 chickens. Like a lot of history here, it has vanished into the past.

History: The Hollyhock Hollow Sanctuary, encompassing 138 acres of old farmlands and limestone quarries, is the former estate of Dr. Robert Rienow (also called "the Colonel") and his wife, Leona Train Rienow. Dr. Rienow was a professor of political science at the State University of New York at Albany; Leona was an accomplished writer.

Together the Rienows collaborated on a book published in 1967 by Dial Press entitled *Moment in the Sun: A Report on the Deteriorating Quality of the American Environment*. The authors were concerned about the negative effect that a growing population was having on the environment. Many believe that the book may have been a catalyst for the creation of Earth Day. The Rienows also collaborated on a number of other books including: *The Year of the Eagle*; *Of Snuff, Sin, and the Senate*; *The Lonely Quest: The Evolution of Presidential Leadership*; and *Our New Life with the Atom*.

Dr. Rienow was a founder of the Audubon Society of New York State and of the Eastern Chapter of The Nature Conservancy, the inception of which took place in 1953 on the Rienows' property.

The Rienow house after fire devastated the home in 1988. Photograph by Ron Dobson.

Leona Train Rienow died in 1983 following a stroke. She authored a variety of books, some for children, including *The Bewitched Caverns* and *The Dark Pool*.

In 1988, tragedy struck when Dr. Robert Rienow, age 79, died in a fire that consumed the historic home in which he lived, a house that was built by an unknown Dutch farmer in 1746.

In his will Rienow bequeathed his estate to the Audubon Society of New York State for use as a public preserve. The Audubon Society rehabilitated a two-story building on the property, converting it into offices, which they named the Rienow Memorial Building. The society maintained their headquarters at the preserve until 2013. By 2015 the Rienow Memorial Building had fallen into disrepair; it was razed and cleared away, leaving behind just a 25-by-40-foot cement floor next to the parking area.

In January 2020 the Audubon Society transferred ownership of the sanctuary to the Mohawk Hudson Land Conservancy.

It is a landscape with history that predates the Rienows, however. During colonial times the property was used for farming and grazing, which must have been a major effort because of the meager layer of topsoil that overlies the limestone bedrock.

In the nineteenth century the land became commercially valuable for quarrying because of its limestone. Blocks of limestone were excavated and exported for construction projects, including the Erie Canal and possibly the Brooklyn Bridge.

Limestone kilns were also established for producing charcoal here, and the woods, already significantly cleared away for farming, were further obliterated. The trees that you see today constitute a second-growth forest.

Birds—Considering the Audubon Society's former stewardship of the preserve, it should come as no surprise that over 80 species of birds have been seen at the sanctuary. Sixty of these nest on site, including belted kingfishers, cedar waxwings, barred owls, and great blue herons.

The sanctuary's name comes from the hollyhock, a tall Eurasian plant with large, coarse, rounded leaves and spikes of flashy flowers. ■

Large rocks populate the streambed along Onesquethaw Creek.

PART TWO • CAPITAL REGION

18. JOHN BOYD THACHER STATE PARK
Section I: High Point & Hang Glider Cliff

Location: Altamont (Albany County)
NYS Atlas & Gazetteer, Tenth Edition, p. 82, A1; **Earlier Edition,** p. 66, C1
GPS Parking: 42.676856, –74.047504
GPS Destinations: *Stonehenge formation*—42.677070, –74.046831;
High Point—42.685756, –74.036532; *Hang Glider Cliff*—42.679834, –74.031756
Hours: Daily, dawn to dusk
Fee: None
Accessibility: *High Point*—1.4-mile hike; *Hang Glider Cliff*—2.2-mile hike (or 0.8-mile hike from High Point)
Degree of Difficulty: Moderate
Additional Information: *Trail map*—parks.ny.gov

Directions: From New Salem (junction of Routes 85 & 85A) drive uphill on Route 85 heading southwest for 0.9 mile. Turn right onto Route 157/Thacher Park Road and proceed northwest for 4.5 miles. When you come to Route 256/Ketcham Road, turn right and head northwest for 1.6 miles. Then turn right onto Route 157/Thompson Lake Road and go north for 0.5 mile. At Old Stage Road turn right and head northeast for 0.7 mile. Finally, turn right onto Carrick Road (a dirt road), drive east for 0.3 mile to its barricaded end, and then turn left into a sizeable parking area after 250 feet.

From Altamont (junction of Route 156 & Main Street & Prospect Terrace) follow Route 156 uphill, going southwest, for 1.8 miles. Turn left onto Old Stage Road and proceed southeast for 1.2 miles. When you come to Carrick Road turn left and follow it for >0.3 mile east to its end, then turn left and head north for 250 feet into a parking area.

Description: High Point and Hang Glider Cliff are two overlooks located in a more recently acquired section of the John Boyd Thacher State Park. John Boyd Thacher (1847–1909) was mayor of Albany, a New York State senator, a writer, book collector, and manufacturer. Following his death in 1914, the land was donated to New York State by his wife, Emma Treadwell Thacher. Since then, additional lands have been acquired, bringing the total parklands to 2,155 acres. The park encompasses six miles of limestone cliffs and is considered to be one of the richest fossil-bearing sites in the world.

The most prominent section of the park, known as Indian Ladder—a hiking trail at the base of the Helderberg escarpment—was discussed in detail in our previous book *Trails with Tales: History Hikes through the Capital Region, Saratoga, Berkshires, Catskills & Hudson Valley*.

18. JOHN BOYD THACHER STATE PARK

Highlights: Areas of karst • Stonehenge formation • High Point • Proximity to historic caves • Hang Glider Overlook • Abandoned cement structure • Abandoned quarry

Hike: From the parking area, walk over to the nearby Fred Schroeder Memorial Kiosk. The kiosk and the memorial trail are named for a regional philanthropist and nature lover who along with his family made generous financial contributions to Thacher Park. An intriguing Stonehenge-type formation lies a hundred feet to the left of the kiosk.

Stonehenge—This rock formation near the kiosk is impressive and sure to raise the questions of who built it and why. We consulted with the Altamont Historical Society, but no one seems to know who put the huge slab stone pieces together, even though it seems evident that heavy equipment must have been used. Until several decades ago one large, horizontal slab rested on two opposing rock columns until it cracked near one end and collapsed inward.

At some time in the past, a building must have stood on this huge expanse of flat, pavement-like bedrock, because if you look closely you will notice bits of glass, bricks, and mortar scattered about. It is not known who used this site or for what purpose, but there is evidence that some quarrying was done off of the Perimeter Trail extension of Carrick Road.

A modern-day Stonehenge.

From the kiosk follow the red-blazed Fred Schroeder Memorial Trail as it leads northeast through a deciduous forest, slowly heading downhill. In 0.5 mile you will come to a junction with the now abandoned, white-blazed W-2 Trail that enters to your right. (The W-2 Trail can still be followed, but is fading away quickly as the forest seeks to reclaim it.)

Turn left and follow the Fred Schroeder Memorial Trail as it heads steadily downhill for 0.2 mile. It will take you to a lower plateau and to an intersection called the "Four Corners." The GPS reading here is 42.680011, -74.039682. Visible to your left are old rock walls.

Continue straight ahead (north), now following the white-blazed W-3 Connecting Trail. You will come to the aqua-blazed Long Path/red-blazed Fred Schroeder Memorial Trail in <0.4 mile, just after you pass by a small area to your right where the bedrock has collapsed to form a tiny sinkhole.

Turn right onto the Long Path/Fred Schroeder Memorial Trail (a sign here states, "High Point Cliff. 0.3 mile") and proceed east. After 0.2 mile you will pass by a 5-foot-deep area of collapsed bedrock to your right. This pit, as well as multiple fissures in the bedrock along the trail, illustrates how easily limestone can be eroded by surface conditions.

In another couple of hundred feet, you will reach a junction. Go left, following a trail that takes you to **High Point** within 150 feet. The views are breathtaking and

High Point, overlooking the village of Altamont.

expansive from here. Several private homes along Leesome Lane can be seen below, including one with its own pond. To your north is the village of Altamont; to your southeast, perpendicular to High Point, is the Hang Glider Overlook (which this hike will reach shortly).

Walk back from the cliff for less than 100 feet and bear left onto the aqua-blazed Long Path/red-blazed Fred Schroeder Memorial Trail, which leads to Hang Glider Road in 0.8 mile. (Note: a fainter, less traveled path goes off to the left just before you reach the Long Path/Fred Schroeder Memorial Trail. This path leads south, staying fairly close to the escarpment edge.)

For this hike, follow the established Long Path/Fred Schroeder Memorial Trail south. It pulls slowly away from the escarpment ridge, then parallels it. This part of the hike takes you near an area where two famous caves are located—Wynd Cave and Livingston Cave. Neither is visible from the trail or close to it, nor are they easy to find if you detour to look for them. Interested hikers should contact the Helderberg-Hudson Grotto (a local caving organization) through their Web site, caves.org/grotto/hhg/about.php.

Livingston Cave—In *Underground Empire: Wonders and Tales of New York Caves*, Clay Perry, a writer for the *Berkshire Eagle* and a 1940s explorer, gives an account of hiking to Livingston Cave, which involved "rock climbing, falling down, boring through dense brush, and tripping over loose rocks and each other, as we did a side-hill dodger stunt, clinging close to the sheer cliff and going halfway around the High Point bluff, which rises almost 1,000 feet above the village [Altamont]. ... We came, finally, to a fine *porte-cochere* sort of entrance. ... The cavern is a tunnel that branches three ways—west, northwest, and southwest." Mike Nardacci, writing decades later in *Guide to the Caves and Karst of the Northeast*, states that the cave "itself is formed in Manlius limestone and has about 300 feet of passage. It consists of one main joint-controlled passage and one side crawl."

Wynd Cave—Perry writes that Wynd Cave is named for the Wynd brothers, whose activities in the nineteenth century were nefarious. It is for this reason that the cave is also known as the Wynd Brothers Robber Cave. Nardacci states that Wynd Cave is the slightly longer of the two caves and more easily accessible because it is located on top of the escarpment. Wynd Cave was visited by Professor Theodore C. Hailes, whose name is associated with Hailes Cave and the Hailes Cave picnic area in the main part of John Boyd Thacher Park.

After heading south for 0.4 mile (halfway to Hang Glider Road), you will come to a junction where the red-blazed Fred Schroeder Memorial Trail goes off to your right and the aqua-blazed Long Path continues straight ahead. Take neither trail. Instead, turn left onto a well-established unmarked path that provides a scenic shortcut to Hang Glider Cliff. Almost immediately you will pass by an informal trail coming in on your left, which is the unmarked path that connects to High Point.

Within 0.2 mile the path takes you down into a deep notch and then back up to the opposite side as it passes through a scenic area of towering pine trees and a forest floor carpeted with pine needles. In another <0.2 mile you will come out onto a large grassy open area at an exposed part of the escarpment. You have arrived at the *Hang Glider Cliff.*

A short, inclined cement ramp extends toward the rounded edge of the cliff. This site provides a launch ramp for hang gliders and paragliders. The Hang Glider Cliff flight record is 71 miles nonstop all the way to Walton, New York. From here there are superb views of Altamont off in the distance, with the High Point cliffs some distance away to your left.

A plaque on the cement launch reads, "Fly Forever Dad." Just below, in smaller letters, are the initials "ECS, Jr." and "1919–1992." A fair amount of research has been done by others to learn who the person was and who installed the plaque, but so far the identities of both remain a mystery.

Once you have finished enjoying the magnificent views from Hang Glider Cliff, follow the magenta-blazed Hang Glider Road Trail southwest. In 0.4 mile you will pass by the aqua-blazed Long Path/Indian Ladder Trail (to your left) and then, in another 0.1 mile, the Long Path (to your right). Soon after, you will reach a junction where the white-blazed W-5 Cross-Over Trail enters on your right.

Hang Glider Cliff (people actually do hang-glide from here).

18. JOHN BOYD THACHER STATE PARK

If you wish to take a short diversion from the Hang Glider Cliff Road, follow the white-blazed W-5 Cross-Over Trail north. In less than 0.1 mile you will begin to see the ***World's End Sinkhole*** to your left, an extensive depression in the earth.

This sinkhole is named for the World's End Gun Club that previously used this area. There is no easy way to bushwhack into the sinkhole, particularly during the summer when the area is filled with lush growth and thickets. It's far better to wait until late fall or early spring to explore this unusual land feature. A stone wall heads off perpendicularly from the road into the woods here, which provides an excellent guide into the sinkhole. At the bottom of the sinkhole, you will discover several inaccessible caves where water flows in after heavy rainfall.

In another <0.05 mile along the W-5 Cross-Over Trail, a rusted but fairly intact automobile is encountered, a reminder that these lower roads were once used by cars. A sign entitled "Gasoline Alley" has been installed on a tree next to the wreckage.

Return to the magenta-blazed Hang Glider Road and continue southwest. Take note of the small creek to your right. This is the stream source for the World's End Sinkhole. After a few moments you will come up to the yellow-blazed Perimeter Trail, so-named because it marks the southwest border of the park. Turn right onto the Perimeter Trail and head northwest. Carrick Road and the parking area are only 0.5 mile from here.

Along the way, after 0.4 mile, look for a metal post to your right whose tip has been painted red. The post marks the start of the former, now abandoned, white-blazed W-2 trail (whose other end was passed by earlier in the hike). If you follow that trail northeast for >0.05 mile, off in the woods to your left will be an abandoned 10-by-12-foot cinder-block building that was once used by the local rod & gun club. You will find the structure to be surprisingly intact, lacking only a door and roof. As far as we know, this is the last intact structure in the Carrick Road part of Thacher Park.

Return to the Perimeter Trail and continue northwest. Just before you reach the end of the road, look for an open pit to your left that harkens back to the days when the High Point area was quarried. Follow a gravel path next to the pit uphill for views of a second, upper part of the quarry.

Back on the Perimeter Trail, hike for another minute and you will reach the barricaded end of Carrick Road and the parking area. ∎

PART TWO • CAPITAL REGION

18. JOHN BOYD THACHER STATE PARK
SECTION II: UPPER MINELOT CREEK

Location: New Salem (Albany County)
NYS Atlas & Gazetteer, Tenth Edition, p. 82, B1; **Earlier Edition,** p. 66, CD1–2
GPS Parking: *Paint Mine Area*—42.651440, –74.014944;
Beaver Dam Road—42.638513, –74.016958
GPS Destinations: *Parking Lot Falls*—42.650652, –74.014697;
Lower Falls—42.649670, –74.015084; *Secret Cascade*—42.648220, –74.016374;
Upper Cascade—42.645371, –74.014340; *Cistern*—42.645604, –74.018459;
Disappearing stream—42.643305, –74.015230; *Stone foundations on east side of Saw Mill Road*—42.643170, –74.014820; *Stone foundations on west side of Saw Mill Road*—42.642595, –74.015472; *Minelot Pond*—42.640971, –74.015853;
Pancake Rock—42.639849, –74.017171
Hours: Daily, dawn to dusk
Fee: None
Restrictions: Dogs must be leashed.
Accessibility: *Saw Mill Road*—0.9-mile hike; *Cistern*— <0.3-mile hike; *Trail along Minelot Pond*— >0.3-mile hike; *Trail to Solitary Rock*— <0.4-mile hike (round-trip)
Degree of Difficulty: Easy to moderate
Additional Information: *Trail map*—thacherparkrunningfestival.com

Directions: From New Salem (junction of Routes 85 & 85A) head southwest on Route 85 for 0.9 mile. When you come to Route 157 near the top of a long, winding hill, turn right and drive north for <3.8 miles. Turn left at the entrance to the Paint Mine Area and park after 0.05 mile near the end of the parking area.

From Altamont (junction of Route 156 & Main Street & Prospect Terrace) follow Route 156 uphill, going southwest, for 3.3 miles. Turn left onto Route 157/Thompsons Lake Road and head southeast for 1.8 miles. When you come to Ketcham Road, turn left and proceed east for 1.6 miles. Turn left onto Route 157 again (which is now Thacher Park Road) and go southeast for 0.7 mile. Finally, turn right into the entrance for the Paint Mine Area and park.

Description: This hike takes you along a section of John Boyd Thacher Park that follows Minelot Creek south from the Paint Mine parking area up to Minelot Pond, a sizeable marshland pond. Along the way you will see a variety of interesting features including gorges, waterfalls, swamplands, a beaver dam, beaver lodge, old stone foundations, limestone formations, and a disappearing stream—all located along the

18. JOHN BOYD THACHER STATE PARK

abandoned, 0.9-mile-long Saw Mill Road (now part of the Long Path) between Route 157 and Beaver Dam Road.

Highlights: Waterfalls • Limestone ridges • Caves & underground streams • Old foundation ruins • Swamp • Pancake Rock • Solitary Rock

Hike & History: From the Paint Mine parking lot follow the path closest to Minelot Creek, passing by an 8-foot-high cascade as you climb up to the next higher level. Continue following the path as it takes you along the edge of a gorge to an overlook, where a 15-foot-high cascade (Lower Cascade) can be seen below. The path then immediately comes out onto Saw Mill Road, a name that old maps have given to this road because a sawmill once operated next to it. (For the sake of clarity, we also will call the road between the Paint Mine parking area and Beaver Dam Road, "Saw Mill Road.") This road once extended all the way down to Meadowdale, continuing through the rock-cut blasted out in 1821 that is now the west entrance to Indian Ladder. This lower part of the road was known as Indian Ladder Road.

Opposite from where you came out onto Saw Mill Road is a lime-blazed park road that leads south for 0.2 mile, passing by an abandoned park building to your right as well as dilapidated picnic tables and unused fireplaces, ending at a cul-de-sac from where the road continues as a trail. This is clearly an abandoned part of the park.

Back on Saw Mill Road, proceed south for <100 feet. Turn left onto the aqua-blazed Long Path/red-blazed park road, immediately crossing over a footbridge spanning Minelot Creek. A number of small cascades falling over ledges can be seen upstream. After 50 feet turn left onto a short path that leads to an overlook above the Lower Cascade that you saw a moment ago from the top of the gorge.

The Lower Cascade looks considerably shorter than it did when you saw it from above. It is all a matter of perspective. Because the cascade is fairly elongated, it appears taller when seen from higher up.

While you're at the overlook, be sure to look upstream to see a 6-foot-high cascade not far downstream from the footbridge. If you wish to see the Lower Cascade from its base, there is a short but steep path that takes you down to the bottom. Much to our surprise we saw that a picnic table had been placed next to the base of the cascade.

Return to Saw Mill Road, which is now marked by aqua, red, and lime blazes, and proceed south for 200 feet until you come to a tiny creek carried under the road by a drainpipe.

Secret Cascade is rarely visited since no path leads to it. The waterfall is not difficult to reach, however, and involves an easy bushwhack of no more than 0.1 mile. Simply follow the tiny creek from the road, heading west through the woods until you reach a deep-cut gorge in the escarpment to your left where several minor cascades, including the 8-foot Secret Cascade, can be seen. Judging by a plethora of abandoned stone fireplaces scattered about in the woods, this area was not so secret in years past. At one time it served as part of a picnic grove, likely accessible from the lime-blazed park road that you passed by earlier.

Return to Saw Mill Road by following the creek back downstream. As long as you stay by the creek, there is no danger of getting lost or disoriented during this short bushwhack.

Continue south on Saw Mill Road until you come to a second drainpipe going under the road. To your right is a fairly well-defined ravine with a seasonal cascade. Unfortunately, the ravine is choked with blowdown, making conditions generally unfavorable for viewing the cascade.

Starting here, Saw Mill Road begins to climb steadily, staying close to Minelot Creek. A gorge soon forms on your left and deepens to 50 feet, narrowing as it becomes increasingly more defined. A wooden fence has been placed where part of the side wall of the gorge has dropped away. Fifty feet beyond this fence is a short spur path that takes you to an overlook of a sizeable cascade at the intersection of two deep-cut gorges.

Continue up the road as you parallel the waterfall-producing stream to your left. When you reach the red-blazed/yellow-blazed road, turn left, immediately

The Magic of Minelot Creek—Although this section of Minelot Creek often appears bone-dry except following periods of intense rainfall or spring's snow-melt, there is still a significant volume of water running by you. The reason you can't see it is because the stream is flowing underground. The bedrock under Minelot Creek, like much of the area, is made of limestone, an extremely soluble rock that is easily eroded, allowing for underground passages and caves of various sizes.

To check out this phenomenon first-hand during the drier months of the year, follow Minelot Creek upstream for <100 to the spot where the creek suddenly disappears, pirated away underground. Minelot Creek serves as a reminder of just how honeycombed Thacher Park is with its caves and other karst topography. Bear in mind, however, that if you are visiting in the early spring or after significant rainfall, what you will see is Minelot Creek brimming with water and flowing along its streambed, its underground system simply overwhelmed by the volume of water flowing from Minelot Pond.

18. JOHN BOYD THACHER STATE PARK

Old stone ruins near Minelot Pond.

crossing over a drainpipe carrying the stream. In 50 feet turn left again onto a tiny, well-worn path.

Junction of two canyons—The well-worn path takes you to the end of a narrow spine where two deep-cut canyons come together, forming an inverted "V." The waterfall to your left, plunging over the top, is the one you just saw a moment ago from Saw Mill Road. This is one of the most spectacular spots in the park, rivaling any that you see along the Indian Ladder Trail, High Point, or Hang Glider Cliff.

Return to the red-blazed/yellow-blazed road and turn left. After walking another 25 feet you will come to a totally unexpected and seemingly completely out-of-place object for such a wooded area—a manhole cover. The manhole cover is part of the park's water system that was created in 1924. The pipes brought water down from nearby Thompson Lake and furnished it to the park's former Olympic swimming pool (near where the park's general offices are located today), restrooms, and other park facilities.

Continue past the manhole cover, crossing over an earthen bridge that divides the easternmost gorge into two sections. A large drainpipe, buried below the surface, carries the stream under the road and releases it into the gorge, producing a small cascade. As soon as you pass by a wooden fence, turn left and follow an informal path along the top of an escarpment for several hundred feet. In places you will glimpse sections of a 6-inch-diameter pipe running along the side of the escarpment, part of the park's early water lines. In a moment you will come to a spot where you can look to your left to see the rocky spine between two canyons that you stood on moments ago.

Retrace your steps back to Saw Mill Road.

PART TWO • CAPITAL REGION

Minelot Pond, the pond source for Minelot Falls.

As you start walking south on Saw Mill Road, take note again of the waterfall-producing stream running next to the road. Follow the stream with your eyes to where it goes under the road, emerging to your right from a rocky spring. You are looking at Bobby Rock Spring. On a good day, 20,000 gallons of water flow out of it. In the past, a nearby cistern would collect and store the water.

In <0.05 mile you will come to the white-blazed W-1 Road (earlier called Suto Road), which enters on your right. Follow it past the marshy north end of Minelot Pond and up to the top of a hill in <0.3 mile, where a 60-foot-by-35-foot, rectangular-shaped building can be seen. The building serves as a water storage unit (cistern) for the park. Although the road continues beyond this point, the land is posted and is off-limits to the public. Before leaving, take a moment to walk around the water-storage facility, whose size is impressive.

Head back down the W-1 Road to Saw Mill Road and turn right. In another 100 feet you will come to Minelot Creek just before an unmarked road, to your left.

From the creek bed, bushwhack up to Saw Mill Road, just a short distance away. When you reach the point where Saw Mill Road momentarily divides as it goes uphill (only to rejoin a moment later), look for a 15-foot-long, 30-foot-wide stone foundation to your left, ~25 feet from the road.

Steam-powered sawmill—It was in this general area that a portable, steam-powered sawmill once operated on land leased from Henry van Zandt. Italian immigrants were employed for manpower. A steam-powered sawmill engine worked by turning water into steam and then using steam pressure to push a piston back and forth inside a cylinder that would drive a connecting rod and flywheel to power a buzz saw or vertical saw. Although the sawmill on Saw Mill Road didn't need to be on a stream in order to draw power from a waterwheel, like earlier sawmills did, it still had to be reasonably close to a source of water for generating steam.

Where Saw Mill Road momentarily divides, bear right and head uphill. Almost immediately to your right you will see a short, descending path that leads to the northeast end of Minelot Pond where a breached cement dam, augmented by a beaver dam, has reduced the flow of water leaving the pond. Were it not for the beavers, the pond's water level would be considerably lower than it is today.

Continue uphill on Saw Mill Road for a few more feet until you reach the top of the first hill. Then bear right onto a well-worn path that leads in 50 feet to a high bluff overlooking Minelot Pond.

Minelot Pond is the headwaters of Minelot Creek, a stream that has produced most of the cascades you have visited along the hike, as well as 116-foot-high Minelot Falls, which is in another section of the park along the Indian Ladder escarpment.

Look for birdhouses set into the marshy areas, and note the limestone cliffs that look down from the opposite side of the pond. Depending upon the time of year, Minelot Pond will either look like a sizeable wetland pond or a vast marshland with a tiny pond. The pond sits in a large, crater-like bowl, perhaps the remains of an old sinkhole.

There are a number of intriguing geological points of interest in this area—Daddy Longlegs Cave (on state land), Witches Hole (on private land), and Forgotten Cave (on state land), as well as two rock formations that we will be seeing shortly.

Instead of returning immediately to Saw Mill Road, follow a well-worn informal path that goes along the top of the Minelot Pond escarpment. By walking this path, you will quickly realize just how big Minelot Pond/marshland is.

In 0.05 mile the trail passes through a large stone wall. The wall is a reminder of just how hard and tenaciously early settlers worked to farm the land or use it for grazing—neither of which likely worked out all that well considering the limited amount of topsoil covering the limestone bedrock. Look for a beaver lodge in the pond not far from the stone wall.

Now take a look to your left through the trees. What appears to be a towering bluff at first glance is actually the 25-foot-high back side of a medium-sized landfill (one that you will pass by later when you return via Saw Mill Road).

Forging ahead you will enter an area filled with evergreens and then, in another moment, ascend to the top of the escarpment and up to a junction where you can either go right, left, or straight ahead. Proceed straight ahead on a path that, along with the path to the right, forms a 0.4-mile loop that takes you past an isolated, 8-foot-high, 10-foot-long rock that we have dubbed "Solitary Rock." Upon closer examination you will see that Solitary Rock is actually a rock slab and that it lies within a stone's throw from Beaver Dam Road.

The loop takes you back to the junction at the top of the escarpment. This time, take the trail that goes left, following it north momentarily along the edge of the escarpment and then east across an area of fractured bedrock. You will come to "Pancake Rock," to your left, in <0.1 mile.

Pancake Rock is a fanciful name that we have given to this odd-looking rock formation that, with a liberal dose of imagination, looks like a stack of large pancakes. The rock is ~4 feet high and probably as many feet wide, and it is definitely part of the bedrock. It would appear that the bedrock surrounding Pancake Rock

Pancake Rock is an odd erosional remnant.

18. JOHN BOYD THACHER STATE PARK

was gradually eroded away until only this one surviving remnant remained. You will see that a stone wall comes up to Pancake Rock from both sides. Apparently an early settler decided to take advantage of the odd-shaped rock and incorporate it into the stone wall he was fashioning.

From Pancake Rock follow the path through the woods for 100 feet to Saw Mill Road. Turn right and walk north on Saw Mill Road for <0.1 mile to the barrier just before Beaver Dam Road. Old maps show that this junction was once called Smith's Corners, named after Benny Smith, who moved to this location prior to 1850 and established an all-in-one grocery store, blacksmith shop, and post office. A sizeable cellar foundation is visible to the right of the barrier.

Turn around and walk north on Saw Mill Road. In 0.2 mile you will pass by the landfill on your left. Years ago, before the landfill, beehives were kept here, and many years before that, this was the site of a two-story house owned by Henry van Zandt. Van Zandt, who had previously lived with his parents, William and Margaret Van Zandt, in a nearby log cabin on Beaver Dam Road, built a more substantial house here for himself. After Henry's house was razed, it was still possible to see the foundation ruins for a number of years until the landfill covered it completely.

From the landfill keep walking north. In <0.2 mile, you will pass by the blue-blazed road that enters on your right. After another 25 feet bear left and bushwhack into the woods for 30 feet. You should end up next to the fairly intact stone ruins of an old cellar that measures ~7 feet by ~8 feet. This structure may also be associated with the stream-driven sawmill that operated in the general area.

Continue north on Saw Mill Road again, essentially retracing your steps, returning to the parking area in 0.5 mile. ■

PART TWO • CAPITAL REGION

19. JOHNSON HALL STATE HISTORIC SITE
WILLIAM JOHNSON STATE HISTORIC SITE

Location: Johnstown (Fulton County)
NYS Atlas & Gazetteer, Tenth Edition, p. 65, B7; **Earlier Edition,** p. 79, D5
GPS Parking: *Johnson Hall State Historic Site*—43.015632, –74.383323;
Sir William Johnson's grave site—43.006444, –74.373149
GPS Destinations: *Johnson Hall State Historic Site*—43.016278, –74.383384;
The Lookout—43.014054, –74.382842; *Sir William Johnson Statue*—43.012434,
–74.380765; *Sir William Johnson's grave site*—43.006590, –74.372986
Hours: *Grounds*—Dawn to dusk; *Johnson Hall*—Reservations must be made in advance. Seasonal tours are conducted Wednesday through Sunday, 10:00 AM—3:00 PM.
Fee: *Grounds*—No charge; *Johnson Hall*—Admission charged (call or check Web site)
Accessibility: *Paved walkway*—0.4-mile walk; *Paved walkway & earthen trail*—0.6-mile walk
Degree of Difficulty: Easy
Additional Information: Johnson Hall, 139 Hall Avenue, Johnstown, NY 12095; (518) 762-8712

Directions: *Johnson Hall*—From Johnstown (junction of Route 29/Main Street & Route 30A/Comrie Avenue) drive west on Route 29/Main Street for 0.7 mile. At the traffic light, instead of continuing straight onto Route 67, bear right, following Route 29/West State Street northwest for 0.5 mile. Bear right at a "V" onto Hall Avenue, past

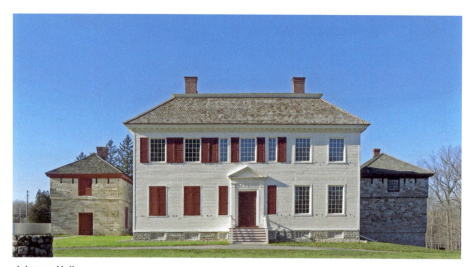

Johnson Hall.

19. JOHNSON HALL STATE HISTORIC SITE

the statue of Sir William Johnson to your left, and continue northwest for another 0.3 mile to the parking area.

William Johnson's grave site—From Johnstown (junction of Route 29/Main Street & Route 30A/Comrie Avenue) drive west on Route 29/Main Street for <0.6 mile and park to your right as soon as you pass by Market Street. William Johnson's grave site is by the southeast corner of St. John's Episcopal Church, near the corner of West Market Street and North Market Street. You will pass by the church on your drive to Johnson Hall.

Description: Johnson Hall is the historic estate of Sir William Johnson (1715–1774), his consort, Molly Brant (~1736–1796), a Mohawk, and their eight children. While living here, Johnson became the most influential person in the colonial Mohawk Valley. By establishing good relations with the Six Nations of the Iroquois, Johnson was able to secure their allegiance to the British during Great Britain's battle with France over control of colonial North America. For this, Johnson was later appointed Superintendent of Indian Affairs.

Highlights: Historic Johnson Hall • Two accompanying stone houses • Cayadutta Creek • "The Lookout" • Johnson's grave site

Hike: *Walking the grounds around Johnson Hall*—Standing in front of Johnson Hall, you will see an attractive stone well about 60 feet from the house. We suspect that the well postdates Johnson's time here. An old painting of Johnson Hall depicted at the kiosk shows the front of the house with an assemblage of guests, but with

Johnson Hall as it may have looked in 1772, by E. L. Henry.

no well in the picture. It was in this area, within a circle of locust trees planted by Johnson, that council meetings were held with Native Americans. In Johnson's time the well (as was typical in those days) would have been located in the cellar.

There were lighter moments, too; it wasn't just a place of serious council meetings. Fairs were held at Johnson Hall, with everyone—whites and Native Americans, men and women, and young and old—participating. There were sports, races, and games, and even a contest to see who could make the funniest face.

In the Johnson Hall State Historic Site brochure, a map entitled "Archeological evidence for structures at Johnson Hall ca. 1770" shows that Johnson's office where he conducted most of his business was not located inside Johnson Hall, but rather was in a separate building just south of Johnson Hall not far from the west end of today's parking area.

From the front of Johnson Hall, walk north, heading downhill. Take note that Johnson Hall is built on the side of a small hill that quickly descends to the top of a 30-foot-high bank overlooking Cayadutta Creek. If you are visiting during the regular season, a number of history plaques are scattered at strategic places along the lawn. (When we revisited in late November, the signs were gone, so it may be that they are only displayed seasonally). The first plaque provides information about the "Indian Trade House," where trading took place between the colonists and Native Americans.

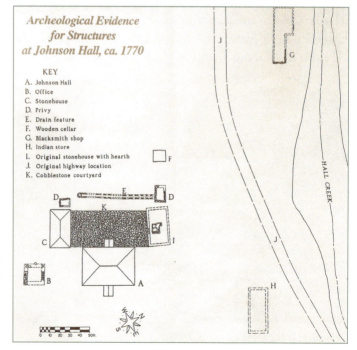

Archaeological recreation of Johnson Hall. New York State Historic Site brochure.

19. JOHNSON HALL STATE HISTORIC SITE

Large millstones are relics from past gristmills.

Walk northwest, paralleling Cayadutta Creek, for >100 feet to the next history marker to read about the "Wash House," which historians believe may have been located in this area, not far from the creek. Water was brought up from the stream, and clothes and linens were boiled and agitated in large kettles that rested on a hearth. Then they were hung to dry. The work was hot and labor-intensive, and particularly unpleasant during the warm summer months.

A little farther northwest are two pairs of large millstones, relics from the days when Cayadutta Creek provided hydropower. The millstones were used for grinding wheat and other grains. The millstones that you see here were undoubtedly gathered from nearby sites.

It's worth noting that millstones came in pairs. The lower millstone, called a bedstone, is stationary and remains motionless. The upper millstone, called the turning runner stone, is the one that does the actual grinding. You can tell the two apart because the bedstone is slightly convex and the turning runner stone is slightly concave.

What's interesting about this part of the walk is that the flat stretch of land next to Cayadutta Creek was formerly the old Colonial Road. This would have been the way you would approach Johnson Hall back in the eighteenth century.

Continue to the northwest end of the property. You will see a tiny, rapids-like cascade on Cayadutta Creek just below the stone block bridge where Johnson Avenue crosses the stream.

Cayadutta Creek is a medium-sized stream that rises on the side of Bleecker Mountain and eventually flows into the Mohawk River by Fonda. Along its route the stream passes directly by Johnson Hall. *Cayadutta* is from a Native American language and means "rippling waters" or "shallow water running over stones."

Tributaries to Cayadutta Creek include Hall Creek, Hale Creek, and Mathew Creek. Hall Creek, rising today out of the Peck Hill State Forest, provided sufficient waterpower for Sir William Johnson to have a sawmill erected next to the stream, and later a gristmill.

According to John J. Vrooman in *Forts and Firesides of the Mohawk Country*, "Other small buildings across a small creek [the Cayadutta] housed some fifteen slaves who worked the land." Sir William Johnson had 60 enslaved Africans working on his property. He was not only the largest slave owner in Fulton County, but may very well have been the largest slave owner in New York State. Even his Mohawk consort, Molly Brant, had her own slave, named Jenny.

From here walk uphill, heading southwest. The next history marker provides information about the cobblestone courtyard located behind Johnson Hall, one that historians have reconstructed as best as they can. It was here that slaves and servants worked, supervised by an overseer, and where they sometimes even slept.

The plaque states: "The courtyard would typically have served as an area for domestic activities and its hard surface would have prevented this high traffic area between the support buildings from becoming a muddy quagmire. Native visitors were also familiar with the courtyard as it was the location of several councils held with Sir William, including one in the dead of winter early in 1768." It was at this council that Sir William became quite ill.

From the courtyard, walk toward the northern stone house. An informational plaque there explains that a wooden outbuilding at this spot probably served as a root cellar, used to help preserve food. The cellars were usually underground or partially underground and stored nuts, fruits, vegetables, and other foods that might endure in the cool dry cellars for periods of time with a little care.

The *Northern Stone House*, also known as a blockhouse, is a reconstruction, the original having been destroyed by fire in 1866. It was built for defensive purposes but never had to be used to ward off an attack. Historians conjecture that it may have been used as servants' quarters, for periodically housing small detachments of British troops, and even for cooking.

Two blockhouses, both about twenty feet from the sides of Johnson Hall, were built in 1763 after word came that Chief Pontiac, an Ottawa leader, had taken up arms against the British. Although Johnson had tremendous influence over the Six Nations of the Iroquois, his influence over the Ottawa was minimal at best, and so Johnson was forced to take precautions. What became known as Pontiac's War lasted from 1763 to 1766, but it never did involve Johnson.

Secret passages (now blocked up) led to the two stone houses. If the main house were under attack, Johnson and his entourage could have rushed into the block-

19. JOHNSON HALL STATE HISTORIC SITE

houses safely without being exposed to musket fire and arrows. Then, protected by the heavy stone walls of the stone houses, they could have fired weapons through the loopholes and driven off a much superior force of attackers.

Just downhill, behind the north side of the stone house, is the last plaque, which tells about the "Road to Stoneraby"—the main road to Johnson Hall. In the eighteenth century the route was called the "Road to Stone Arabia."

Blacksmith's Shop—Any great estate in the eighteenth century had to have a blacksmith's shop. Horses needed to be shod; repairs to carriages and wagons had to be made. Various implements had to be fashioned, some of which were used for trading with Native Americans. Historians estimate that the blacksmith shop at Johnson Hall was 60 feet by 24 feet, which included living quarters for the smith. An archaeological recreation of the Johnson Hall estate shows that the blacksmith's shop was located north of Johnson Hall, next to Cayadutta Creek and probably close to where Johnson Road crosses over the creek.

Privies—In the eighteenth century, privies were known as "necessaries." There were two at Johnson Hall, and both were set on limestone foundations. One was six feet square; the other was six feet by ten feet. Archaeologists have determined that the privies were located directly behind each of the blockhouses and were partially flushed by a stone drain that ran parallel to the courtyard between the privies. Servants and slaves had the unenviable job of not only dumping chamber pots into the privies, but also cleaning out the privies on a regular basis.

Trail Walk—From the parking area next to the Johnson Hall kiosk, follow a 4-foot-wide path that leads to the southwest corner of the property and then head southeast. In 0.2 mile you will come to a large, 3-foot-high, semicircular, stone-cemented structure with two stone benches. It is called *"The Look-out,"* an appropriate name for a structure that once looked out onto fields and distant forests. Today, the views are not quite the same. The view from The Look-out now is of Route 29 and a grouping of residential homes called "Trackside Homes."

A bronze plaque affixed to a medium-sized boulder in front of The Look-out reads: "This look-out built by Mrs. Charles B. Knox [Rose Markward Knox] 1928. From nature's noble watch-tower the pioneer settlers defended their homes, dreamed their dreams and caught the vision of their vast new world. Eternal vigilance is the price of liberty."

Rose Markward Knox was the wife of Charles B. Knox, a creative businessman who discovered a method for granulating gelatine, making it easier for cooks to use the product in their homes. Knox went on to establish the Charles B. Knox Gelatine Co. in Johnstown in 1891. When Charles died in 1908, the business was inherited

PART TWO • CAPITAL REGION

"The Lookout" now looks down over roads and houses instead of fields.

by his wife, Rose Markward, who proved to be more than equal to the task of running and developing the business. Under her tutelage the business grew and became more and more profitable.

Rose went on to publish a booklet entitled *Dainty Desserts for Dainty People* that is still regarded as one of the best manuals on how to make desserts, salads, and gelatine candies. She is held in esteem as one of America's foremost businesswomen of the early twentieth century.

From The Look-out, continue southeast for another 0.1 to the southernmost part of the walk, where a history plaque entitled "Landscaping of Johnson Hall" mentions that after nearly two centuries of changing ownership, only 20 acres of the original 700 acres of the estate remain. The plaque reads: "The Johnstown Historical Society, trustees of Johnson Hall in the early years of state ownership, posted bids in 1926 for landscape design for the Hall's then desolate park grounds. A proposed 'General Plan' established a figure 8 layout of paths and benches circling open lawns. This early-twentieth-century landscape has been restored to allow visitors to once again enjoy a stroll through a portion of Johnson Hall's grounds." It's worth

Portrait of Sir William Johnson.

19. JOHNSON HALL STATE HISTORIC SITE

noting, however, that no one really knows how the original grounds were laid out because no sketches were ever made of the grounds in the eighteenth century.

From here the path U-turns and heads back northwest to the parking area in 0.2 mile. However, it is only a 250-foot walk farther southeast to reach the statue of Sir William Johnson that you drove by when entering the grounds. The life-sized marble statue on granite risers was erected in 1904 by the Aldine Society of Johnstown, New York. The Aldine Society was a ladies social and study organization whose mission was to promote education, good works, and charitable activities.

It is a walk of only <0.3 mile back to the parking area from here.

History: *Johnson Hall* was the centerpiece of Sir William Johnson's 700-acre working estate. He selected the site for his house in 1762, and by 1763 the home was sufficiently constructed for Johnson to move in. Prior to that, he had lived at Old Fort Johnson along the Mohawk River outside of Amsterdam. Johnson employed the services of a Boston-trained carpenter named Samuel Fuller to head the project. Fuller took his design from those he had seen in a Georgian building design book. Although Johnson Hall today is within the city limits of Johnstown, in the 1700s it was at the edge of the frontier.

As you enter Johnson Hall there are two large rooms to the right—a front dining room and, in the rear, Johnson's library, where he is said to have died. To the left of the entrance are a drawing room and a bedroom. An inconspicuous stairway leads

Statue of Sir William Johnson at park's entrance.

PART TWO • CAPITAL REGION

Sir William Johnson's grave. St. John's Episcopal Church.

down to the kitchen and storage area, where Johnson stored his supply of wine, while a much larger and more ornate stairway leads up to the second floor, where more bedrooms are located. Above that is an attic, where an overflow of guests or family could be bunked.

Johnson ran a bustling estate with mills, shops, barns, an "Indian store," stone office, bakery, smokehouses, well houses, and dwellings for servants and tenants. He even had bark houses built specially for chiefs from the Six Nations when they came for council meetings or for other special gatherings. Johnson's estate included a 2.5-acre garden where herbs, roots, vegetables, and fruits were grown, as well as an orchard consisting of plum trees, apple trees, and pear trees.

One of Johnson's most prized and unusual possessions was his "Cabinet of Curiosities," which consisted of a variety of notable objects gleaned from the colonies.

Johnson Hall was well situated at the approximate confluence of six major Native American trails. One important trail ran from the mouth of Caroga Creek east to the Cayadutta, and then northeast through Lake George and Lake Champlain to Canada. Other trails headed east from Cayadutta Creek to Saratoga Springs, westward to West Canada Creek near Hinckley, and south to the Mohawk River at Fonda and Tribes Hill. Not surprisingly, all of these old trails are now modern roads.

Soon after Johnson died in 1774, Molly Brant took her children and returned to her native village in Canajoharie, leaving Johnson's eldest son, John (son of Sir William and his earlier common-law wife, Catherine Weisenberg) in charge of the estate. John Johnson stayed loyal to the British during the American Revolutionary War and had to flee with his family to Canada.

19. JOHNSON HALL STATE HISTORIC SITE

Following the end of the Revolutionary War, the property was seized and subsequently auctioned off to Silas Talbot, a naval officer and American Revolutionary War hero. Johnson Hall remained in private ownership through many individuals and families until 1906, when New York State acquired the property from the estate of John E. Wells. It has been a State Historic Site since then, and a National Historic Site since 1960.

Sir William Johnson was born in 1715 in Ireland and came to the United States sometime around 1738 to look after his Uncle Peter Warren's property. Because most of the people in the Mohawk Valley region at that time were Native American and spoke the Mohawk language, Johnson applied himself and soon learned the language well enough to be able to speak fluently with the natives. In doing so he established a long-lasting friendship with the Mohawks. Johnson's Native American name was *Warraghegagey*, which translated as "bringing two peoples together." This relationship proved to be an asset in currying favor with the Six Nations of the Iroquois, winning them over to the side of the British in the ongoing territorial war with the French.

For his efforts in helping to win the ensuing French & Indian War, which included providing leadership at the Battle of Lake George and capturing Fort Niagara, Johnson was made a baronet and awarded the tract of land that became the Johnson Hall estate. That acquisition made him the second-largest landowner in British North America.

Johnson's paramour, Molly Brant, was a Mohawk, and together they had eight children. Molly was the brother of Joseph Brant, a famous Mohawk military and political leader who was closely allied with Great Britain before, during, and after the American Revolutionary War. Prior to his involvement with Molly Brant, Johnson had a common-law wife, Catharine (also spelled Catherine) Weisenberg, a German girl with whom he had one son (John) and two daughters. Catharine died early on in the marriage. It is said that Sir William named the city of Johnstown in 1762 after his son John.

Sir William Johnson died in 1774 when he was "seized of a suffication." He was buried with honors under the altar of St. John's Episcopal Church in Johnstown. There were two St. John's Episcopal churches prior to the present one. The first church was built in 1767, but at a different location; the second church, erected in 1771, was built on the spot now occupied by the present church. When the second St. John's Episcopal Church was destroyed by fire in 1836, however, and a new church promptly built on the same site, Johnson ended up left out in the cold outside of the church. Why? Although his burial site had not changed, the orientation of the church had, and the new alignment left Johnson outside of its walls. ∎

PART TWO • CAPITAL REGION

20. CHRISTMAN SANCTUARY PRESERVE

Location: Delanson (Schenectady County)
NYS Atlas & Gazetteer, Tenth Edition, p. 81, A10; **Earlier Edition,** p. 65, BC7
GPS Parking: 42.743196, –74.128689
GPS Destinations: *Main waterfall*—42.739253, –74.128417; *Stream crossing*—42.740664, –74.125099; *Christman Memorial*—42.741341, –74.125712; *1931 plaque*—42.743218, –74.123885
Hours: Daily, dawn to dusk
Fee: None
Accessibility: *Blue-blazed trail*—0.8-mile hike, starting from kiosk; *Red-blazed trail*—1.1-mile hike; *Yellow-blazed trail to lean-to*—0.1-mile hike; *Yellow-blazed connecting trail*—0.05-mile hike
Degree of Difficulty: Moderate
Additional Information: Christman Sanctuary, 3281 Schoharie Turnpike, Delanson, NY 12053; The Nature Conservancy, Eastern New York Chapter

Directions: From Duanesburg (junction of Route 7/Duanesburg Road & Route 20/Western Turnpike) proceed southwest on Route 7/Duanesburg Road for 0.8 mile. Turn left onto Weaver Road and head south for 1.0 mile. When you come to the Schoharie Turnpike, turn left and drive northeast for 0.7 mile, then turn right into the parking area for the Christman Sanctuary.

Description: The Christman Sanctuary Preserve encompasses 120 acres of land. Its centerpiece is a 30-foot-high waterfall that is formed on the Bozen Kill, a medium-sized stream that produces a series of waterfalls as it cascades from one ledge to the next.

Highlights: 30-foot waterfall • Multiple smaller cascades • Christman Memorial Boulder • Red pine plantation • Lean-to

Historic postcard—Included in this chapter is the front and back of an antique postcard of historical value. The front shows the "Falls on Bozenkill Creek near Delanson, N.Y.," which today is called Bozen Kill Falls. There is a swimmer near the base of the waterfall, as well as two near the shore. The most interesting feature of the card, however, is its back side. Here, we have a note written by none other than W.W. Christman, posted August 1908. The note reads: "Cousin Clint: Will C. Jr. is coming up to see you next Friday if nothing happens. If he proves to be a nuisance send him

20. CHRISTMAN SANCTUARY PRESERVE

home on the next train. W. W. Christman". How unusual to come across a more than 110-year-old postcard of a waterfall sent by the very person whose name is now associated with it! As for Will Jr., one can only wonder if he ended up getting sent back home on the next train.

The front of Christman's postcard.

The back of Christman's postcard.

Hike: From the kiosk at the parking area, follow a path southeast for >0.1 mile across an overgrown meadow that is gradually reforesting. Be prepared for walking through shallow mud periodically despite the presence of numerous boardwalks that have been placed to help prevent further erosion. As soon as you reach the edge of the woods, bear right (straight) onto the 0.7-mile-long blue-blazed loop trail and follow it south as it takes you in 100 feet across a footbridge spanning a tiny stream that rises from a nearby pond and quickly becomes a tributary of the Bozen Kill.

PART TWO • CAPITAL REGION

The 30-foot-long *Plant Bridge* (a footbridge) crossing the tiny stream was constructed in 2004 with the help of many volunteers and was dedicated to the memory of Doris Saunders Plant, 1921–1999, wife of Henri Tredwell Plant. Henri Plant was a long-time member of the Mohawk Valley Hiking Club and is best remembered for spearheading the fight to preserve the Christman Sanctuary when New York State authorities began to consider having I-88, a freeway connecting Schenectady to the southern tier, cross directly over the top of the sanctuary's 30-foot-high waterfall. Environmentalists eventually won, and I-88 was redirected to its present location. Plant continued to advocate for the sanctuary, serving as a steward for more than 30 years, dying in 2012 at the age of 90.

Continue south on the blue-blazed trail for ~0.2 mile. Just as you begin to approach the Bozen Kill gorge, straight ahead, the trail turns sharply left. Follow it downhill for 100 feet and then turn sharply right onto the yellow-blazed trail (pay close attention here, for the yellow-blazed trail can be easily missed). Follow the yellow-blazed trail southwest as it leads between a dramatic narrow cleft in the bedrock and then, a moment later, under a 4-foot-long rock overhang. A plaque embedded in the side wall here reads: "To have experienced this sanctuary is to know it is very special. Thus, it is fitting that it is maintained and protected with the help of an endowment dedicated to my dearly loved wife Doris Saunders Plant. 1921–1999. She too was very special. Henri T. Plant. 2004."

The Plant Bridge under construction in 2004.

20. CHRISTMAN SANCTUARY PRESERVE

From the overhang continue following the trail downhill, assisted by steps and a hand-line that accompanies you along the descent because of the drop-off of considerable height on your left. By the time you reach the bottom, you will have passed by two small cascades. Be sure to look across the stream at the north bank to see where a sizeable chunk of the rock wall has sheered off, leaving huge pieces in the creek. Erosion continues to take place in the preserve and is unstoppable.

A third cascade, a two-tiered 10-footer, lies just ahead and is the second largest cascade in the sanctuary.

The *Bozen Kill*—The waterfalls in the Christman Sanctuary are formed on the Bozen Kill, a medium-sized stream that rises from Duane Lake and the wetlands near Delanson and flows into the Watervliet Reservoir, where it emerges as the Normans Kill. The word *Bozen* is Dutch for "noisy" and *Kill* is Dutch for "stream." Enjoined, the two words thus mean "noisy stream," an apt description of the Bozen Kill as its waters continuously chatter through the sanctuary, dropping from ledge to ledge.

In another 200 feet the yellow-blazed trail dead-ends at a large pool of shallow water in front of the sanctuary's 30-foot-high main waterfall. We would be remiss if we didn't voice our suspicion that the waterfall is not actually quite 30 feet in height, unless you count the cascade directly above it. Also, although this waterfall is called Bozen Kill Falls by many people, a much larger waterfall lies farther downstream on private land and is listed on topo maps as Bozen Kill Falls. Perhaps it is not a problem to have two identically named falls in such close proximity if one fall is inaccessible to the public.

Directly upstream from the park's Bozen Kill Falls are three smaller falls. You can see the first of the three while standing below. They are all located near the edge of the park's boundary.

This is a very scenic location—one of the loveliest spots in the Capital Region—and further enhanced by the massive, 50-foot-high walls enclosing the gorge and waterfalls, turning this part of the sanctuary virtually into a box canyon.

In times of heavy rainfall or following snowmelt, a slender cascade also appears on the south wall of the gorge, downstream from the main fall.

Further adding to the enjoyment of this site is a large, open-faced, Adirondack-style lean-to near the main fall. The lean-to was built by the Mohawk Valley Hiking Club (MVHC) in 1934. Since then, the club, which was founded in 1929, has maintained a tradition of enjoying a Thanksgiving breakfast annually at the lean-to.

Return to the blue-blazed trail and from there continue downhill for ~0.1 mile. Soon the trail, which had moved slightly away from the stream, approaches the Bozen Kill again.

The lean-to next to Bozen Kill Falls was built in 1934 by the Mohawk Valley Hiking Club.

When you reach a very distinctive, 3-foot-high ledge fall, look closely and you will see that the red-blazed Plantation Trail starts here, crossing the Bozen Kill at the top of the cascade. We have listed a GPS coordinate for the crossing to make sure that its location is clearly identifiable. Under most conditions it should be easy to cross here. However, do not attempt a crossing if the Bozen Kill is running high and fast or if you're at all unsure of your footing, for there is a 3–4-foot drop-off to your left.

The Red-blazed Plantation Trail—Once you cross over the Bozen Kill, follow a path uphill for 100 feet to a junction. Turn left and follow the red-blazed Plantation Trail as it parallels the stream. Within 0.1 mile the trail pulls away from the stream and soon begins paralleling a limestone ridge to your left. Shortly thereafter the trail gradually descends to a swampy area and then climbs steeply, leading you through a forest of red pines. Eventually you will see pastures to your left—indications of how the land looked in the days when it was farmed.

After a while the trail returns you to the Bozen Kill at a higher elevation, now directly above the main waterfall and its three upper companion cascades, offering a view of the waterfalls from the opposite side of the gorge.

The trail leads right along the top of the gorge here. Extra caution should be exercised on this short section of the hike, and we would not recommend that young children accompany you here—a 50-foot drop-off is only a foot or two away. In less than 0.05 mile the trail descends quickly.

20. CHRISTMAN SANCTUARY PRESERVE

An unusually large rock wall.

A hundred feet before you reach the stream crossing, you will walk through a very well defined 3-foot-high stone wall—one of the highest and most intact walls that we have seen on any of our hikes.

Follow the spur path across the Bozen Kill and return to the blue-blazed trail, turning right.

Back on the blue-blazed trail, in 100 feet you will cross over a tiny tributary of the Bozen Kill that enters on your left. This is the same stream that you crossed earlier via the footbridge at the beginning of your hike.

In another 50 feet turn left onto a yellow-blazed connecting trail and follow a series of rock steps uphill. You will come to the Christman Memorial, to your left, in less than 200 feet.

The ***Christman Memorial***, located on the opposite side of a tiny stream, consists of a medium-sized boulder with two plaques affixed to it. The plaque on the left reads: "W. W. Christman. May 10, 1865–Feb 26, 1937. When you went we grieved, the lack. Then softly fell the evening of content. The wind had changed. We would not wish you back." The plaque on the right reads: "Catherine Bradt Christman. May 2, 1867–Feb 2, 1946. First reader, critic, and wife. A new life springs phoenix-like upon the ashes of the old."

Two stone-slab benches face the boulder, giving hikers a chance to rest and meditate on the beauty of this sanctuary,

From the Christman Memorial follow the yellow-blazed trail to its intersection with the blue-blazed trail, 150 feet ahead. Turn left and head uphill on the blue-blazed trail, completing the loop, and then exit from the sanctuary on the same path that you took earlier from the parking area.

History: The genesis for Christman Sanctuary began during the Blizzard of March 1888 when William Christman and his wife Catherine decided to feed starving birds by scattering grass and weed seeds across the deep snow. This grew into a winter bird-feeding program. When he was 59 years old, Christman began to convert his land into a preserve, setting out a 60-acre plantation of pine and other trees.

In 1931 the Mohawk Valley Hiking Club erected a plaque on a cairn of stone rocks cemented together. They placed it along the Schoharie Turnpike near a white house 0.2 mile east of today's parking area. It reads: "In honor of Mr. and Mrs. W. W. Christman, I give, bequeath, devote, devise, shelter to every bird that flies."

In 1970 The Nature Conservancy acquired the original 97 acres of land of the Christman Sanctuary from Lansing and Lucille Christman, son and daughter-in-law of William and Catherine. It was also around this time that a battle began between environmentalists and the state in a fight to keep the state from routing I-88 through the property.

The environmentalists won that battle, and since then the sanctuary has grown to 120 acres of land.

William Weaver Christman was born in 1865 on the 105-acre Christman family farm. Although Christman worked as a farmer all of his life, he was also a nature writer and poet. In 1933 he wrote *Wild Pasture Pine*, which was awarded the Burroughs Medal in 1934 by the John Burroughs Memorial Association. He also wrote *Song of the Helderhills* in 1926 and *Song of the Western Gateway* in 1930. Perhaps his most telling book was *The Untillable Hills*, which may give some insight into what he thought about farming in this region. Christman corresponded with John Burroughs and Walt Whitman, and even once entertained Robert Frost and his wife.

One of Christman's sons, Henry, was also a writer. Henry authored the well-regarded book *Tin Horns and Calico*, a history of the Anti-Rent War.

The Christman Preserve is a Registered National Historic Landmark and is listed in the National Register of Historic Places as the "Christman Bird and Wildlife Sanctuary." Reportedly it was one of the earliest such sanctuaries in the United States. ■

21. NORMANSKILL FARM

Location: Normanskill (Albany County)
NYS Atlas & Gazetteer, Tenth Edition, p. 82, B4; **Earlier Edition,** p. 66, CD3
GPS Parking: 42.634894, –73.800126
GPS Destinations: *Pappalau Icehouse ruins*—42.634823, –73.800727; *Whipple Bridge*—42.635897, –73.800218; *Yellow Brick Road*—42.634782, –73.798618; *Community gardens*—42.634067, –73.807994; *Artificial section of the Normans Kill*—42.632799, –73.807587; *Normans Kill Cascade*—42.633007, –73.797838; *Normansville Community Church*—42.633503, –73.798823
Hours: Dawn to dusk
Fee: None
Restrictions: Dogs must be leashed.
Accessibility: *Normans Kill to woods*—0.7-mile walk; *Loop hike*—1.8-mile hike; *Whipple Bridge Loop*—0.3-mile walk
Degree of Difficulty: *Normans Kill to woods*—Easy; *Loop Hike*—Moderate; *Whipple Bridge*—Easy
Additional Information: Friends of the Normanskill Farm—organization formed in 2003 to ensure the preservation and promotion of this pastoral setting in urban Albany

Directions: From Albany near Washington Park (junction of Route 443/Delaware Avenue & Route 20/Madison Avenue), drive southwest on Route 443/Delaware Avenue for ~2.0 miles. Just before you start to cross over the Delaware Avenue bridge that spans the Normans Kill, turn left onto Mill Road and follow the road downhill, west, for 0.2 mile to a parking area on your left for the Normanskill Farm.

Description: The Normanskill Farm, once a significant dairy farm, is now a park owned by the City of Albany. The park includes historic buildings, historic ruins, and a downsized working farm. The Normans Kill, a major stream, is a constant companion for most of the hike.

Highlights: Normanskill Farm Hiking trail along Normans Kill • Historic "yellow brick road" • Whipple Bridge • Pappalau Icehouse ruins • Albany's largest community garden • Historic village of Normansville • Artificially created section of the Normans Kill

Hikes: *Part One: River Walk*—The trailhead begins at the southwest end of the parking area and heads northwest, following between the bank of the Normans Kill to your left and Mill Road (a dead-end park road) to your right. The part of the

Normans Kill next to the parking area contains tiny ledges and rapids, causing the stream to chatter incessantly in the background.

The *Normans Kill* is a sizeable stream that flows out of the Watervliet Reservoir and into the Hudson River south of Albany near the Port of Albany. Some believe that the name comes from a Norwegian (a Norman) immigrant named Albert Andriessen Bradt, who initially tried raising tobacco by the Normans Kill and then, when that failed, proceeded to build two sawmills.

Other past names for the stream include Petanock, Tawasenths ("place of the many dead"), and Godyn's Kil. The section of the stream by the Normanskill Farm has banks of clay and a streambed primarily composed of slate.

Leaving the parking area, you will immediately pass between old ruins—sections of the Pappalau Icehouse that have survived for over a century. Some sections are still standing upright. We paced off the main foundation ruins and found the dimensions to be around 60 feet by 30 feet.

Upstream from the icehouse, a 4–5-foot-high dam earlier spanned the Normans Kill, creating an impoundment. During the winter, ice was harvested from the artificially-created pond. No trace of the dam remains today.

In <0.1 mile the trail goes past several farm buildings on your right. The first

---

The **Pappalau Icehouse** was one of hundreds of icehouses that once operated on or near the Hudson River. This business was run by the Pappalau family—Vincent (a German immigrant born in 1835) and his sons, Harry, Edward, William, and George.

Ice harvesting was a big industry before the advent of modern refrigeration. In a typical winter the Normans Kill by January or February would have frozen to a depth of 14–16 inches, thick enough for the harvesters to begin work. First, horse-drawn scrappers would remove snow and debris from the section of the river to be harvested. Next, holes would be drilled 20 feet apart, and lines would be cut connecting the holes to create a checkerboard pattern. Then the cutters would get to work carving up the ice sheets into blocks. The blocks would be floated through open-water channels to steam-driven conveyer belts, which would then carry the blocks into the icehouse where they could be stored. Most likely the Pappalau Icehouse was painted white or yellow to reflect heat during the hot days of summer. Icehouses were generally double-walled with insulation between the walls. Despite all precautions, however, ice would inevitably begin to melt. Some icehouses experienced as much as a 50 percent loss of their product from melting. In well-insulated icehouses, the loss could be kept to a minimum, sometimes to as low as 20 percent.

Some icehouses were so large that they could hold up to 60,000 tons (see chapters "R. & W. Scott Icehouse" and "Falling Waters"). Shipments of ice were made not just locally and to New York City, but to places as far away as the Caribbean and even India. In 1870 a ton of ice could sell for as much as $20, a considerable amount of money in those days.

In the early 1900s the Pappalau Icehouse caught fire at about 4:30 AM just as Edward Pappalau was loading a wagon with ice blocks to make deliveries. The fire worked its way quickly through the sawdust/straw-insulated walls of the building, burning off the exterior housing. Two of the other brothers, William and Harry, and their families had to be rousted from their home near the icehouse; the heat was so intense that it blew out the windows of their house. Over 8,000 tons of ice were left exposed to the sun and warm air, and the brothers were forced to declare their business a total loss.

The end was just as inevitable for the rest of the ice-harvesting industry. The industry began to go into decline following World War I with the advent of modern refrigeration and had all but vanished by the 1930s.

The ruins of the Pappalau Icehouse overlook the Normans Kill.

one, on the opposite side of Mill Road, is the Tenant House (circa 1830). This is followed by the Blacksmith Shop (circa 1830), between the trail and Mill Road, and then the Hog Barn (circa 1920), also between the trail and Mill Road. In days gone by, the front part of the Blacksmith Shop housed the forge (which was restored in 2007 and dedicated to Patrick J. Grossi, the blacksmith who designed the forge), and the back part of the house was where ice for the farm was stored. Because of significant erosion caused by inland tropical storms over the last decade, work was done in 2012 to shore up the bank next to the blacksmith shop.

Across the river along the opposite bank is the 12-acre Normans Kill Preserve East, owned by the Mohawk Hudson Land Conservancy. Its trails parallel the south side of the river and provide views of the Normans Kill and Normanskill Farm from a different perspective.

In >100 feet, the trail used to cross over a footbridge spanning a tiny stream, but the footbridge is no longer structurally safe and has been closed off. The path now bypasses the footbridge and continues along the bank of the Normans Kill. In a moment you will come to a fenced-in garden and orchard (which earlier was home to beehives) on your right and, opposite, a rusted, hulking piece of farm machinery. At the end of the garden on your left is a stream-gauging station that measures water level and rate of flow. In the past we would see a slack zip-line here that environmentalists used to get sediment readings from the river. The shed with a solar panel on its top serves as a base of operations for the environmentalists.

At various locations along this hike, you will note that paths occasionally lead down to the river; these are used by fishing enthusiasts.

Around 0.3 mile from the parking area, you will pass by a National Grid gas transmission plant to your right. Take note of the unmarked dirt road that comes in next to the transmission plant and steadily descends from the northeast corner of the farmlands. Later you will be returning on that road.

Around this point you will pass over a gas line corridor and then under power lines. The path comes out to the road for a moment and then returns to the bank of the Normans Kill. You will immediately pass by a Beacon Institute weather station, which is part of the River and Estuary Observation Network that monitors air temperature, wind speed and direction, precipitation, barometric pressure, and relative humidity.

It's worth keeping in mind that this part of the Normans Kill was artificially created in 2000 after the rampaging stream undercut a section of the bank in Delmar next to Route 443 and had to be rerouted. The forest has yet to reclaim this modified part of the landscape, leaving the artificial channel easily distinguishable by its lack of mature trees and the secondary growth along its banks.

21. NORMANSKILL FARM

Up ahead, on the opposite side of the Normans Kill, can be seen a small wooden footbridge crossing a stream near the east border of the Normans Kill Preserve West. The Normans Kill Preserve West is another section of land along the Normans Kill owned and operated for public use by the Mohawk Hudson Land Conservancy. Access to its 1.0-mile-long trail is from Normanskill Boulevard off of Delaware Avenue in the Town of Bethlehem.

For a short distance the trail and Mill Road nearly merge as they run side by side. To your right, next to an artificially created mound, is the Normanskill Farm Dog Park, where dog owners can bring their pets to romp freely about within the confines of a gated play area.

Just west of the dog park is the Capital District Community Gardens (CDCG), a private nonprofit organization that has operated since the 1970s. It works with local residents to improve neighborhoods through gardening and greening projects, and it is the largest community garden in Albany. On the Normans Kill side of Mill Road opposite the gardens is a small, slowly deteriorating pavilion with a picnic table.

Once you pass by the gardens, Mill Road turns into a well-worn path that continues along next to the Normans Kill. Look carefully and you will see the line of demarcation at which point the Normans Kill changes from an artificial channel back to a natural stream. In 0.2 mile from the Community Gardens, you will reach the edge of the woods. Follow the trail into the woods to reach a tiny, rapids-like

The Day the Normans Kill Bank Collapsed—In May 2000 heavy rains caused a 400-foot-long linear section of the Normans Kill's south bank in Delmar to collapse, destroying Anthony Battaglia's Delaware Avenue vegetable stand in the process and threatening to collapse Delaware Avenue. In order to determine the solidity of the underlying soil, geologists rigged up a 5,000-pound drill to obtain deep soil samples. The National Guard was called in to help, and Black Hawk helicopters were even pressed into service.

It took six months and over $25 million for the site to be stabilized, the Normans Kill to be rerouted, and Delaware Avenue to be reopened to traffic.

Because much of the land is sand over clay, the steep terrain promotes landslides when the ground becomes too saturated with water. It is hoped that no further landslides will occur (at least not in the foreseeable future), thanks to the remediation efforts, but it should be noted that more erosion was spotted behind Hoffman's Car Wash on Delaware Avenue in 2012, and there was a substantial landslide into the Normans Kill at the Normanside Country Club in 2015.

cascade. Directly opposite, on the south side of the Normans Kill, is another part of the 30-acre Normans Kill Preserve West.

After <200 feet the trail turns right and climbs uphill steeply. Just before the top of the gorge is reached, the trail takes you north along the steep embankment. In <0.05 mile you will reach the highest point on the trail. From here the trail descends to a lower, 25-foot-high promontory where the Normans Kill changes direction abruptly, turning from southeast to southwest. Look below to see a huge pile of downed trees and brush that has been washed up and captured by this elbow turn. There is no reason to follow a steep path to the bottom of this bluff unless you want to be close to the river, for the path essentially dead-ends by the pile of debris.

After savoring the view, follow the path to your right and head east for >100 feet, then downhill following a wide grassy path within a wider power line corridor. At the bottom of the hill to your left is a sign that reads: "Take a break. Welcome to the hiker's rest. As always, carry in/carry out. 1.5 miles to club house. 1.2 miles to Farm." The sign was erected while Gerald D. Jennings was mayor of Albany (1994–2013). Perhaps a bench or pavilion was located by the sign at one time to provide a resting stop, but if so, it is long gone. There is no place to rest here at "the hiker's rest."

Should you continue west for another 0.05 mile from the "hiker's rest" sign, you would reach the southeast end of the Capital Hills at Albany Golf Course (previously known as the Albany Municipal Golf Course).

To head back east, scamper back up the wide path that you just descended. It is a *very* steep climb to the top. Before you reach the summit, turn left and follow a path that leads along the edge of the woods. In <100 feet you will pass by an easily missed trail on your left designated as "Ski Path" (it was earlier indicated by the letters "R11," and is actually an old road that has devolved to the size of a path). The trail dead-ends in <0.2 mile where the earth has washed out around a drainpipe. There is little reason to take this path, for it is eroding away and probably will be gone entirely in another decade. We had a hard time imagining any skier negotiating the trail.

Back on the main trail, continue on past the "Ski Path" uphill along the edge of the woods for 0.1 mile to an old farm road at the northeast corner of the open farm fields. From here take in the expansive views of the Normanskill Farm, the Normans Kill, and Delaware Avenue, which are clearly visible in the distance. It's hard to believe that you are only 0.4 mile away from the New York State Thruway at this point.

Follow the old farm road downhill for <0.4 mile to Mill Road (where the National Grid gas transmission plant is located). Along the way you will be following a fairly deep ravine to your left that gradually disappears by the time you reach

21. NORMANSKILL FARM

A surviving section of the "Yellow Brick Road."

Mill Road. Turn left and follow Mill Road for 0.3 mile back to the parking area.

Part Two: Yellow Brick Road Walk—From directly opposite the parking area, follow a wide path uphill for 0.05 mile to the Whipple Bowstring Truss Bridge. The bridge, which is open to pedestrians throughout the year but to cars only seasonally, spans a deep ravine formed by a stream that rises near Whitehall Road and South Main Street. The bridge connects the farm property to Normanskill Road, which is part of the old Yellow Brick Road. The farmhouse and buildings that you see to your left (west) are part of the Albany Police Department mounted unit and their K-9 training area. It is off-limits to the public except for special events.

Take a moment to look down from the bridge into the ravine, which is surprisingly deep for having been made by such a seemingly insubstantial stream. The stream continues south, goes under Mill Road, and then flows into the Normans Kill next to the east side of the parking lot.

Walk across the Whipple Bridge and turn right, following Normanskill Road downhill to Mill Road. You will notice near the junction of Normanskill Road and Mill Road that a large area of yellow bricks has been left exposed on the otherwise paved highway. This is the Yellow Brick Road that was originally part of the Delaware Turnpike system constructed in the early nineteenth century. At one time the road continued across Mill Road and then crossed over the Normans Kill via the "Yellow Brick Road Bridge," connecting Albany with Normansville. That bridge, however, has been abandoned for many years, and in 1990 was closed off to vehicular traffic for safety reasons.

To safely get to the tiny hamlet of Normansville, just across the river, go back

PART TWO • CAPITAL REGION

The cast- & wrought-iron **Whipple Bowstring Truss Bridge**, designed by Squire Whipple (1804–1888), was built by Simon DeGraff in Syracuse in 1867 and moved to its present location in 1899 when the Delaware Avenue Turnpike was rerouted. Whipple was the first to correctly analyze the stresses involved in a bridge truss.

This Whipple bridge, which spans a deep ravine, is the only remaining Whipple bridge in vehicular service out of more than a 150 that were built, and was placed on the National Registry of Historic Places in 1971. Most of the other Whipple bridges spanned various sections of the Erie Canal and were obliterated after the canal was abandoned in the early 1900s. You can still visit an Erie Canal Whipple bridge at the Vischer Ferry Nature & Historic Preserve near Clifton Park; that bridge has been converted into a footbridge.

Of around 150 similarly made bridges, the Whipple Bridge at the Normanskill Farm is the last to still accommodate vehicular traffic.

up to Delaware Avenue, drive 0.2 mile past the west end of the Delaware Avenue Bridge and take the first left onto Old Delaware Avenue, which leads southeast and downhill to the hamlet of Normansville in 0.3 mile. Park by the Normansville Community Church.

The hamlet, which now consists of two dead-end streets, was once known as Upper Hollow to differentiate it from nearby Kenwood, which was called Lower Hollow. In earlier days the upper dead-end street (Rockefeller Road) continued

21. NORMANSKILL FARM

Bridges over the Normans Kill—In 1805 a 100-foot-long wooden bridge spanned the Normans Kill Gorge and was part of the Delaware Turnpike (a toll road). In 1869 a freshet washed that bridge away (not an uncommon event for bridges of that era). Soon afterward the Town of Bethlehem—the Delaware Turnpike having been discontinued—build an iron bridge to take its place.

The 156-foot-long Yellow Brick Road Bridge was built in 1884 and was paved with—you guessed it—yellow bricks. Although since paved over, sections of bricks still show through today.

In 1929 a newer, wider, much higher Delaware Avenue bridge, called the Normanskill Viaduct, was built over the Normans Kill 60 feet higher up in the gorge than the bridge it replaced. In 1994 it was dismantled and replaced by the current Delaware Avenue Bridge, which is just upstream from where the old one stood.

What remains of the 200-year-old Yellow Brick Road (Normanskill Drive) is historically significant, for it is one of the few of its type that has survived into the twenty-first century.

Local lore has it that L. Frank Baum incorporated the concept of the yellow brick road into *The Wizard of Oz* after reading Edgar Allen Poe's account of this Albany road.

southwest toward Elsmere.

The Normansville Community Church, located at the start of Rockefeller Road, dates back to the 1700s. The Victorian-style home located uphill from the east end of the Delaware Avenue Bridge is the former residence of the Harder family, who ran the Albany City Paper Mill just north of the public bathing beach in Normansville. Proceed to the left of the church and follow Mill Road for 0.1 mile to its end. Along the way you will have great views of the Normans Kill Gorge as well as of a 4–6-foot-high cascade that can be seen once you are 100 feet beyond the last house on your left.

If you proceed to the right of the church and follow Rockefeller Road south for 0.3 mile, you will come to a barrier. Walk around the barrier and continue southwest, now heading uphill. You may begin to wonder why this perfectly drivable road is closed. The answer is reached in 0.2 mile. The Rockefeller Road Bridge is gone. In the vast space between the two bridge abutments, and at some distance below, is the Albany County Helderberg-Hudson Rail Trail, a 9.0-mile-long, paved, multipurpose trail that runs between Albany and Voorheesville. If you wish to continue farther, the rail trail can be accessed from the end of the bridge abutment via a steep spur path on your left before you reach the end of the bridge.

History: Archaeologists have identified prehistoric Native American encampments in the immediate vicinity of the Normanskill Farm that were occupied thousands of years ago.

In Henry Wadsworth Longfellow's epic poem, "The Song of Hiawatha," the following lines are about the Normans Kill valley, the summer home of the Mohicans:

> *In the vale of Tawasentha,*
> *In the green and silent valley,*
> *By the pleasant water-courses,*
> *Dwelt the singer Nawadaha.*
> *Round about the Indian village*
> *Spread the meadows and the corn-fields,*
> *And beyond them stood the forest,*
> *Stood the groves of singing pine-trees,*
> *Green in Summer, white in Winter,*
> *Ever sighing, ever singing.*

The Mohicans engaged in trade with the early white settlers at Fort Nassau, but then were roundly defeated in battle and ultimately displaced by the more aggressive Mohawks (see "Hudson River Skywalk: Thomas Cole House to Olana" for details about the climactic fight between the Mohicans and the Mohawks).

In 1637, Albert Andriessen Bradt, an early settler whom the Dutch called "Norman" because he was Norwegian, obtained water privileges on the stream and erected two mills farther east toward the Hudson River. Gradually the stream became known as "Norman's Kill" (with *kill* a Dutch word for "creek"). His neighbors were a fur trader named Teunis C. Slingerlands and a miller and farmer called Pieter Winne.

In the 1800s a sawmill and the Pappalau Icehouse were established along the north bank of the Normans Kill just west of the Normanskill Farm's parking lot.

The area also began to be farmed in the 1800s. The main farmhouse was built ~1850, and then was enlarged between 1895 and 1900. A further addition was made in 1920. In 1900, Mark Stevens established the Normans Kill Dairy Farm. This enterprise soon turned into a conglomerate run by C.P. Stevens and included a bottling plant in Albany, a skimming station in Westerlo, additional dairy farmlands along Route 9 in Glenmont, and a milk-receiving station in

21. NORMANSKILL FARM

Washington County, where extra milk was purchased for bottling.

The company maintained a traditional image until 1955, when its horse-drawn wagons delivering milk in Albany were finally replaced by motorized vehicles. The bottling company survived until the early 1960s, at which time it was razed to make room for the Empire State Plaza. The Normans Kill Dairy Farm remained in the Stevens family until the late 1970s. By then all the cows had been sold off. In 1975 Crowley Foods purchased the Normanskill Farm name.

In 1980 the City of Albany, spearheaded by Mayor Erastus Corning, purchased the property for recreation and open space preservation. However, farm activity didn't end. A lease agreement with the city allowed the land to be used for cattle farming. Stoffels Glenview Farm (owned by James D. Frueh) and Frueh Bros. Farm are names mentioned on a side gate along Mill Road, as is the Tivoli Lake Preserve & Farm, which uses the property as a winter residency for its animals.

Today the park is overseen by the City of Albany's Parks & Recreation Department. Part of the farm and some of the buildings are used by the Albany Police Department for their K-9 unit and for their mounted horse unit. The main farmhouse is occupied by the farm manager. Outbuildings from the farm include a blacksmith shop (near the icehouse ruins), a pig barn (next to the blacksmith shop), a poultry shed, a main hay barn, and a main livestock barn.

Just back up the road from the parking area, at the east end of the lower bridge on the Yellow Brick Road, is where the Hinkel Hotel, bar, and restaurant once stood. The Hinkles operated a little showboat and would take guests out for short rides between the lower dam in Normansville and the upper dam by the Pappalau Icehouse. ■

Two bridges across the Normans Kill—one new, one old.

PART TWO • CAPITAL REGION

22. SCHUYLER FLATTS CULTURAL PARK

Location: Watervliet (Albany County)
NYS Atlas & Gazetteer, Tenth Edition, p. 82, A5; **Earlier Edition,** p. 66, C4
GPS Parking: 42.706750, –73.710722
GPS Destinations: *Schuyler Burying Ground*—42.706581, –73.709004; *Historic Schuyler House*—42.706197, –73.708578; *Path to River Walk*—42.705410, –73.708730; *Arbor*—42.704231, –73.710273; *Clinton's Ditch*—42.704973, –73.713437
Hours: Dawn to dusk
Fee: None
Restrictions: Dogs must be leashed; park rules are posted.
Accessibility: *Schuyler Flatts*—0.7-mile trek along wide, paved walkway wheelchair accessible; *Bikeway Extension*—0.5-mile walk
Degree of Difficulty: Easy

Directions: From I-787 take Exit 7W for Route 378/Watervliet and proceed southwest on Route 378/Menands Bridge Road, bearing right where the sign directs you toward Watervliet. Turn right onto Route 32/Broadway and drive northeast for 0.4 mile. When you come to the sign for Schuyler Flatts Cultural Park, turn right and drive northeast for 0.1 mile to the main parking lot next to the two-story-high shelter/pavilion.

Description: Schuyler Flatts Cultural Park is a small, self-contained, 12-acre park offering a little something for everyone. The land, originally a floodplain, was used by Native Americans for growing crops. It was occupied by the Schuyler family from the 1700s through the early 1900s. A section of the Erie Canal went through part of the estate.

Highlights:
Original site of a historic cemetery whose graves were later moved to the Albany Rural Cemetery • Site of the historic Schuyler House • Freshwater tidal wetlands east of the park and bikeway • Outline of the original Erie Canal ("Clinton's Ditch")

The Walk: *At the pavilion*—Two, 4-foot-high stone blocks, each with a plaque, can be seen next to the pavilion. One stone block contains the original plaque that was mounted on the historic Schuyler House until the house burned to the ground in 1962. This new display was dedicated in 2002 by the Town of Colonie Historical Society. The other stone plaque informs you that you will be walking through the Schuyler Flatts Archaeological District, a site that became a National Historic Landmark in 1993.

There is also a sign by the pavilion stating that the land is owned by the Open Space Institute (OSI), an organization dedicated to land conservation and environmentally sound land use planning. Funding to create the preserve was made available through the Lilia Acheson & Dewitt Wallace Fund for preserving the Hudson Highlands.

Inside the pavilion are two large informational plaques—"Schuyler Flatts Cultural Park," which provides a concise timeline of events that occurred on the Flatts, and "Schuyler Flatts in the French & Indian War."

From the pavilion/kiosk—Walk east toward the Hudson River along a paved walkway. You will pass by two more stone blocks, one of them dedicated to Jean Olton, who was the town historian and a passionate preservationist instrumental in saving many of Colonie's cultural treasures. Continue straight ahead at a fork. In 0.1 mile you will see a sign to your left that reads, "The Old Schuyler Burying Ground."

According to 1874 records, the *Old Schuyler Burying Ground* contained more than 50 graves. Most of those interred had died from epidemics in the 1830s and 1840s, and many were children under the age of ten. By 1920 the Old Schuyler Burying Ground was in such a state of neglect that the remaining Schuyler descendants requested that the graves be moved to the nearby Albany Rural Cemetery and reinterred close to the General Philip Schuyler monument. General Schuyler served with distinction as a commander during the Revolutionary War, became a U.S. Senator, and was the father-in-law of Alexander Hamilton.

An old photograph of the Schuyler House.

Continue east along the paved walkway for another hundred feet to reach the site of the former *Schuyler House*, to your right. Large stone blocks believed to date back to 1649 are arranged in a rectangular outline to give a general sense of how the house was laid out.

Walk through the stone blocks as if you were strolling through the house, and exit on the south side. A walkway makes a tiny circle here where two more history plaques can be read. One is entitled "The Colonial & Revolutionary Wars"; the other one, nearby, reads "Arent van Curler & Fr. Jogues at the Flatts in 1643."

During the colonial wars in North America involving France, Britain, and Spain, which lasted from 1689 to 1763, Schuyler Flatts was in constant danger of being attacked from the north by the French and their Native American allies. For this reason the Schuyler House was fortified by a stockade in 1747 that was large enough to hold 100 soldiers. This fortification not only served to protect the Schuyler home from attack, but helped provide a defense of Albany. The Schuyler House also played a significant role during the Revolutionary War, providing an encampment for the Patriots in 1775 and 1777.

Arent van Curler & Father Jogues—Arent van Curler, grandnephew of Kiliaen van Rensselaer, future founder of Schenectady, and an early resident of Schuyler Flatts, was instrumental in helping Father Isaac Jogues (pronounced "zhog"), a French Jesuit missionary and soon-to-be martyr, escape from the Mohawks in 1642 when the captured priest was brought by his abductors to Beverwijck (a fur-trading community slightly north of Fort Orange). And what did Father Jogues do after he was rescued? Within a couple of years he went back to his missionary work among Native Americans and was killed at a Mohawk village near present-day Auriesville, New York. A statue of Father Jogues can be seen at the Auriesville Shrine, erected in 1922 by the Order of the Alhambra.

Walk east across the grass to reach the paved walkway near the edge of the woods, and then proceed south. In a moment you will come to a spur path that takes you to a tertiary section of the Bikeway.

Bikeway Extension—This 0.5-mile-long extension of the bikeway takes you along the Little River—a tiny tributary of the Hudson River that rises in the hills west of Schuyler Flatts. Walking along this part of the bikeway affords the opportunity to be close to a freshwater tidal wetland—a globally rare ecological community—physically connected to the Hudson River. Although these wetlands are flooded daily by tides, the salinity level of the water is near zero because of the creek's distance from the Atlantic Ocean and because fresh water is steadily introduced by the stream. As a result you are likely to see such wetland plants as pickerelweed, spatterdock, arrowhead, wild rice, water-willow, cattail, and buttonbush.

22. SCHUYLER FLATTS CULTURAL PARK

An aeriel view of seventeenth-century blocks outlining the shape of the Schuyler House.

Turn right and follow the pathway south for >0.1 mile to its dead end at The Village One Apartments for views of the wetlands to your left, which become more extensive as you head south. Or turn left and follow the walkway north for <0.4 mile. What's notable about this part of the walk is that both the Little River and I-787 approach much closer as the space between the two narrows. Before the walkway ends at the corner of Broadway and Fourth Street, you will see to your right the Little River flowing out into the Hudson River through two large culverts.

It's virtually impossible to imagine today how the land next to the Little River may have looked during the Schuylers' time. The creation of I-787 has totally transformed the landscape between Schuyler Flatts and the Hudson River.

Follow the spur path back up to the park and continue south on the paved walkway. In 0.1 mile you will come to the next history plaque, on your left, entitled "The Native People." By the time that Henry Hudson sailed up the Hudson River in 1609, Native Americans had been hunting, fishing, and cultivating the land in this area for 12,000 years. The idea that Hudson "discovered" the river that would eventually bear his name is rather ludicrous.

Continue on the paved walkway, now heading southwest. Within 100 feet you will see to your left a number of large wooden structures just beyond the edge of the woods. A short, informal path leads to them. These structures, including lean-tos, a teepee (which is not a Native American form of lodging indigenous to this region), and a number of other structures, are all made out of trimmed branches. Whether or not this section of the park has anything specifically to do with Schuyler Flatts or its history, it makes for a fascinating diversion and should not be missed.

PART TWO • CAPITAL REGION

Clinton's Ditch—a tiny section of the original Erie Canal.

Back on the paved walkway, after walking through a white-painted arbor and continuing west for 0.2 mile you will reach the park's southwest corner where huge stone blocks can be seen outlining the shape of "Clinton's Ditch"—part of the original Erie Canal completed in 1825. The canal was 4 feet deep and 40 feet wide. Although it was considered a marvel of engineering in its time, the canal proved inadequate within a couple of decades and had to be replaced by the enlarged Erie Canal (see following chapter, "Erie Canal Ruins").

From Clinton's Ditch, continue following the paved walkway as it leads north back to the pavilion and parking area.

History: Schuyler Flatts was born at the end of the last ice age when a 160-mile-long body of water called Lake Albany, spanning the distance from Newburgh to Glens Falls, formed and then disappeared thousands of years later. It left behind at the Flatts a substantial area of flat, fertile lands—a floodplain nourished by the Hudson River when it periodically would overflow its banks. Because the land was rich in nutrients, nomadic groups of early Native Americans began visiting the area to hunt and fish and to gather nuts and edible plants. By 1200 a semi-permanent village had been established. The land was cleared for farming, and corn was grown and stored in pits. These early people called themselves *Muhheakunnek*, meaning "people of the ever-flowing waters." In time they became known as the Mohicans.

Fast-forward to the seventeenth century and the arrival of Europeans. Initially the property was part of a 1630 land purchase by Kiliaen van Rensselaer for his Rensselaerswyck patroonship. In 1642, Arent van Curler, a grandnephew of Kiliaen, built a house on the Flatts that served as a trading post. The house was 120 feet long

22. SCHUYLER FLATTS CULTURAL PARK

and sheltered farm laborers, with a section set aside for the farm animals. It had a cellar 20 feet long by 28 feet wide.

During this period of time, the Dutch were able to turn a nice profit by trading European goods to Native Americans in exchange for beaver skins. Van Curler's house partially collapsed in 1668, and that had an impact for a short time on trade relations.

In 1670 the house was rebuilt by Richard Van Rensselaer, who was another member of the patroon's family. Subsequently it was purchased by Philip Pieterse Schuyler in 1672 for 700 beaver pelts and 1,600 guilders, and for the next two and a half centuries it remained in the Schuyler family. The most notable Schuyler to live in the home was Pieter Schuyler, who became the first mayor of Albany in 1686.

During the colonial wars that lasted from 1689–1763, the house was fortified by a stockade in 1747 to make it less vulnerable. This perimeter encompassed an area large enough to contain 100 soldiers. The house also became a center of colonial military and social life, a place where troops could gather in the process of moving north or west to attack the French. It was here that Lord Howe was entertained while on his way to Ticonderoga in 1758.

During the American Revolution the house was occupied by the Patriots in 1777 while readying themselves for the Battle of Saratoga.

With the need to expand travel and commerce westward through the Mohawk Valley, part of Schuyler Flatts was dug up in 1823 to create a waterway for the original Erie Canal. This version of the Erie Canal was completed in 1825, enlarged later, and ultimately abandoned when the New York State Barge Canal was completed in 1918.

In 1910 the Schuyler family moved out of the estate, finally selling the house in 1929, and then the remainder of the property in 1948. From 1910 to 1948, the land at Schuyler Flatts was rented out for farming and carnivals. It became known as Beattie's Field, after Guy and Mary Ann Killough Beattie, who lived there for a period of time. In 1949 a carnival operator named James E. Strates bought the Beattie farm and made Schuyler Flatts the home for his traveling carnival and circus.

In 1946 the mansion was sold to Charles Rivenberg, who operated the house as the Sunnycrest Nursing Home until it went out of business in 1959. From 1960 on, the historic house remained abandoned until it burned down in November 1962.

In 1993 the Schuyler Flatts Archaeological District was designated a National Historic Landmark.

The town park that you see today was established in 2002. It has many uses today, including as the site of an annual Civil War Heritage Days encampment. ■

PART TWO • CAPITAL REGION

23. ERIE CANAL RUINS

Location: Cohoes (Albany County)
Fee: None
Hours: Dawn to dusk
Note: This hike is divided into four sections. Consult each section for information on parking, GPS and Gazetteer locators, accessibility, degree of difficulty, and additional information for that section.

Description: The first three sections in this chapter take you to various parts of the old Erie Canal in Cohoes where fairly intact locks can be viewed close-up. In addition you will see partial ruins of the Juncta where the Erie Canal and Champlain Canal were joined, as well as a very intact weigh station where boats were weighed and charged a toll based upon tonnage. The fourth section takes you to a replica of a giant mastodon, whose skeleton was found in an enormous pothole when the site for Harmony Mills #3 was being excavated.

Highlights: Cohoes Falls • Sections of the original Erie Canal ("Clinton's Ditch") • Surviving locks from enlarged sections of the Erie Canal • Historic Harmony Mills • Reconstructed Cohoes mastodon

23. ERIE CANAL RUINS

General History of the Erie Canal: The history of the Erie Canal takes place in two phases. The original Erie Canal was 40 feet wide and 4 feet deep. It extended all the way from Albany to Buffalo, a distance of 363 miles, and contained 83 locks, each being 90 feet long and 15 feet wide. Eighteen aqueducts were required to carry boats and barges across rivers, the Mohawk River being the principal river that had to be crossed.

Construction on the canal began in 1817 and was completed in 1825. Part of this accomplishment is attributed to Canvass White, who came up with a way to make hydraulic cement (cement that will harden under water) in America, instead of importing it at great cost from England. At its time the Erie Canal was the second-longest canal in the world, surpassed only by the 1,100-mile-long Jing-Hang Grand Canal in China. There were many opponents of the canal's construction who called it, derisively, "Clinton's Ditch" and "Clinton's Folly"—references to New York Governor Dewitt Clinton, who was a major advocate for the canal.

Nevertheless the canal proved to be an immediate success and played no small role in making New York "the Empire State." By surmounting 70-foot-high Cohoes Falls, the Erie Canal provided a doorway into western New York, opening up the entire state for industrial development and settlement.

Speed was never a defining attribute of the canal system, however. Boats generally traveled at an average rate of three miles an hour. It took ten days to go from Albany to Buffalo.

The original canal quickly became obsolete and was deemed inefficient. It simply was not big enough and deep enough to accommodate the increasing number of ever-larger and heavier boats and barges traveling the canal. Eleven years later, in 1836, work began on enlarging the canal. The first work at enlargement of the canal was done in eastern New York, where demand was the heaviest.

To accomplish the task, a new route was laid out in Cohoes using 16 double locks (which allowed two boats to be accommodated simultaneously), a reduction of 3 locks from the original 19. Each of these locks measured 110 feet in length and was 18 feet wide. These are the locks that you will see on your tour. The work in this area was completed in 1842.

It took another 20 years, however, for the canal enlargement to be completed across the entire state. But efficiency had definitely been improved. There were fewer locks to cause congestion, and thirteen miles of the original length had been eliminated.

Unfortunately, the glory days of the Erie Canal were numbered despite all of the improvements that had been made. With the advent of the locomotive, canals could no longer compete with the rail system's high speeds, lower costs, and greater efficiency. Gradually, traffic on the canals diminished.

PART TWO • CAPITAL REGION

In 1918 the Erie Canal was completely abandoned with the inauguration of New York's newest system—the New York State Barge Canal. The barge canal essentially canalized the Mohawk River through a system of dams and locks. No aqueducts were needed. The Barge Canal is still in use today, over a century later, although more for luxury crafts and boats than for commercial transportation. ∎

Erie Canal Locks 14–18.

23. ERIE CANAL RUINS

Section I
Cohoes Falls and Locks 18, 17, 16, 15 and 14

Location: Cohoes (Albany County)
NYS Atlas & Gazetteer, Tenth Edition, p. 66, E5; **Earlier Edition,** p. 66, B4
GPS Cohoes Falls Parking: 42.785436, –73.711249
GPS Destinations: *Lock 18*—42.784871, –73.711507; *Lock 17*—42.782617, –73.709874; *Lock 16*—42.780189, –73.706068; *Lock 15*—42.778369, –73.703400; *Lock 14*—42.774855, –73.704420; *Power Canal Park*—42.779827, –73.703825; *Johnston Mansion (Longview)*—42.777164, –73.704602
Accessibility: *Lock 18*—Roadside; *Lock 17*— <0.2-mile walk; *Lock 16*— >0.4-mile walk; *Lock 15*— >0.5-mile walk; *Lock 14*—0.7-mile walk; *Power Canal Park*—1.6-mile walk; *Round trip*— ~2.2-mile walk
Degree of Difficulty: Easy to moderate

Additional Information: Cohoes Visitor's Center, 58 Remsen Street, Cohoes, NY 12047, (518) 237-0078; Spindle City Historic Society, formed in 1994 ("Spindle City" is the nickname for Cohoes)

Directions: Take I-787 to its northern terminus at the City of Cohoes. From the junction of I-787 & Route 32, cross over Route 32 and drive northwest on New Courtland Street/North Mohawk Street for ~1.0 mile. Turn left into the parking area for Cohoes Falls Overlook Park.

Walk & History: Section I takes you from Cohoes Falls to a series of locks, one after the other, and then back up through the Harmony Mills Historic District to where you started. From the parking area, walk across North Mohawk Street to the Cohoes Falls Overlook Park. A paved walkway takes you across a bridge spanning the power channel that leads to the hydroelectric plant and directly to a breathtaking lateral view of Cohoes Falls. At times, when conditions are safe, the lower section of the park is opened so that visitors can descend to the bottom of the gorge for close-up views of Cohoes Falls and the Mohawk River. From Cohoes Falls, return to the parking area. In the back of the parking area, on the side of the hill to your left, is Lock 18.

Lock 18 is a fairly well-preserved double lock that was listed on the National Register of Historic Places in 1971. Several on-site history plaques illustrate how Lock 18 and the other locks worked by using hydraulic pressure instead of complicated machinery to open and close their massive doors. For this reason the gates were always slightly angled upstream to take advantage of water pressure.

PART TWO • CAPITAL REGION

Cohoes Falls is a massive waterfall, 70 feet high and nearly 1,000 feet wide, lying virtually at the terminus of the Mohawk River (New York's second-largest river) just upstream from the Mohawk's confluence with the Hudson River at Peebles Island. At one time Cohoes Falls rivaled Niagara Falls as New York's premier natural attraction, having the obvious advantage of being in an area of high population density and accessibility as opposed to Niagara Falls, which was tucked away in a less-visited corner of the state.

In *Glacial Geology of the Cohoes Quadrangle*, James H. Stoller, a twentieth-century geologist, writes that Cohoes Falls ...

... then falls 70 feet over a precipice of rock. The water does not descend abruptly as a vertical sheet but flows over the steeply inclined rock declivity [i.e., downward slope]. The slope of this declivity corresponds in general to the dip of the rocks but in the middle portion of the falls the rocks have been worn and broken so that the angle of the fall is less than that of the dip and in places the falling water has the character of a cascade. At about one-third of the width of the river from the left bank there is a projecting mass of smooth rock over which little water passes. At the inner side of this mass the volume of falling water is greater than elsewhere and at the base there is a deep pool of water occupying a depression worn into the rocks.

Cohoes Falls was one of the main reasons for the Erie Canal's creation. There was simply no way for boats and barges to bypass the immense waterfall. In the end it took a total of 16 locks to lift boats and barges high enough to surmount the waterfall.

Cohoes Falls was itself transformed. The Mohawk River was dammed >0.5 mile upstream from the falls and a power chanel created that brought water down to Harmony Mills. This significantly reduced the flow going over the falls. Later, when Harmony Mills ceased operations, the power channel was used to drive the turbines at the Brookfield hydroelectric plant (an aging facility that still remains in operation today). When the New York State Barge Canal was completed in 1918, additional waters were pirated off from above Cohoes Falls to maintain a constant level of water in the Waterford Flight of Locks. Cohoes Falls has been significantly enfeebled. What you see today is not what Native Americans and early European settlers saw when they visited the falls centuries ago.

23. ERIE CANAL RUINS

Cohoes Falls from William Cullen Bryant's 1874 Picturesque America.

Erie Canal wending its way through Cohoes. Postcard circa 1900.

PART TWO • CAPITAL REGION

Walk along the west wall of Lock 18 and then down and around to Rioux Court, a tiny street that immediately takes you to Church Street. Proceed northeast on Church Street for 0.1 mile, turn right onto Orchard Street, and head southeast for >0.1 mile. When you come to the junction of Orchard Street and Erie Street, bear right and walk across an open field for close-up views of Lock 17.

Lock 17 is mostly intact except for its north wall. Adjacent to the lock is a private home that originally belonged to the lock tender. According to sources, lock tenders usually were married men because it was believed that single men were not as reliable. The tenders' wives and children often became unpaid assistants by virtue of being in the same household.

From the junction of Erie Street and Orchard Street, head southeast on Erie Street for 0.1 mile and then bear right onto Harmony Street. An escarpment forms on your right. You will notice a paved walkway to your left, which is part of the Cohoes Heritage Trail. Follow this walkway south. In <0.2 mile you will pass by the ruins of **Lock 16** to your left. Only the uppermost capstones of the double-chambered lock protrude from the earth; the bulk of the lock lies buried under the ground.

Below, to your left, is a section of the Harmony Mills complex. On the south side of North Mohawk Street are Mill West B (where the offices for The Lofts are), Mill West D, and Mill West F. On the north side of North Mohawk Street stands the awesome Harmony Mill #3—1,185 feet long, 70–76 feet wide, and 5 stories high, capped with a mansard roof. In its time, two 800-horsepower Boyden turbines provided all the power that was needed for the mill to function.

Locks 13 & 14. Postcard 1910.

23. ERIE CANAL RUINS

Continue past Lock 16 for ~150 feet to reach Vliet Street. Along the way take note of the brick buildings to your right that were once domiciles for the Harmony Mills workers. At one time, over 6,000 men, women, and children were housed in a variety of dormitories, multi-family tenement houses, and single-family homes.

Cross over Vliet Street and head southeast on the paved walkway. The pavement quickly turns to gravel and becomes a towpath lined with rectangular stone blocks. In 0.1 mile you will reach Lock 15, on your left.

Lock 15 is a fairly well-preserved double lock, but probably receives fewer visitors than the locks near Cohoes Falls. Look for a small house on the east side of the lock, which was once the lock tender's residence.

The large building downhill, next to North Mohawk Street, is Harmony Mill #4. Originally it was the Van Benthuysen Paper Mill until it was bought by Harmony Mills and remodeled. It produced cotton bags for shipping fabrics made by the mills.

While walking along this section of the towpath, think about how the canal and pathway were literally blasted out of the side of a hill.

Continue southeast. In 0.05 mile you will see to your left a more recent path that crosses down and up the canal ruins, running perpendicular to the towpath. Pay close attention to the side of the canal along here, for two old feeder canal foundations that once channeled water into the main canal are visible. The pit containing the canal is quite wide in this section. Farther ahead, the entire canal pit has been filled in with earth, and this continues for a short distance.

"Longview"—On top of the hill to your right is the Johnston Mansion, which was constructed in 1866. It was called "Longview" for its sweeping views of the Hudson and Mohawk valleys. The three-story Italianate mansion was built for David John Johnston, who served as superintendent of the Harmony Mills Company, literally overseeing it from his home.

In <0.3 mile from Vliet Street, you will reach the end of the towpath and the beginning of Standish Place (a tiny side street). Immediately on your left is a path that leads over to *Lock 14*, but there is not a lot to see there—essentially disheveled blocks of stone and a lock that has been significantly filled in.

There is a more promising view of the lock, however. Walk down Standish Place for several hundred feet. Then, just before you reach Cohoes Bowling (a low-lying building on your left), look back to see what remains of Lock 14's front.

Follow Standish Place downhill and turn left onto Route 470/Ontario Street. Walk east for >0.2 mile, bear left onto Mohawk Street, and then left again onto New Courtland Street/North Mohawk Street. Ahead of you now will be the Harmony Mills complex.

PART TWO • CAPITAL REGION

As you head northwest along the sidewalk, you will pass by Harmony Mill #4 on your left and then come to a stone-laid walkway to your left that goes down and then comes back up 500 feet later. A history plaque at the beginning of the walkway tells you that you are at Power Canal Park.

Power Canal Park—Try to imagine that where you are standing now was once the original Erie Canal (Clinton's Ditch) and then later the power channel for Harmony Mills. You would be treading water here over a century ago.

Follow the walkway down to a lower level. You will see gated ducts to your left in the stone side wall that were once conduits from the power channel to Harmony Mill #2.

The next history plaque along the walkway provides information about the Erie Canal.

Water from the Mohawk River was ultimately diverted through a series of gates and dams into seven different channels, which used the water six different times before releasing it back into the Mohawk River.

The third history plaque reads "Developing an Industrial Empire" and furnishes information about Peter Harmony and the wealthy industrial capitalists who created the Harmony Manufacturing Company in 1836. Under Peter Harmony's guidance, however, the mill failed to make a profit and was sold in 1850 to Thomas Garner of New York City and Alfred Wild of Kinderhook. They brought on an experienced weaver named Robert Johnston, and the mill became a financial success. A larger-than-life-sized bronze statue of Thomas

Power Canal Park.

23. ERIE CANAL RUINS

Garner, installed in 1875, can be seen in a niche at the center of the Harmony Mills #3 tower.

An 1866 photograph of the Johnston Mansion is displayed on this history plaque. The mansion, known as Longview, is associated with David John Johnston, who managed the mill and was the son of the mill's first manager, Robert Johnston.

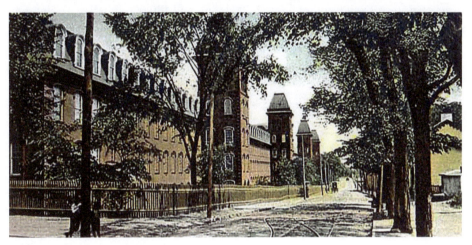

Harmony Mill #3. Postcard circa 1900.

When **Harmony Mills** opened in 1872, it was the largest cotton mill complex in the world. It was nicknamed Mastodon Mill because of the mastodon skeleton that was found buried in a nearby pothole. The mill continued to operate until 1988 when its main tenant, Barclay Home Products, went out of business. Mill No. 2 burned down in 1995; then, in 1998, Mill No. 1 suffered extensive damage from a fire.

A developer named Uri Kaufman purchased the complex in 2000 and began over the years to convert the mill buildings into 340 high-end luxury apartments known as The Lofts at Harmony Mills.

In 1971 Harmony Mill No. 3, the centerpiece building, was listed on the National Register of Historic Places, followed by the entire Harmony Mills Historic District in 1978. In 1975 Mill #3 was designated as a National Historic Mechanical Engineering Landmark by the American Society of Mechanical Engineers. Sections of the complex, including some of the housing that was constructed for the millworkers, were placed on the register of National Historic Landmarks in 1999.

The fourth history plaque, entitled "The Harmony Mills," relates information on the Johnstons.

Although it's startling to read that children under nine worked long hours in the mills, it was not an uncommon occurrence in this Charles Dickens era.

Mill #3's operation was almost beyond belief. Thirteen miles of belting powered by water-driven turbines drove 2,700 looms and 130,000 spindles. Twelve-foot pulleys driven by enormous gears ran 2-foot-wide leather belts throughout the mill. One belt, stretching up to the fifth floor, was 200 feet long.

You will encounter the fifth history plaque as you come back up to sidewalk level. The plaque expounds on what constitutes "A Company Town," which Harmony Mills certainly was. The mill had its own police force, repair crews, sanitation men, even paving crews. It was also very involved in the community schools and churches.

The last history plaque is located in a tiny, sidewalk-level alcove halfway between the two ends of the park. This plaque is of particular interest, for it shows what the original Harmony Mill and subsequent Mills #1–#5 looked like. The plaque emphasizes that what you are seeing below are the "…stone arched exits of the hydro tunnel that carried water released by the turbines at the back of Harmony Mill #2." Harmony Mill #2 no longer exists, but many of the other mills do. Harmony Mill #3, just up the street on the right-hand side, remains a showpiece of late-eighteenth-century architecture.

Return to the Cohoes Falls parking area—When you come back up onto the main sidewalk from the history plaques to Vliet Street, continue northwest on New Courtland Street/North Mohawk Street for 0.5 mile, walking through the Historic Harmony Mill District and past School Street (leading to the old Cohoes Falls Overlook Park) to return to the parking area by Cohoes Falls. ■

23. ERIE CANAL RUINS

Section II
Locks 9 & 10 and the Old Juncta

Location: Between George Street & Alexander Street
NYS Atlas & Gazetteer, Tenth Edition, p. 66, E5; **Earlier Edition,** p. 66, BC4
GPS Parking: 42.766111, –73.702991
GPS Destinations: *Lock 10*—42.764688, –73.702432; *Lock 9*—42.762040, –73.702018; *Juncta*—42.763616, –73.698978
Accessibility: *Lock 10*—0.1-mile walk; *Lock 9*—0.3-mile walk; *Juncta*—0.7-mile walk; *Round trip*—1.0-mile walk
Degree of Difficulty: Easy to moderate

Directions: Heading north on I-787, continue past Exit 9E for 7 East/Troy/Bennington for 0.7 mile and turn left at the traffic light onto Tibbits Avenue. Head west for 150 feet.

Heading south on I-787 from Cohoes (junction of Routes 32 & I-787), turn right onto Tibbits Avenue after ~1.8 miles and proceed west for >150 feet.

From either direction, turn right onto Route 32/ Cohoes Road and drive north for 1.0 mile, then turn left onto Main Street, proceeding northwest. After <0.2 mile turn left onto George Street and go southwest for <0.2 mile. Park either in front of George Street Park or along the dead-end street next to its west side. The park is open daily from 7 AM–9 PM.

Walk & History: From the west side of George Street Park, follow a stone block path south that leads past

Locks 9, 10 & the Juncta.

the playground area. In less than 0.05 mile you will begin to see sections of the old canal to your left as you leave the playground behind.

After 0.1 mile look to your right to view an area where a stream has cut a noticeable ravine. This tiny stream, called Eagle Nest Creek, parallels the walkway momentarily and then disappears into a culvert. At one time the stream served as a feeder canal for the Erie Canal. Several paths lead down into the ravine here, but none go for any distance. Although it's hard to imagine how this place once looked, you are in the area where *Lock 10* operated. One wall of the lock remains, but that is all that has survived, at least above ground.

In another 0.1 mile you will come to Spring Street, which runs between Locks 9 & 10, separating the two. Continue south on the towpath for a short distance farther to reach Lock 9.

Lock 9 lies virtually next to the towpath, on your left, and it is a real beauty—an almost completely intact double lock. Be sure also to notice the house next to the lock, which at one time belonged to the lock tender but has been modified over the years since.

Continue south on the stone-block towpath as it leads past the west side of the lock. In another 300 feet you will come to Alexander Street. The path officially ends here, although an informal path continues south from Alexander Street for another 0.1 mile before ending at a fenced-in section of private land. Although no locks are contained in the section south of Alexander Street, traces of the canal itself remain, particularly near the end of the trail. The part of the canal closest to the Alexander Street Park was filled in years ago with debris from the Cohoes Memorial Hospital after it was demolished.

Lock 9 is surprisingly intact.

23. ERIE CANAL RUINS

Return to Alexander Street, walk east to Lincoln Street, turn left, and go north for 0.1 mile. At Spring Street turn right, head east for 0.1 mile, and then left onto Route 32/Saratoga Road. In <0.1 mile look for a historic marker on your right that recounts information about the Juncta, which was where the Erie Canal & Champlain Canal were enjoined (hence "juncta" for "junction").

Remnants of *The Juncta* can be found ~150 feet away from Route 32 and nearly next to I-787. The downside here is that the Juncta can only be viewed by peering through a chain-linked fence behind a presently vacant lot. The Juncta can also be viewed from I-787, but only in passing, since there is no place for cars to pull over and take a closer look.

In its heyday the Juncta was a hub of commercial activity. It was here that canal men could buy supplies, food, hardware, livestock, animal feed, and virtually anything else they needed for the trip. There were even hotels where boatmen could rest or sleep.

From the Juncta, continue north on Route 32/Saratoga Street for 0.1 mile, bear left onto Main Street, and then left onto George Street, returning to your car within 0.2 mile from Main Street.

There are two other surviving parts of the Erie Canal nearby in Cohoes that can be glimpsed but not accessed. Neither is particularly interesting in itself, but they are remnants of history worth preserving. One site is across George Street Park opposite the dead-end road next to the park. Stand at the dead-end road that runs behind the Heritage Baptist Church and you will see a side wall less than 50 feet away from the road (GPS 42.766419, −73.703467).

The other remnant is very close by. You can either walk or drive to it. Go to the west end of George Street and turn right onto Central Avenue. Head north for <0.2 mile. When you come to the Cohoes Fire Department at 25 Central Avenue, look to your right toward the back of the south side of the fire department and you will see a canal wall that remains standing (GPS 42.768514, −73.703971). ∎

The Juncta—junction of the Erie Canal & Champlain Canal.

CAPITAL REGION

Section III

Weighlock, Maplewood Historic Park

Location: North end of Watervliet across from 26th Street
NYS Atlas & Gazetteer, Tenth Edition, p. 82, A5; **Earlier Edition,** p. 66, BC4
GPS Parking: 42.736767, −73.700365
GPS Weighlock: 42.736749, −73.700136
Accessibility: Roadside
Degree of Difficulty: Easy

Directions: Heading north on I-787, continue past Exit 9E for 7 East/Troy/Bennington for 0.7 mile and turn left at the traffic light onto Tibbits Avenue. Head west for 150 feet.

Heading south on I-787 from Cohoes (junction of Route 32 & I-787), turn right onto Tibbits Avenue after ~1.8 miles and proceed west for >150 feet.

From either direction turn left onto Route 32/Cohoes Road and drive south for 0.9 mile to reach Maplewood Historic Park and the weighlock. Look for a historic marker in front of the weighlock.

History: *The weighlock*, which was used to levy tolls on barges carrying produce and merchandise, is a surprisingly well-preserved relic from the nineteenth century. It measures ~160 feet long, 30 feet wide and, because it has not been completely buried under fill, is ~3–4 feet deep. The block foundation of the weighlock station (where the weighing was done) can be seen next to the lock a few feet to the east.

The historic weighlock is located in tiny Maplewood Historic Park.

23. ERIE CANAL RUINS

A photograph of the weighlock with its striking Greek Revival exterior is displayed on a stone block by the lock.

This weighlock was a departure from the ones before it. Up until 1850, boats were weighed by measuring the volume of water they displaced. The more water displaced, the more the boat operators were charged. This weighlock incorporated a new hydraulic system using scales. Each boat that entered the lock would come to rest on a wooden cradle as the water was drained from the lock. The weigh-master, moving a center balancing weight along the beam, would then determine the tonnage of the boat by subtracting out the known weight of the boat when empty. The proper tariff would then be applied accordingly.

Although the weighlock building endured from 1850 to 1915, it had already ceased operations by the late 1800s after New York State abolished tolls in an effort to help the canals better compete with the railroads. ■

Block foundation of the Weighlock Station next to the lock.

Section IV
Cohoes Mastodon

Location: Cohoes Public Library, 169 Market Street
NYS Atlas & Gazetteer, Tenth Edition, p. 66, E5; **Earlier Edition,** p. 66, BC4
GPS Parking: 42.772394, –73.699280
GPS Cohoes Public Library: 42.772104, –73.699390
GPS Cohoes mastodon historic marker: 42.782955, –73.706942
Accessibility: Inside library
Degree of Difficulty: Easy
Additional Information: Cohoes Public Library, 169 Mohawk Street, Cohoes, NY, (518) 235-2570

Directions: From Cohoes (junction of Bridge Avenue/Columbia Street & I-787) drive northwest on Columbia Street for 0.1 mile. As soon as you cross over railroad tracks, turn right onto Mohawk Street and proceed north for 0.1 mile. Bear right either onto Van Rensselaer Street or Canvass Street and head north for 0.1 mile to the parking area in front of the library entrance.

History: A life-sized replica of the Cohoes mastodon (also spelled "mastodont") can be seen at the Cohoes Public Library. It was constructed in 1922 by Noah T. Clare and Charles P. Heidenrich at the behest of the New York State Museum.

The Cohoes mastodon is an impressive behemoth to behold. It stands 8.5 feet high (as measured to its shoulders) and is 15 feet long, with tusks that extend 4 1/2 feet. It is believed to have been a male who died at age 32 after its skull was pierced by the tusk of another mastodon. Presumably the two opponents were locked in mortal combat, perhaps over territory, food, or mating. The Cohoes mastodon also engaged in an earlier battle when it was 11 years old (during a period called "musth" when raging hormones produce highly aggressive and combative behavior between competing males). The mastodon sustained bone injuries that stunted the growth of its tusks and also led to chronic malnutrition. It never lived long enough to reach the average life expectancy of 50 years for a mastodon. When alive, the creature weighed 8,000–10,000 pounds, or roughly 4–5 tons. Scientists estimate that it died over 11,000 years ago at a time when the last ice age was approaching its end.

In their heyday the mastodon ranged from Alaska to Central Mexico. Their only predators were saber-toothed tigers and humans. The word mastodon is derived from the Greek words *mastos*, meaning "breast," and *odous*, meaning "teeth."

23. ERIE CANAL RUINS

To clear up a common misunderstanding, the mastodon was not the same as a mammoth, but rather another proboscidean that belonged to the genus *Mammut*.

The bones of the Cohoes mastodon were found inside two large potholes in 1866 by workmen excavating rock at the site of Harmony Mill #3. The skeleton rested on a bed of clay and broken shale covered by fifty feet of muck and peat. The bones were initially displayed loosely and unassembled in the Harmony Mills office. Later they were exhibited at the Troy County Fair and a number of other places. Eventually the bones were purchased by New York State, and in 1867 the almost complete, assembled skeleton was put on display at the State Cabinet of Natural History on State Street. The exhibition was transferred to the museum in the State Education Building, in the "Geological and Agricultural Hall." In 1976 the skeleton was relocated to the lobby of the new Cultural Education Center, and in the early 2000s repositioned to its present location near the south end (rear) of the museum. ∎

Replica of the Cohoes mastodon.

PART THREE
SARATOGA REGION

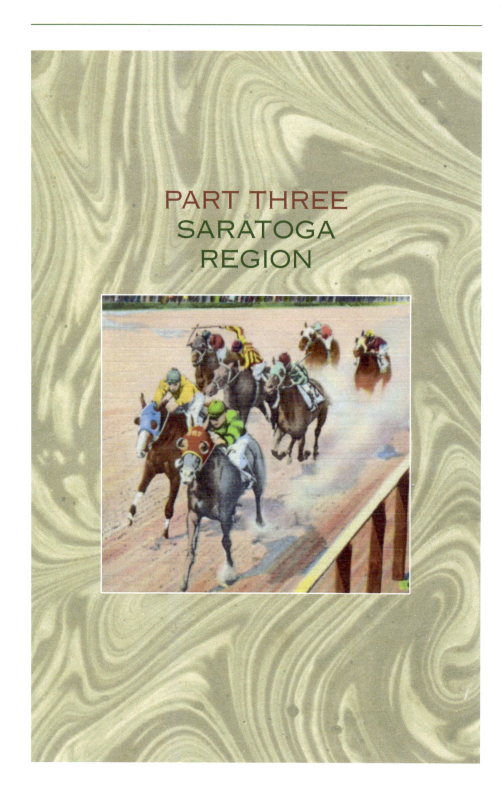

24. SHENANTAHA CREEK PARK

Location: Northwest of Round Lake (Saratoga County)
NYS Atlas & Gazetteer, Tenth Edition, p. 66, C4; **Earlier Edition,** p. 66, A3
GPS Parking: 42.964428, –73.824524
GPS Destinations: *Flaxseed mill ruins*—42.965861, –73.821106; *Indian mortars (general area)* –42.965705, –73821121; *Cascade*—42.960125, –73.822494
Hours: 7:30 AM–sunset
Fee: None
Restrictions: No alcohol, hunting, or littering; dogs must by leashed
Accessibility: *Mill ruins and post-glacial erosional features*—0.1-mile hike; *Malta Trail*—0.7-mile hike; *Cascade*—0.2-mile walk
Degree of Difficulty: *Malta Trail to mill ruins & post-glacial erosional features*—Easy; *Malta Trail to end*—Moderate; *Cascade*—Easy
Additional Information: Shenantaha Creek Park, 376 East Line Road, Malta, NY, 12020; disc-golf course map—discap.net/courses/Shenantaha-creek

Directions: Driving north on the Adirondack Northway (I–87), take Exit 11 for Burnt Hills & Round Lake and drive west on Round Lake Road for ~1.0 mile. At a traffic light bear right onto Eastline Road/Route 82 and proceed north for 2.0 miles, turning right into Shenantaha Creek Park.

Driving south on the Adirondack Northway (I–87), take Exit 12 and drive west on Route 67 for 1.4 miles. Bear left onto Eastline Road/Route 82 and proceed south for 0.5 mile, turning left into Shenantaha Creek Park.

From either direction, follow Solotruck Lane east for <0.3 mile to the parking area at Shenantaha Creek Park.

Description: Shenantaha Creek Park combines hiking with history and throws in a little bit of geology for good measure. The park is close to residents of the Capital Region, yet unknown to many people and visited by fewer still. It contains the ruins of an old flax mill and post-glacial erosional features (potholes) believed to have been used by Native Americans for grinding corn.

Ballston Creek has cut out a deep gorge in the park with walls as high as 25–30 feet.

Highlights: Ruins of old flaxseed mill • Indian mortars (bowls worn into the rock) • Ballston Creek and its deeply cut ravine • 20-foot-high elongated cascade • Paved, multipurpose trail for walkers, joggers, and bikers • Disc-golf course

PART THREE • SARATOGA REGION

Barbara Delaney sizes up a large boulder at Shenantaha Park.

Hike: *To Indian mortars and flaxseed mill ruins*—From the parking area, follow a paved walkway north that quickly passes between pavilions A and B and then by a playground area to your right. Once you are beyond the playground, head straight across the field toward the woods and then bear right, following the edge of the woods east. The hike begins from the southeast end of a field where two historical markers stand, thirty feet apart at the edge of the woods, each one directly in front of a trail. The red-blazed Malta Trail begins here.

Malta Trail—Start by taking the red-blazed Malta Trail to the left of the Indian mortars historical marker and follow it down a spine of land, quickly descending to the bottom of a ravine where Ballston Creek makes an appearance. One or two large boulders can be seen in the streambed by the creek. The river turns sharply here as the trail follows along, paralleling it. Within <0.1 mile from the start, you will reach the ruins of the flaxseed mill on your left and near the creek. Two sections of a stone wall foundation remain partially intact. The stone wall next to the creek is the better preserved of the two and measures 4 feet high and 15 feet long. We paced off the dimensions of the foundation and estimate that the structure was at least 20 feet wide by 25 feet long. It is easy to walk by this site without realizing what it is unless you know in advance what to look for.

Continue following the Malta Trail as it slowly pulls away from the streambed. In 200 feet you will come to disc-golf basket #12. Turn right here, following the Malta Trail as you enter a field of small boulders along a gently sloping hill. A number of smaller paths go off to the right and lead to different parts of the boulder field. This is an area well worth taking the time to explore, for a number of the boulders here contain post-glacial erosional features (potholes). One very

24. SHENANTAHA CREEK PARK

distinctive potholed boulder lies next to the trail about 50 feet uphill from the disc-golf basket.

Indian Mortars—Historians believe that the glacially formed holes in the rocks uphill from Ballston Creek were used by Native Americans as vessels for grinding or crushing substances like grain with a pestle.

Although post-glacial erosional features may seem like quite a novelty, in reality they occur fairly frequently in eastern New York. Many can be seen in the bedrock by Cohoes Falls. The largest ones that we are familiar with are located farther west in the Mohawk Valley on Canajoharie Creek in Canajoharie and on Moss Island at Little Falls (see *Adirondack Trails with Tales* for detailed information about these two Mohawk Valley sites).

Flaxseed Mill—In the late 1700s a settler named Jonah Starr erected a flaxseed oil mill off Eastline Road that operated from 1795 to 1825. He dammed Ballston Creek and used its waters to power an overshot waterwheel. Starr also ran a farm at the same time.

In the mid-1800s Starr's mill was acquired by Samuel Clark and a Mr. Lindley of Schenectady. The mill was overseen by James Clark, a relative of Samuel. From here on the mill became known as the Clark & Lindley Oil Mill.

According to John Coffman (spouse of Town Historian Jane Coffman), at one time an old "people bridge" over Ballston Creek must have connected the mill with Route 67, thereby eliminating a long trek on an old road (now gone) that entered off of the Eastline-Jonesville Road.

The stone foundation ruins of a flaxseed mill next to Ballston Creek.

One of a number of post-glacial erosional features.

As you leave the field of boulders behind, be sure to keep Ballston Creek to your left and try to stay fairly close to it for the rest of the hike. In <0.05 mile you will pass by disc-golf basket #11, off in the woods to your right. This is a good reference point, because from here the trail immediately veers right and begins following along the top of the bank of Ballston Creek. There are very steep, 25-foot drop-offs to the left, so use caution.

Soon you will find a row of stones along the top of the high bank, as if placed to make the trail more clearly defined. When you come to where a side trail descends left to the stream level, continue straight ahead, pulling away from Ballston Creek slightly. After >100 feet turn left and follow the trail, unmarked momentarily, through a stone wall and then down through another field of small-to-medium-sized boulders.

When you reach Ballston Creek again, follow the Malta Trail, now visibly marked, as it parallels the creek at some height above it. Soon the trail takes you down into a ravine deeply cut by a tributary. As you reach the streambed, take note of a small, dissected spine of land to your left that goes up to the top of a promontory. This isolated spine of land has been cut out on one side by Ballston Creek and on the other side by the unnamed stream. A short path leads up to the top of the promontory, but be careful—there are considerable drop-offs to your left and to your right.

Past this unique landform, the trail immediately leads down to the bottom of the ravine and then takes you along the edge of Ballston Creek for 100 feet. From here the Malta Trail follows next to Ballston Creek through a large expanse of uniformly flat land. Pay particular attention to a 30-foot-high vertical wall of black shale on the opposite side of Ballston Creek. This is the only time you will see a rock wall like this one along the trail.

You might wonder why there is so much space between the opposing banks of the creek here since Ballston Creek is not that large a stream. That is because Ballston Creek is not what it appears to be …

Ballston Creek, despite its diminutive size today, was once many times larger and more powerful and was thus able to cut a deep gorge. Some geologists believe that today's Ballston Creek was actually part of an earlier route used by the Mohawk River to reach the Hudson River. According to that theory, the Mohawk River, following this route from Schenectady, would have gone through Ballston Lake (which does have a river-like look to it), down Ballston Creek, through Round Lake, and then along the Anthony Kill into the Hudson River at what is now Mechanicville. What altered the Mohawk River's course was a pirate channel that slowly developed in Rexford and diverted the flow of the river east toward Cohoes instead of northeast toward Mechanicville. It may be for this reason that a myriad of rounded rocks populate the Indian mortar area. They were formerly part of a streambed.

After you cross a second tiny tributary to Ballston Creek, look up at the escarpment to your right to see a deep-cut ravine that has been partially walled up near the top with cement blocks topped by logs. This was done many years ago in order to shore up the railroad bed that has now become the paved multipurpose Zim Smith Trail.

Although you can follow the Malta Trail for another <0.05-mile, it dead-ends suddenly near the edge of the creek where "no trespassing signs" are posted. We spent some time looking to see if the Malta Trail inconspicuously turned before the dead end and climbed up the steep escarpment to the Zim Smith Trail, but we saw no evidence for that or of the Malta Trail being a loop trail.

You will need to backtrack on the Malta Trail to the disc-golf course and from there return to the parking area.

Although these directions should be quite clear, take note that the creation of multiple informal paths, as well as an 18-hole disc-golf course, has obscured the main trail at times, turning the area into a patchwork of paths. Just keep on the lookout for red markers and, if all else fails, remember that you want to stay relatively close to Ballston Creek through the entirety of the hike.

Cascade—From the parking area, walk south on the Zim Smith Trail for ~0.2 mile. Look to your right when you come to a fenced-in spot to see a 20-foot-high

PART THREE • SARATOGA REGION

An elongated cascade can be seen along the Zim Smith multiuse rail-trail.

elongated cascade. At the bottom of the cascade, below where you are standing, the stream is conducted under the Zim Smith Trail and exits from the other side at the bottom of the cement block wall that you saw earlier from near the end of the Malta Trail.

Zim Smith Trail—The 20-mile-long asphalt pedestrian trail is part of a rail-trail that extends from Ballston Spa to Mechanicville. It is one of forty trails in New York State designated as a National Recreation Trail by the United States Department of Interior.

The Zim Smith Trail follows the former bed of the Rensselaer & Saratoga Railroad (which later merged with the Delaware & Hudson Railroad), a rail line that took passengers from Troy to Ballston Spa, a distance of 25 miles. It was the third railroad to be chartered in New York State.

24. SHENANTAHA CREEK PARK

The trail is named for Zimri "Zim" Smith, a retired United States Air Force colonel who died in 1994. Smith took an active role in historic preservation in Saratoga Springs and founded the "Friends of Saratoga Battlefield," a not-for-profit volunteer organization dedicated to supporting the mission of the Saratoga National Historical Park.

History: Many centuries before Jonah Starr, an early flaxseed mill owner, was born, the site was occupied by Native Americans. Mohicans and Mohawks used nearby Kayaderosseras Creek as a water trail when traveling between the Mohawk Valley and the St. Lawrence Valley. Located between these two destinations, the area encompassing Ballston Creek became a seasonal encampment where Native Americans would grind corn and nuts to supplement their diet, and also use as a base camp to hunt game.

Shenantaha is a Native American word for "deer water," a term suggesting that game has always been plentiful around the creek.

The genesis for Shenantaha Creek Park came about in 1993 when the town board directed the Ruhle Road Park Committee to look into establishing a 56-acre park along Ballston Creek. This was done, and in 1995 an additional 5 acres of land were purchased to provide ready access to the land, which otherwise was landlocked to vehicles. The park officially opened in 1997.

Historical markers have been erected by the edge of the woods at the trailhead, not only to provide essential information on the flaxseed oil mill and the Indian mortars, but to serve as a reminder of just how fortunate we are to live in a region where history and geology intertwine, and where trails have many tales to tell. ■

PART THREE • SARATOGA REGION

25. LESTER PARK

Location: West of Saratoga Springs (Saratoga County)
NYS Atlas & Gazetteer, Tenth Edition, p. 66, A3; **Earlier Edition,** p. 80, D3
GPS Parking: 43.092297, –73.848133
GPS Destinations: *Lester Park*—43.092297, –73.848133; *Kiln at north end of park*—43.092472, –73.848417; *Hoyt's lime kiln on opposite side of Petrified Sea Gardens Road*—43.091994, –73.848217; *Hoyt's quarry*—43.091517, –73.848580
Hours: Dawn to dusk
Fee: None
Restrictions: Removal of artifacts is not permitted.
Accessibility: *Lester Park & kilns*—Roadside; *Quarry*—150-foot walk
Degree of Difficulty: Easy

Directions: From Saratoga Springs (junction of Routes 9/50 & 29 West) drive west on Route 29 for 3.2 miles and turn right onto Petrified Sea Gardens Road.

From Rock City (junction of Route 29 & Rock City Road) drive east on Route 29 for ~3.7 miles and turn left onto Petrified Sea Gardens Road.

From either direction drive north on Petrified Sea Gardens Road for ~1.2 miles. When you come to Lester Park, pull over to your right and park off-road.

Note: On the drive along Petrified Sea Gardens Road to Lester Park Road, take note of two large stone columns to your right at 0.5 mile. They mark the entrance to the former world-famous Petrified Sea Gardens (closed since 2006).

Description: Lester Park is practically an informal outdoor museum, with exposed bedrock displaying a half-billion-year-old form of plant life, an old limestone quarry, and two kilns.

Highlights: Stromatolite reef • Foundations of old kilns • Hoyt limestone quarry

Hike: Lester Park's main feature is the stromatolite reef contained in the exposed bedrock next to the road. You can spend as much time as you like walking on the bedrock and studying these life forms of great antiquity.

When you are finished exploring the stromatolite bed, walk to the northwest end of the bedrock and look straight ahead. You will see the crumbling ruins of an old kiln, virtually clinging to the side of the embankment. A good part of the kiln has collapsed and now lies in large pieces along the sloping embankment. What we found odd was that no sign had been placed next to the kiln to alert visitors to its presence.

25. LESTER PARK

Stromatolite reef beds.

At the southeast end of the exposed bedrock is a path that leads down the embankment for 50 feet to the edge of a tiny stream. On the opposite side of the stream are old stone walls from bygone days when the land was farmed. To your left and a short distance north upstream is the stone foundation of the collapsed kiln.

The main kiln at the park lies diagonally across the road from the exposed section of bedrock. It dates back to the late 1800s and, to our laymen's eyes, looks like a double kiln (if such a thing exists). A plaque next to the kiln provides relevant information.

Hoyt's Lime Kiln—The kiln belonged to the Hoyt Family, who occupied the area in the late 1800s. Unlike many quarries, which carved out blocks of limestone to be used for construction projects such as the Erie Canal, the limestone obtained from this quarry was excavated and used as agricultural lime. There was a good reason for this. Vast tracks of nearby land contained sandy soil that would not support crops. Adding lime to the soil markedly increased the land's fertility.

The kiln stands roughly 12 feet high above the road and will likely last for decades to come since its interior is mostly filled in with earth.

Lime kilns work by the calcination of limestone (calcium carbonate) to produce quicklime (calcium oxide). A high temperature is required, upward of 1,800°F. But if the temperature is too high, then an unreactive "dead-burned" lime is produced, so delicacy and close monitoring of the process are required.

Lime kilns are lined with bricks in order to withstand the intense heat required for the conversion of limestone into quicklime.

PART THREE • SARATOGA REGION

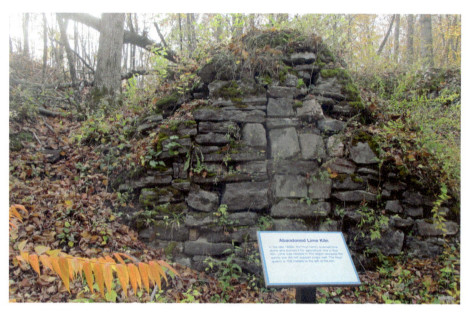

A roadside kiln lies directly opposite the stromatolite reef beds.

From just south of the kiln, follow a wide path that leads west for ~100 feet into the interior of a good-sized quarry. The quarry's most notable feature is a nearly vertical 20-foot-high wall of limestone directly in front of you. You will discover that the quarry is much larger than it first appears.

An interpretive sign explains how the name Hoyt came to be applied to a particular kind of limestone that is only found in this quarry and in certain parts of the southeastern Adirondacks. The sign also points out that, "A number of late-Cambrian age fossils are found only here and in Poughkeepsie, New York."

The quarry is maintained by Skidmore College.

History: Although Lester Park encompasses 3 acres of land, most of what people see is the roadside exhibit, a slab of exposed bedrock roughly 100 feet long and 30 feet wide. This stromatolite reef rests at the top of a 25-foot-high embankment. A small creek flows through the woods below. Lester Park is a smaller version of the Petrified Sea Gardens that once operated nearby.

The park was established in 1914 in memory of Willard Lester, Esq. Lester, who was born in Saratoga Springs in 1852, became a New York State attorney in 1877. For the early part of his life, he was less involved in law and more occupied with the management of a number of hotels, including the Grand Union Hotel and Windsor Hotel in Saratoga Springs. Later he took up real estate law and did very

25. LESTER PARK

well, becoming the director of the First National Bank of Saratoga Springs. Fortunately, Lester also took a turn toward philanthropy and donated the property that became Lester Park to the New York State Museum. The park is considered to be one of the oldest outdoor science parks in the United States and is listed as one of the top 100 sites in North America by the American Geological Institute.

It was here that James Hall, considered the father of American geology, first described the genus *Cryptozoon*. Donald W. Fisher, New York State paleontologist from 1955 to 1982, wrote a paper about the stromatolites entitled "Algae from Antiquity—the 'cabbages' of Saratoga, a 500 million year old paleontological rarity."

Lester Park was considered too small to be managed by the NYS Office of Parks, Recreation & Historic Preservation, and so was taken over by the New York State Museum. It is classified a "scientific reservation," just as is Starks Knob, north of Schuylerville (see *Trails with Tales* for more information on Starks Knob). In fact, these two may be the only designated scientific reservations in New York State.

There are three informational plaques by the stromatolite reef. The northernmost (left) sign provides a timeline, visually illustrating just how ancient these fossil remains are. The middle sign recounts how stromatolites came into existence. The southernmost (right) sign shows a picture of how stromatolites may have looked.

Stromatolite beds are not commonly found throughout the world. The most prominent sites in the United States are at Glacier National Park in Montana and the Capitol Reef National Park in south-central Utah.

Geology: The round grey shapes you see in the bedrock are called stromatolites, meaning "layered stones." They were formed over 488 million years ago (for perspective, dinosaurs became extinct only 65 million years ago).

Stromatolites were created by cyanobacteria mats or vast colonizations of blue-green algae that formed layer upon layer. The fossil remains are easy to spot because they look like heads of cabbages that have been sliced in half.

In *Geological Excursions*, James H. Stoller, professor emeritus of geology at Union College, writes, "The mode of life of these plants of ancient time may be compared to that of corals living in the tropical seas of today. They were fixed organisms living in shallow sea waters. They multiplied by budding. They extracted the elements of lime from sea water and secreted the skeletal structures of their bodies. From their skeletal remains in long course of time limestone reefs were formed." Of particular interest is that stromatolites were a major factor contributing to the production of oxygen in the atmosphere, thus helping to make oxygen-breathing life on land possible. For a period of ~2 billion years, they were the dominant form of life on this planet.

PART THREE • SARATOGA REGION

Fossil remains of stromatolites.

In addition to stromatolites, you can also see fossils of snails, trilobites, and brachiopods interspersed in the bedrock. Trilobites were marine bugs that once crawled along the bottom of tropical ocean floors. Millions of years ago this area of upstate New York was located near southern Brazil. Plate tectonics moved the landmass to its present spot.

Hoyt limestone, which is featured at Lester Park, is composed of alternating beds of limestone and dolomite (an anhydrous carbonate mineral). Generally the rock is dark in color, often black, and thick-bedded. It is in these beds that the *Cryptozoon* formed. In *Geology of Saratoga Springs & Vicinity*, a New York State Museum Bulletin published in 1914, H.P. Cushing and R. Ruedamann write, "In 1879 Dr. C. E. Wolcott first described an Upper Cambic fauna from limestone of that age in the vicinity of Saratoga. ... In 1899 [John M.] Clarke and [Charles] Schuchert first assigned a name to this formation, calling it the Greenfield formation." The name didn't stick, however, for that particular name had already been assigned to a type of limestone found in central Ohio. Bemoaning that fact, Cushing and Ruedamann continue by saying, "The name Saratogan was preoccupied. Under the circumstances there seemed no alternative but to apply to the formation the name of the [Hoyt] quarry at which it is best and most fully shown. Unfortunately, the farm has changed hands and the quarry is no longer locally known as the Hoyt quarry. But no other name suggests itself as suitable, and we are therefore proposing the name Hoyt limestone for the formation ... ." ■

25. LESTER PARK

Petrified Sea Gardens—The 25-acre Petrified Sea Gardens was once a popular attraction for tourists visiting Saratoga Springs. In fact, it is said that the famous paleontologist Stephen Jay Gould, who visited the site in his youth, was so inspired that he devoted his life to the field of paleontology.

For years the park was run as a commercial attraction by Robert F. Ritchie, who owned the property. This explains why some residents of Saratoga County still think of the Petrified Sea Gardens as Ritchie Park. When the property was acquired by the D.A. Collins Construction Co./Pullette Stone Co., the new owners allowed the park to remain open, and a group of volunteers under the auspices of Friends of the Petrified Sea Gardens took over and ran the attraction under a 501(c) (3) not-for-profit designation.

In 1967 the Petrified Sea Gardens was designated a Natural National Landmark and, in 1999, a National Historic Landmark.

Despite these designations and its international fame as a fossil site, the park ceased operations in 2006 and has not reopened.

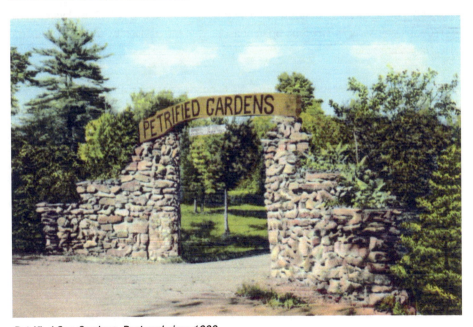

Petrified Sea Gardens. Postcard circa 1980.

PART THREE • SARATOGA REGION

26. VICTORY WOODS

Location: Schuylerville (Saratoga County)
NYS Atlas & Gazetteer, Tenth Edition, p. 67, A6; **Earlier Edition,** p. 81, D5
GPS Parking: 43.098839, –73.594156
GPS Destinations: *Saratoga Monument*—43.098561, –73.593302; *Victory Woods*—43.094050, –73.592112
Hours: *Victory Woods*—Open daily, sunrise to sunset
Saratoga Monument—Interior open from Memorial Day weekend to Labor Day, Wednesday–Sunday, 9:30 AM–5:00 PM, and Labor Day to Columbus Day, weekends only, 9:30 AM–5:00 PM
Accessibility: 1.0-mile loop trail begins at the Saratoga Monument; fairly level terrain; handicapped-accessible boardwalk starts at the end of Monument Drive and is intended for persons with disabilities who display a handicapped parking sticker on the windshield of their car.
Fee: None
Degree of Difficulty: Easy
Additional Information: Saratoga National Historical Park, 648 NY 32, Stillwater, NY 12170; nps.gov/sara; *Restrooms* open seasonally in the pavilion by the parking area; *Trail map*—nps.gov

Directions: From the village of Schuylerville (junction of Routes 4/32 & Route 29 East/Ferry Street), drive southwest on Routes 4/32 for >0.1 mile. Turn right onto Burgoyne Street/Route 338 and proceed west for >0.6 mile. When you reach Cemetery Road, turn left and then immediately left into the parking area by the Saratoga Monument.

From Saratoga Springs (junction of Route 29/Lake Avenue & Route 5/Broadway), drive east on Route 29/Lake Avenue for <10.0 miles. Turn right onto Route 338 just before descending into Schuylerville and proceed south for 0.6 mile. Then turn right onto Cemetery Road and immediately left into the parking area for the Saratoga Monument.

Description: This hike through history takes you from the Saratoga Monument through the Prospect Hill Cemetery with its tombstones and majestic old pines, and then over to Victory Woods where an expansive boardwalk guides you through a marshy area replete with plaques describing the historic British encampment and the events that took place here.

Highlights: Saratoga Monument • Historic Prospect Hill Cemetery • Encampment site of the British Army • Old breastworks

26. VICTORY WOODS

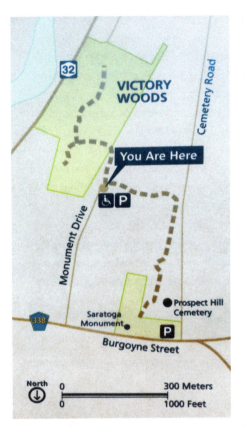

Hike: Before undertaking the hike, take a moment to familiarize yourself with the map of Victory Woods at the pavilion by the parking area.

Starting at the pavilion, walk east for several hundred feet to the Saratoga Monument. The monument is well worth a stroll around its exterior even if the interior happens to be closed at the time of your visit. A new parking area and entrance to the monument were constructed in 2005.

From the Saratoga Monument, walk south over to the *Prospect Hill Cemetery*. Look for Major Nathan Goodale's tombstone by the trailhead. Goodale is remembered for his act of bravery in capturing General Burgoyne's supply boats at the mouth of Fish Creek—a sizeable stream that enters the Hudson River from the west between Victory Woods and Schuylerville.

During the next 0.3 mile you will be walking through an historic cemetery where some of the tombstones date back to the early 1800s. For the first 0.1 mile a dirt road takes you south along the eastern perimeter of the cemetery. The road then veers right, heading up to the spine of the hill, and then resumes its southward course. Along the way you will pass by a plaque on your right that provides historical information about the cemetery.

In 1777 the area by the Prospect Hill Cemetery was a vast fortified encampment containing 6,000 British soldiers. Eighty years later, in 1865 when the Battle of Saratoga was but a distant memory, the remaining walls of this 1777 fortification were knocked down and the Prospect Hill Cemetery created. The cemetery occupies a high point, resting at an elevation of over 320 feet.

We suspect that few soldiers associated with the Battle of Saratoga are buried here given the fact that the cemetery was created over three-quarters of a century after the battle was fought.

Several hundred feet beyond the plaque, the road takes you between elegant rows of tall pines. When you come to the south end of the cemetery, turn left and

PART THREE • SARATOGA REGION

Saratoga Monument—The Saratoga Monument is an impressive 154.5-foot-high granite obelisk with 188 steps in a staircase that connects 5 levels, culminating in a viewing platform at the top. The first 2 levels contain a total of 16 bronze relief plaques depicting various scenes from the American Revolution. Work was begun on the monument in 1877 when a cornerstone was laid containing 21 newspapers, a U.S. flag, Bennington Battlefield Monument documents, a 1777 silver coin with the image of King George III, an 1877 U.S. silver dollar, and a memorial to the opening of the N.Y. & Canada Railroad. The monument was completed in 1878 and officially dedicated in 1912, the 135th anniversary of General John Burgoyne's surrender to General Horatio Gates in 1777, considered to be the turning point of America's Revolutionary War.

Note the three bronze statues: a statue of General Philip Schuyler faces the east, where his estate was located; a statue of Colonel Daniel Morgan, commander of Morgan's Riflemen, faces the west, where his corps positioned itself to entrap the British; and a statue of General Horatio Gates faces the north, toward where the British forces had advanced from Canada. The south niche has been deliberately left vacant. It was to hold a statue of General Benedict Arnold, but Arnold's acts of heroism in the Patriot cause, including his pivotal role in the Battles of Saratoga, were overshadowed by his later betrayal of his country.

The impetus for the creation of the Saratoga Monument began in 1856 when the Saratoga Monument Association was formed. Planning was interrupted by the Civil War, but then was restarted in 1872. In 1877 an architect named Jared C. Markham was chosen to lead the project, and work commenced, culminating in the monument's completion in 1878.

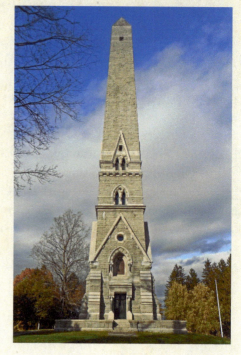

The Saratoga Monument is at the head of the Prospect Hill Cemetery

26. VICTORY WOODS

Strolling through Prospect Hill Cemetery.

follow a path downhill to the actual beginning of the Victory Woods walkway at the southeast end of the cemetery. By now you will have gone ~0.3 mile.

The wide, pressed-stone walkway takes you east for <0.1 mile to the south end of Monument Drive, where parking is available for drivers with disabilities. The boardwalk trail begins here, starting from a wooden deck and observation area.

The 0.1-mile-long boardwalk trail is ingeniously constructed, allowing you to walk through a marshy area without getting wet, muddy, or disturbing the historic terrain. The walkway is shaped like a giant "U," nearly taking you back to your starting point, but not quite. In addition there is also a pressed-stone walkway that extends from the boardwalk midway and heads south for 0.1 mile to the end of the park, from where a connecting path joins Herkimer Street in another 0.05 mile.

Now for the walk through Victory Woods…

At the very beginning, a history plaque sets the solemn mood by stating, "You've been robbed of your heritage"—a reference to the fact that the site has been picked clean over the years by relic-seekers, an activity that is now illegal.

Long before the British temporarily occupied this site, over a 7,000-year period Native Americans, including Algonquians and, later on, the Iroquois, regularly

PART THREE • SARATOGA REGION

camped in this area. Whatever artifacts these first Americans may have left behind are gone.

Look to your left and you will see a swampy body of water that perhaps was more pond-like 245 years ago. Shallow ponds, naturally enough, have a tendency to fill in more quickly than deeper ones as centuries pass.

After walking along the boardwalk for >0.05 mile, you can continue straight along the walkway or bear right onto a stone-paved path.

Continue straight for the moment, immediately coming to a history plaque on your right that reads, "Burgoyne hopelessly surrounded." The plaque recounts what happened as the days began to unfold and Burgoyne found himself increasingly outmaneuvered in a stratagem by the Patriots that later became known as "corking the bottle."

Several hundred feet farther, a history plaque on your left tells of "The Last Ditch Defense," detailing how earthen defenses were made—trenches were dug and the displaced earth piled up high in front to create breastworks. Burgoyne's fortified camp was big, the size of 80 football fields. It's worth taking a moment to note that the site occupied by Burgoyne is at the top of a steep hill. If you are under attack, having the high ground is always of paramount importance.

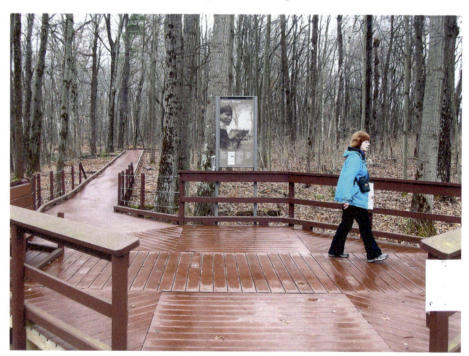

Exploring Victory Woods via elevated boardwalks.

26. VICTORY WOODS

In >50 feet you will come to the end of the boardwalk. More earthen mounds can be seen, merely vague shapes now. There is a picnic table on the deck for those who wish to relax and take in the surroundings. The history plaque at this site talks about the almost unimaginable terror of facing cannon fire. Some of the cannonballs weighed as much as 24 pounds; flying at a velocity of hundreds of miles an hour, they could smash through anything in their path. The 138 cannons seized here by the Patriot army were later used against the British. This was a fortunate confiscation by the Americans because at that time no North American factory could produce comparable weapons.

Head back now, turning left onto the stone-pressed walkway you passed by earlier. You will come to a history plaque in several hundred feet that recounts "The Stench of Failure." It was October 1777—cold, wet, and muddy. All grass was gone, and the oxen and horses that had been brought into the fortification were dying from starvation, producing a terrible stench. Such was a soldier's life in this compound.

In another couple of hundred feet, you will arrive at a history plaque set 50 feet off to the left—"Two Brothers Meet Again" (GPS 43.091793, −73.591087). This tells the story of how Patrick Maguire, serving with the British 9th Regiment, unexpectedly met his brother, a soldier with the Patriots, as they stood on opposite sides of Fish Creek. They ran into the middle of the river and embraced each other. Up until that moment, neither knew that they were fighting on opposite sides.

If you are visiting this spot when the foliage is sparse, Route 32 is easily discernible below, down the side of the hill. The 5-story-high building that you see off of Route 32 is Victory Mills, erected in 1918 by the American Manufacturing Company. It was listed on the National Register of Historic Places in 2009. An earlier version of the mill was built in 1846 by the Saratoga Victory Manufacturing Company. Fish Creek is also visible, looking more substantial where the waters have backed up behind the dam. It was from high points of ground such as this, on the opposite side of Fish Creek, that the Americans launched their cannon fusillade at the British.

In another few hundred feet you will come to the point where the road turns sharply. A history plaque here reads, "The Loyalists Leave Early." When it became apparent that the British forces were trapped, hundreds of Loyalists were afraid that if they stayed to surrender they would be mistreated by the Patriots. Under cover of night they succeeded in bluffing their way out past the Patriot line and made it to the British camp at Lake George, a trek that took four days.

Our journey ends here, and you return back along the same path, or you may continue south on the path from here for another 0.2 mile until you reach the north end of Herkimer Street in the village of Victory.

PART THREE • SARATOGA REGION

History: When you undertake this walk, you are strolling across the grounds where General John Burgoyne spent his last days before surrendering to colonial forces in 1777. The Battle of Saratoga has often been cited as the turning point in the American Revolutionary War.

The 22-acre Victory Woods Park was opened to the public in June of 2010.

The land forming the nucleus of the park was originally donated to the Saratoga National Historical Park by the Victory Mills Packaging Company in the 1970s, but no further action was taken until 1991 when Joe Finan, Superintendent of Saratoga National Historical Park, lobbied for funding for an archaeological assessment of the site. Money to do so was finally obtained in 2004.

It was quickly realized then, if not fully known already, that Native Americans had been living in this area for millennia before the Battle of Saratoga. Unfortunately, archaeological surveys have uncovered very few eighteenth-century or earlier artifacts. Most had already been grabbed by nineteenth- and twentieth-century curiosity-seekers who looted the woods of historical treasures. Because of this dearth of surviving material, researchers have been unable to pinpoint the exact locations where Burgoyne's various regiments were camped. It drives home the point that history can be obliterated forever if effort is not made early enough to preserve it.

Although looting took place, the large earthworks have remained essentially undisturbed. To ensure that the site not be further disturbed or destabilized, an ADA-accessible boardwalk was set into place through Victory Woods' swamp. Clark Dalzell, the ground and trail foreman, and his crew spent three summers constructing the boardwalk that goes over land owned by both the park and the Town of Victory. ■

PART FOUR
TACONIC & BERKSHIRE REGIONS

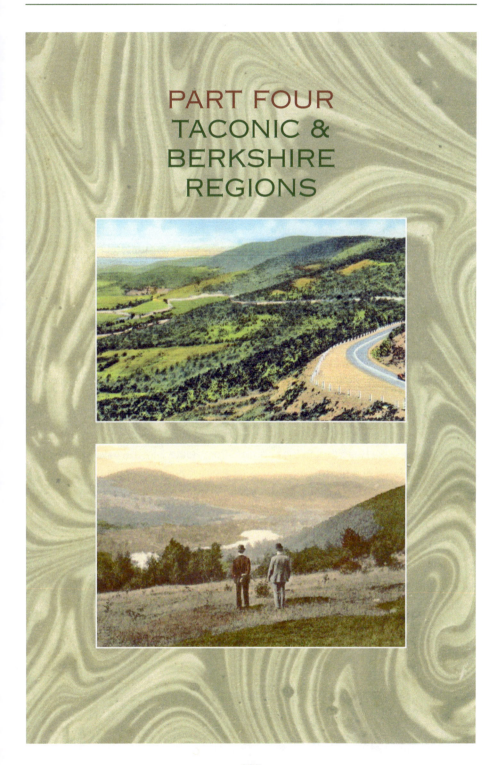

PART FOUR • TACONIC & BERKSHIRE REGIONS

27. DICKINSON HILL FIRE TOWER

Location: Grafton (Rensselaer County)
NYS Atlas & Gazetteer, Tenth Edition, p. 67, E8–9; **Earlier Edition,** p. 67, B6
GPS Parking: 42.790766 –73.433605
GPS Destinations: *Foundation Ruins*—42.791771, –73.426429;
Fire Tower—42.793780, –73.413935
Hours: Dawn to dusk
Fee: None
Accessibility: 1.3-mile hike; 180 feet elevation gain
Degree of Difficulty: Moderate
Additional Information: *Trail map*—nysparks.com; Friends of Grafton Lakes State Park—friendsofgraftonlakes.org

Directions: From the center of Grafton (junction of Route 2 & Long Pond Road), drive northeast on Long Pond Road for ~2.0 miles. On the drive up you will pass by the Grafton Trail Blazers Snowmobile Club at 1.5 miles and past stone ruins and a tiny cemetery in the woods to your right at <1.7 miles. After ~2.0 miles, park off to the side of the road at the junction of Long Pond Road and Firetower Road (unnamed), or in the small space provided for 2–3 cars. Although Firetower Road isn't gated, it is essentially a trail and vehicular travel is not advisable.

Note: it is possible to drive up to the Dickinson Hill Fire Tower from Grafton by taking Babcock Lake Road (Route 87) northeast from Route 2 for 1.6 miles, turning left onto Firetower Road and proceeding north for 1.2 miles, but if your goal is to get out, get a little exercise, and enjoy the great outdoors, that would defeat the purpose.

Description: The restored, 60-foot-high Aermotor LS40 Dickinson Hill Fire Tower rests on top of Dickinson Hill (1,762 feet) above Grafton.

The old woods road leading to the fire tower contains a series of history plaques that provides information on fire towers in general and the Dickinson Hill Fire Tower specifically.

Highlights: Dickinson Hill Fire Tower • History plaques along Firetower Road • Old ruins

Hike: The hike begins from the junction of Long Pond Road and Firetower Road, where you will see a history plaque to your right entitled "From the Ashes of a Million Acres." It reads:

27. DICKINSON HILL FIRE TOWER

In less than a decade from 1899 to 1908, a number of massive fires led to more than a million acres of New York State forests burned. Smoke from the Adirondack fires spread over much of New York State and was visible at times even in New York City. Forest fires from a seven-week period in 1908 cost $3.5 million in losses (approximately $90 million today).

New York began a new focus on prevention. With state and federal funds quickly spent on equipment, a new fire warden program and fire tower construction, the overall cost to fight fires dropped $712 per acre to $65 per acre.

In the nearby Adirondacks, the first six fire towers put up were on Gore Mountain, Snowy Mountain, Hamilton Mountain, West Mountain, Whiteface, and Morris.

Head southeast, uphill, on the Firetower Road Trail for a couple of hundred feet to reach the next history plaque, where a telephone line crosses the trail. The plaque provides information about how fire towers operated. To maximize manpower, they were generally staffed from April through early November, when fires were most likely to occur. Observers would sit in the center of a tiny cabin with a circular panorama map in front of them displaying the landscape that fell within their field of vision. If smoke was sighted, the observer would pinpoint its exact location using an alidade (a tool still used by surveyors and astronomers today for measuring angles and determining directions). The sighting would then be checked against a list of legal burns. If the sighting was not on the list, a fire warden would be dispatched to investigate the matter further.

Turn left and begin heading northeast (the direction that the road will now follow for the rest of the hike). The next history plaque is reached within 150 feet. It is to your right and reads:

> Telephones and towers to save lives: The very first fire observation towers were wooden, open platforms with limited communications abilities, but the design improved quickly. Between 1916 and 1917 a great number of these were replaced by steel towers, which were safer and sturdier for observers 60 feet above the ground.
>
> Although the telephone was invented in 1876, this relatively new technology was only readily available in urban areas in the early years of the 20th century. When added to newly constructed Fire Towers, telephones allowed for rapid response to fires, ultimately saving thousands of acres of forest that would have otherwise burned.

The reason why fire towers initially lagged behind other telephone users was that they were generally located in fairly remote areas where running a telephone line to the outpost was costly and difficult to accomplish.

One technology that fire towers did use from the very beginning was copper wire rods to ensure that the tower—generally the highest object around—was grounded from lightning strikes.

Within <0.05 mile the fourth history plaque is reached, located in a fairly wide open space to your right. A grouping of stones in disarray in the open space suggests that some kind of structure once occupied the site. Look closely and you will notice a path, faintly outlined with stone, that goes off into the woods to your right. It leads in ~150 to a shed, or possibly what was once an outhouse (GPS 42.790265, −73.430035). The history plaque by the trail reads:

Atop a Tower, a Lonely Vigil: Do you enjoy having time alone? If so, this may have been just the job for you. A fire tower observer's days were often long and solitary. Hazards from inclement weather such as high winds and lightning strikes could test the courage of novice observers. In the fall and early winter the unheated cab would make it difficult to spend long stretches on the tower without descending to warm up. For all the challenges presented by this job, in 1959 observers could expect to make $61 per week (valued at $611 today).

Fire towers proved to be destinations for hikers, however, and the observers often not only interacted with the hikers, but in some cases dispensed wallet cards that hikers could use as proof that they had reached the summit and been to the fire tower.

In <0.1 mile you will come to another history plaque. This one gives some personal details about a fire observer named Helen Ellett and her dog, Tippy:

Helen Ellett, a local resident of the Town of Grafton, was one of the first female fire tower observers employed in New York State. Starting in 1943, she spent nearly 15 years of her life as an observer. At the time, it was unusual for a woman to be hired for this sort of work, but as men went off to war, women saw greater opportunities in the workforce.

In early years of her career, Helen made her commute on horseback or with the help of a Ford Model-A automobile. Helen's job was a little less lonely thanks to her dog Tippy and pet raccoon Soggy who kept her company in the cabin of the tower while she kept watch.

27. DICKINSON HILL FIRE TOWER

Helen would sometimes have to remain in her tower for up to twelve hours at a time. She recalled reporting as much as 18 illegal fires in one day.

Readers curious to know more about Helen Ellett can pick up a copy of Randy Kneer's book, *I Remember When: The Untold Story of Helen Ellett*, published by Podskoch Press.

Just ahead, ~0.4 mile from the start, is the Chet Bell Trail, which enters on your left. This leads to the parking area at the northeast end of Long Lake, <0.2 mile from where you parked. The trail was named for the owner of a camp at Grafton.

In another 100 feet an unused road that goes off to your left passes by the stone foundation of an old homestead whose walls are slowly caving in. A fairly large open space lies to the west of the ruins where telephone lines run, paralleling the trail. The abundance of stone walls crisscrossing the landscape suggests that this was once active farmland.

The Firetower Road Trail that you continue to follow is a fascinating one, lined with stone walls, and also lined with much history that survives only through its stones.

In <0.05 mile you will come to a junction where the Spruce Bog Trail, Conklin Pass Trail, and White Lily Trail (that takes you to the east side of White Lily Pond) go off to your right. Virtually on the opposite side of the trail is a sixth history plaque:

A Jack of all Trades: When fire danger was low, the men and women who staffed these towers played many other roles. They might plant trees, cut brush to maintain trails or answer questions posed by hikers or other outdoor explorers. To teach the public about fire safety, they would visit county fairs

Stone ruins near the Fire Tower Trail.

or welcome groups of scouts. During WWII, observers were part of the Aircraft Warning Service and watched for enemy aircraft.

Records show that in 1959, fire observation towers in New York State were visited by 94,983 visitors. Through these interactions with the public, the observers became a vital link to a new generation of people interested in conservation and caring for forests. The fire towers that remain today still serve in that capacity.

It would seem that observers didn't live quite the idle, lonely lifestyle after all.

In another 0.1 mile, "The End of an Era" history plaque is reached. By now you have probably gathered that the signs are spaced out roughly every 0.1 mile to give you a chance to take a breather while incrementally learning more about fire towers. This plaque reads:

> By the 1960s, New York State had ceased the construction of new fire towers. In 1971 more than half of the 101 towers throughout New York State were closed, saving the state $250,000 per year. By the 1970s, private contractors were given the task of patrolling these routes by plane instead of staffing the fire observation towers. In the 1980s, most fires were being reported by the public. By 1990 there were no forest observers remaining in New York. Concerns about liability led New York State to remove a total of 52 towers, but luckily the Dickinson still stood and has since been restored.

No doubt fire detection has the potential to be taken to an even higher level of technology today through the use of orbital satellites. The world, once seemingly so large, has shrunk immeasurably.

Continue following the trail for another 0.05 mile to reach the eighth history plaque, on your right. It makes the ever valid point that "Only YOU can Prevent Forest Fires":

> Several factors contributed toward turning the general public into a major force in fire prevention. The first was education. Campaigns like those involving Smokey Bear increased public awareness of forest fires. The second was opportunity. As remote areas became more accessible and inhabited, there were more eyes on the lookout. The final factor was ability. In recent times mobile phones have made it easier for individuals to report any sightings of smoke they may encounter when in remote areas.

27. DICKINSON HILL FIRE TOWER

The plaque includes a picture of Smokey Bear. You migt wonder how this famous forest-fire-fighting symbol originated. Smokey was born in 1944 when the Forest Service created the familiar jean-wearing bear in a campaign hat, often holding a bucket of water poised to douse an unattended campfire. They named him Smokey Bear, reputedly after "Smokey" Joe Martin, a New York City hero fireman who suffered extensive burns and blindness in 1922 during a rescue attempt.

The first poster image of Smokey was created by Albert Staehle, a well-known illustrator who was popular from the late 1930s into the mid-1960s. In 1947 the slogan "Remember ... only YOU can prevent forest fires" was created by the Ad Council. In 2001 the slogan changed slightly to read, "Remember ... only YOU can prevent wildfires." Why the change from forest fires to wildfires? The reason was partly because wildfires occur in other places as well, such as fields, and not just in forests, but also because not all forest fires are undesirable. Some are controlled burns for conservation purposes. Once you pass by the Smokey Bear plaque, roughly 0.8 mile into the hike, the trail begins climbing steadily and becoming rockier.

At 1.0 mile you will come out onto the drivable part of Firetower Road. A camp will be on your left and a garage to your right. Continue up the road until you come to the top of a rise just past a swampy body of water to your right. Turn right here and follow a gated, unmarked jeep road that leads uphill in <0.1 mile to the Dickinson Hill Fire Tower. Just before you reach the fire tower, you will pass by what remains of the foundation of the ranger's cabin, to your right.

History: The steel-frame *Dickinson Hill Fire Tower*, located on 12 acres of hilly land on the northern slope of the Rensselaer Plateau, was erected in 1924 as part of a chain of fire-detection observation towers and posts. The fire tower stands at 60 feet high with a 7-foot-by-7-foot cabin at its top. A radio repeater tower stands 100 feet away and is significantly taller than the fire tower.

The era of fire towers ended around 1970, including for the Dickinson Hill Fire Tower. New technologies had simply made fire towers obsolete.

In 1998 The Friends of Grafton Lakes State Park (a not-for-profit charitable organization involved in promoting educational and environmental projects in the park), initiated plans to bring the fire tower into the park system even though it was outside of Grafton Lakes State Park's eastern boundary. At that time the land by the fire tower was under the control of the New York State Police, who used the repeater tower to aid in radio communications. In the end the State Police were able to transfer control of the fire tower to the Grafton Lakes State Park, which is under the jurisdiction of the New York State Office of Parks, Recreation, and Historic Preservation.

PART FOUR • TACONIC & BERKSHIRE REGIONS

The Dickinson Hill Fire Tower was erected in 1924.

In 2011 the fire tower was listed on the National Register of Historic Places. At the same time, the Friends of Grafton Lakes State Park began work on restoring the fire tower so that it would be accessible to visitors again. In 2012 the Dickinson Hill Fire Tower officially reopened to the public.

Today, the Dickinson Hill tower is the last remaining fire tower in Rensselaer County.

From the tower's cabin, sweeping views can be obtained of the Adirondack Mountains to the north, Petersburg Pass, Berlin Mountain, and the Green Mountains of Vermont to the east, the Helderbergs and Catskill Mountains to the west, the Taconic range to the south, and the nearby Grafton Lakes.

Grafton Lakes State Park opened in 1971 and encompasses 2,350 acres, including five lakes of varying sizes that were initially created as a watershed to provide drinkable water to Troy and the surrounding area.

The Town of Grafton contains 37 mountain peaks. Its plateau is the fifth largest unfragmented forest in New York State. ■

View of swamplands from the Dickinson Hill Fire Tower.

28. DYKEN POND
DYKEN POND ENVIRONMENTAL EDUCATION CENTER

Location: Grafton (Rensselaer County)
NYS Atlas & Gazetteer, Tenth Edition, p. 83, A8; **Earlier Edition,** p. 67, BC6
GPS Parking: 42.723072, –73.434776
GPS Destinations: *Dyken Pond Environmental Education Center*—42.723256, –73.435244; *Grandfather Rock*—42.731936, –73.432570; *Rock Garden*—42.733735, –73.434052; *Ring Rock*—42.727548, –73.435028; *The Sentinels*—42.726230, –73.435754; *Dyken Pond*—42.722628, –73.431664
Hours: Dawn to dusk
Fee: None
Restrictions: Follow rules and regulations posted at kiosk.
Accessibility: *Long Trail*—2.2-mile hike
Degree of Difficulty: Moderate
Additional Information: *Trail map*—friendsofdykenpond.org

Directions: From Cropseyville (junction of Routes 2 & 351) drive east on Route 2 for 1.5 miles. At the sign for Dyken Pond, turn right onto Route 79/Blue Factory Hill Road and proceed southeast for 2.1 miles. When you come to Madonna Lake Road, turn left and head southeast for another 2.1 miles. As Madonna Lake Road veers left, continue straight ahead on Dyken Pond Road (a dirt road) and head east for >2.2 miles to reach the parking area for the Dyken Pond Environmental Education Center.

From Petersburg (junction of Routes 2 & 22) drive west on Route 2 for ~8.0 miles (or 1.5 miles west of the blinking traffic light at Grafton Lakes State Park). Turn left onto Dunham Road and head southeast for >1.8 miles. When you come to Madonna Lake Road, turn right and proceed southwest for 0.8 mile. As Madonna Lake Road veers to the right, turn left onto Dyken Pond Road (a dirt road) and head southeast for >2.2 miles to reach the parking area for the Dyken Pond Environmental Education Center.

Description: The Dyken Pond area encompasses 594 acres of land, including 134-acre Dyken Pond, and over six miles of trails. The Long Trail takes you past three sets of large glacial erratics, returning you to a time when glaciers were masters of the landscape. Another short trail takes you along Dyken Pond, where scenic views can be obtained.

Highlights: Dyken Pond • Glacial boulders • Rock walls & rock piles • Historic Dyken Pond Environmental Education Center

PART FOUR • TACONIC & BERKSHIRE REGIONS

Hike: *Part One: Long Trail Hike*—From the parking area, walk uphill to the right of the brown farmhouse/Dyken Pond Environmental Education Center. You will see an arrow-like rock pointing the way to the trailhead, which begins where a sign to the right says "Abbt Farm Trail."

Follow the road/path north for <0.2 mile. You will come to a junction where the Abbt Farm Trail goes left. Continue straight ahead on the white-blazed Long Trail/yellow-blazed Otter Creek Trail and proceed northeast for ~0.4 mile. When you come to a fork where the yellow-blazed Otter Creek Trail goes left, continue right on the white-blazed Long Trail.

After hiking north for another ~0.4 mile, you will reach a junction. The white-blazed "Long Trail Short Cut" goes off to the left. Continue right on the white-blazed Long Trail, following a sign that points the way to Grandfather Rock, which you will reach in <0.05 mile.

Grandfather Rock is impressive enough to cause even the most rock-weary hiker to pause momentarily and marvel at how something this size could have been so easily moved by glaciers. The glacial boulder is ~10 feet high and 15 feet long. Grandfather Rock was given its name by staff members of the environmental center. It is borrowed from a Native American practice of naming the oldest or largest being in the forest "grandfather" as a term of respect and endearment.

Grandfather Rock.

28. DYKEN POND

In another 0.3 mile the trail U-turns and begins heading south. You will quickly pass by what we initially thought was the Rock Garden. We drew this conclusion based upon a bench dedicated to "Aldo Leopold. Eagle Project. Justin Hall. Troop 222" that overlooked the site. However, in another couple of hundred feet we came upon an even larger depression. We think now that the second one may be the rock garden that is listed on the park's map.

As pointed out to me by Lisa Hoyt, Director of the Dyken Pond Environmental Education Center, the bench at the previous site is based on a design created by Aldo Leopold (1887–1948) in the late 1800s. Leopold was an American author, philosopher, ecologist, naturalist, scientist, forester, conservationist, and environmentalist, and is regarded as the "Father of Wildlife Conservation."

Rock Garden—Rock gardens by tradition are "artificial mounds or banks built of earth and stones and planted with rock plants." In this respect the rock garden site at Dyken Pond fits the bill, for it consists of a large, somewhat circular depression in the earth framed by a ridge on one side and filled with numerous rocks of all sizes, as well as ferns and moss; little of the vegetation in the depression sprouts to a height greater than one or two feet.

From the Rock Garden continue south for ~0.1 mile. When you reach a junction where the yellow-blazed Otter Creek Trail comes in on your left, bear right, staying on the white-blazed Long Trail.

In another 0.1 mile a second junction is reached. The path to your right leads to the "Old Road," which is the north section of the Abbt Farm Trail. Bear left, remaining on the white-blazed Long Trail. Almost immediately you will see to your right an inchoate rock wall that forms a large oval shape some 50 feet long. It didn't look naturally formed to us. On the other hand neither of us had a clue as to what the purpose of this rock formation would have been.

As if that weren't mystery enough for one day, within <0.05 mile we came upon a 20-foot-long, 2-foot-high pile of rocks on our left so neatly arranged as to form what looked like a rectangle. Once again the purpose of this rock pile eluded us. It seemed too well organized to be just a random pile of rocks, but not long enough to be a serviceable stone wall. Perhaps the pile of rocks was stacked by farmers wishing to get rid of unwanted rocks while plowing their fields, with the intention of building a stone wall at a later time, and that day never came.

Ring Rock is reached in another 0.1 mile. Ring Rock is a 6-foot-high boulder that, unlike Grandfather Rock, does not stand alone. It is surrounded by a retinue of lesser rocks, including a medium-sized boulder directly behind it.

We struck the big boulder with a smaller rock hoping to produce a "ringing" sound, but no harmonious tone issued forth. We later spoke with Lisa Hoyt, who

PART FOUR • TACONIC & BERKSHIRE REGIONS

The Sentinels stand guard over the Mary Oakley McFalls Natural History Trail.

suggested that the name came about because the numerous rocks here form a ring or circle. The ring may have been used by farmers in the past as an enclosure for sheep, fortified by barbed wire strung on top of the rocks.

From Ring Rock, the pink-blazed Old Road is reached in 0.05 mile. Turn left and follow the white-blazed Long Trail south as it joins with the pink-blazed Old Road Trail.

After <0.05 mile turn right onto the Mary Oakley McFalls Natural History Trail and follow it downhill for <200 feet to reach The Sentinels.

The Sentinels—This rock formation consists of a cluster of boulders that features two large boulders and several smaller ones. The Mary Oakley McFalls Natural History Trail goes right between the boulders, which is probably what gave rise to the boulders being called The Sentinels since they seem to act as silent guardians of the thoroughfare. The first boulder, to your left, is about 10 feet high and is quite imposing. The second boulder, approximately 8–9 feet in height, is partially buried in the earth.

Return to the pink-blazed trail and continue south for <0.1 mile. You will come out behind the Dyken Pond Environmental Education Center only 50 feet west of the path that you started out on.

Abbt Farm—The building that serves as the Environmental Educational Center headquarters is the refurbished Abbt farmhouse. The Abbt Farm and Abbt Farm Trail are named for a family of German settlers who farmed the lands in the nineteenth and twentieth centuries. The family had come from downstate New York looking for a better life. During their stay by Dyken Pond, the Abbt family never accessed their farmlands or house via Dyken Pond Road. An earlier version of Dyken Pond Road simply dead-ended ~0.5 mile before the farmhouse. Rather, the Abbts traveled back and forth on the now abandoned Abbt Farm Road, which entered from the north. Nor did Dyken Pond Road look like it does today. Back then, six farms were located along the road. Much has changed over the years.

Part Two: Dyken Pond Hike—From the parking area, walk around a barrier designed to prevent vehicular traffic and continue east along a gravel road for <0.2 mile to reach Dyken Pond. The light-blue-blazed Shoreline Path, going north and south, provides continuous views of the pond. On the day we visited, we were greeted by the call of a loon.

If you follow the Shoreline Path south, you will pass behind several cottages that belong to the Dyken Pond Environmental Education Center. If you follow the path north, you will come to the yellow-blazed Otter Creek Trail in <0.3 mile.

Dyken Pond, also spelled Dyking Pond and Dykeing Pond in years past, is the main headwaters of the Poesten Kill, a sizeable stream that is a waterfall kingmaker—producing 92-foot-high Barberville Falls in Barberville and 175-foot-high Mt. Ida Falls in Troy—before it flows into the Hudson River in Troy.

Dyken Pond began as a small, naturally formed body of water on the Rensselaer Plateau. In 1902 the pond underwent enlargement when the Manning Paper Company erected a dam on the Poesten Kill, increasing the size of the pond to 134 acres by merging Dyken Pond with its neighboring pond, South Long Pond.

In 1973 the Manning Paper Company donated the land to Rensselaer County following the company's move to another location in 1962. The land has been preserved as an educational and recreational nature center ever since. ■

Dyken Pond in the fall.

PART FOUR • TACONIC & BERKSHIRE REGIONS

29. MATTISON HOLLOW

Location: Cherryplain (Rensselaer County)
NYS Atlas & Gazetteer, Tenth Edition, p. 83, B9–10; **Earlier Edition**, p. 67, CD7
GPS Parking: 42.634809, –73.340248
GPS Destinations: *Kilns*—42.640444, –73.324676; *Kronk Brook Falls*—42.641941, –73.318175; *Farm ruins*—42.642623, –73.315963
Hours: Dawn to dusk
Fee: None
Accessibility: *Kiln ruins*—0.9-mile hike; *Kronk Brook Falls*—1.2-mile hike; *Farm ruins*—1.4-mile hike; *Taconic Crest Trail*—2.6-mile hike
Degree of Difficulty: Moderate

Directions: From Petersburg (junction of Routes 22 & 2) drive south on Route 22 for ~8.8 miles until you come to Cherryplain. Turn left onto Cherryplain Square, drive southeast for nearly 0.2 mile, and then turn left again. Within 20 feet bear left again at a fork with George Allen Hollow Road and follow Mattison Hollow Brook Road east for 0.9 mile, paralleling Kronk Brook. Park off to the side of the road just before crossing over Kronk Brook as it is conducted under the road by a large drainpipe.

From Stephentown (junction of Routes 22 & 43) drive north on Route 22 for ~6.1 miles. Turn right onto Fuller Lane and head east for 0.1 mile. Then turn left onto Cherryplain Square and proceed north for <0.2 mile. Turn right and then, after 20 feet, immediately left at a fork, following Mattison Hollow Brook Road east for 0.9 mile, paralleling Kronk Brook. Park off to the side of the road to your left as soon as you cross over the brook.

Description: The hike through Mattison Hollow follows along an old logging road that eventually ascends to the Taconic Crest Trail (see next chapter, "Snow Hole," for more details about the Taconic Crest Trail). The Mattison Hollow Trail parallels Kronk Brook for the entire hike. Along the way you will pass by the faint circular outline of several old kilns, a waterfall, smaller cascades, and the old foundations of a deserted farm.

Highlights: Stone outline of old charcoal kilns with scattered assortment of bricks • Waterfalls on Kronk Brook • Old farmstead ruins—Collins Lot • Historic 1790 home at end of Mattison Hollow Road

Hike: From the southwest end of the bridge, look for a blue-colored sign that reads, "Taconic Crest Trail. Mattison Hollow," and follow the yellow-blazed trail (an old

29. MATTISON HOLLOW

The faint stone outline of a Mattison Hollow kiln.

logging road) steadily uphill, making sure to sign in on the trail register to your right at the beginning of the hike. Because Mattison Hollow is one of several entry points to the Taconic Crest Trail system, most hikers make the trek all the way up to the Taconic Crest Trail near Misery Mountain, but you will not need to do so for this hike.

After you have gone ~0.2 mile, look to your left to take note of an unusual stone wall made of marble that extends down the hillside for ~50 feet.

Within >0.4 mile from the start of the hike, the deciduous forest changes to evergreens. Continue north for another 0.4 mile with Kronk Brook, your constant companion, far below to your left.

As soon as you exit from the pine forest for a second time, at ~0.9 mile, look for a cleared area on your left that goes downhill and then flattens out before reaching the stream. You will see a small ravine here. Follow the slope to the right of the ravine downhill until you near the bottom of the hill, roughly 50 feet up from Kronk Brook. Look for the kiln sites to your right.

The Kiln Sites—Although a bushwhack is required to reach the kiln sites, it is very short, less than 100 feet. Some sleuthing may be required in order to find the kiln remains, but we were able to find two kiln sites without much difficulty even though it was late fall and the ground was covered with leaves. Finding the kilns would be much easier in early spring.

It is worth noting here that one of the faint roads coming down the hill above the Mattison Hollow Trail served as the bed for an inclined railroad, allowing timber from the higher areas to be brought down efficiently while at the same time transporting workers from the base camp to where the forest was being harvested. A funicular, two-car lift system was used.

None of the kilns has survived into the present. To spot the kiln ruins, look for the large circles of rocks—only a few inches higher than the ground—on which the kiln rested. The outline of one ring (more like a semicircle after all these years) is clearly identifiable at one site, but less so at a second site only 25 feet away to the east. There may be other sites covered by leaves.

If you had visited the area during the 1870s and 1880s, you would have seen several beehive-shaped charcoal kilns possibly rising up as high as 20 feet. In order to create charcoal, 30 to 40 cords of wood had to be stacked in the kiln and ignited. The process took roughly two days and worked by super-heating (charring) the wood. The kiln had to be closely monitored to make sure that the fire did not go out or that the wood didn't burn too quickly and be consumed. The residue that remained was charcoal—a black, porous form of carbon that burns at a higher temperature than wood and gives off very little smoke. The kind of smoke that the kiln master looked for was blue smoke, which indicated that proper carbonization was taking place.

The charcoal produced was used in forges to create the high temperatures needed for iron smelting in Troy and Albany, glass making in Sand Lake, and the working of precious metals.

From the kiln site continue east on the yellow-blazed, road-like trail for >0.3 mile to reach Kronk Brook Falls, where the trail zigzags momentarily as it goes from one level to the next to bypass private lands.

Old photograph of the kilns at Mattison Hollow.

29. MATTISON HOLLOW

Kronk Brook Falls.

Kronk Brook Falls is a small but scenic cascade where the stream drops 4–5 feet into a pool of water. The cascade is formed on Kronk Brook, a fairly small stream that rises from the 678-acre Berlin State Forest and flows into the Little Hoosic River. Take note of the posted sign and enjoy the falls from the trail. With a little bit of care, you should be able to get a nice photograph of the waterfall without trespassing on private land.

From Kronk Brook Falls (also known as Mattison Hollow Cascade) follow the yellow-blazed trail east for several hundred feet to where Kronk Brook has cut through a section of rock. A tiny cascade has formed here, but it is the small rock cut that really catches the eye. Downstream from the rock-cut cascade is a footbridge from which a good photograph can be taken.

Continue east on the yellow-blazed trail for another 100 feet. The trail crosses the stream here via a wooden plank, just upstream from the confluence of two brooks. After crossing the stream, follow the path north for 100 feet and you will reach the old farmhouse foundations, to your left.

Farm homestead ruins—The ruins are all that survive from a farmhouse likely belonging to the Collins family. The main foundation is roughly 25–30 feet long and ~20 feet wide. One wall is 5 feet high. A second, separate foundation can be seen nearby. The farm was ideally situated, with a woods road that ran in front of it and a freshwater stream behind it.

Mattison Hollow was named for Job Orlando Mattison (1821–1895), who owned a farm in the hollow and was a cobbler for his extended family. When he was 24 years old, Mattison took a trip on the Erie Canal to visit his cousin in Wisconsin and wrote up brief notes about his experience.

At the end of Mattison Hollow Road, 0.4 mile east of the trailhead, is an historic 1790 house that at one time operated as the Mattison Hollow B & B. ∎

The extensive foundation ruins of the Collins farmstead.

30. SNOW HOLE
HOPKINS FOREST & STATE LAND

Location: North of Petersburg Pass (Rensselaer County)
NYS Atlas & Gazetteer, Tenth Edition, p. 83, A10; **Earlier Edition,** p. 67, BC7
GPS Parking: 42.723150, −73.277822
GPS Destinations: *Overlook near kiosk*—42.724751, −73.276902; *Shepard's Well*—42.730228, −73.270708; *Meteorological site*—42.728391, −73.271054; *White Rock #1*—42.750771, −73.278199; *White Rock #2*—42.753338, −73.280676; *Snow Hole*—42.758863, −73.280646
Hours: Daily, dawn to dusk
Fee: None
Restrictions: No wheeled or tracked vehicles (including bicycles); no camping, fires, horseback riding, fishing, hunting, or collecting flora or fauna; dogs must be leashed
Accessibility: *Shepard's Well Trail*—0.6-mile hike; *Snow Hole*— ~3.0-mile hike
Degree of Difficulty: *Snow Hole Trail*—Moderate to difficult because of length of hike; *Shepard's Well Trail*—Moderate
Additional Information: The Hopkins Memorial Forest kiosk, located 0.1 mile north of Route 2 along the Taconic Crest Trail, provides information about the 2,600-acre forest reserve owned by Williams College and managed by the Williams College Center for Environmental Studies (CES).

Maps are available in the drawer located at the bottom of the kiosk. Maps can also be obtained from The Center for Environmental Studies, Williams College, and from the Taconic Hiking Club.

Directions: *From New York State*—Starting at Petersburg (junction of Routes 2 & 22) drive southeast on Route 2 for ~5.6 miles until you reach the Petersburg Pass Recreation Area on your right at the apex of Route 2.

From Massachusetts—Starting from southwest of Williamstown (junction of Routes 2 & 7), drive northwest on Route 2 for ~4.0 miles until you reach the Petersburg Pass Recreation Area on your left.

Description: Snow Hole is an enormous crevice in the Earth's surface—a place where the earth has split apart, creating an enterable fissure over 30 feet deep.

Excellent views of the Little Hoosic Valley from the crest of the Taconic range are part of what makes this an exciting hike.

PART FOUR • TACONIC & BERKSHIRE REGIONS

Highlights: Huge crevice in the Earth ("Snow Hole") • "White Rocks" overlooks of the Little Hoosic Valley from the Taconic Crest Trail • Well from the former Shepard's Farm • Meteorological site along the Shepard's Well Trail • Views of Mt. Greylock range from the Shepard's Well Trail

Hike: This hike takes you along a ~3.0-mile section of the 35-mile-long Taconic Crest Trail, which runs in a north-south direction from Route 20 outside of Pittsfield, Massachusetts, to Route 346 in North Petersburg, New York. The trail is maintained by the Taconic Hiking Club of Troy, New York. Although several side paths are mentioned along the trek, with the exception of the Shepard's Well Trail they should be considered as possibilities for future adventures and not part of this hike.

The hike begins from the parking area at Route 2's highest point.

Petersburg Pass Ski Center—The parking area at Petersburg Pass looks unnaturally large for just a trailhead and makes you wonder if there was something else here in the past. As it turns out, there was. In 1962, two Sprague Electric Company executives, Francis Wilson and Gilbert Devy, constructed a downhill ski area, which they named the Petersburg Pass Ski Center. Food was served at the Schusskabob Restaurant, located at the site of today's parking area.

Gazing out across the valley from the Taconic Crest Trail.

30. SNOW HOLE

In 1967 the men sold the ski center to a Mr. Deliso, who two years later was forced to close when he ran into financial difficulties. It wasn't long after that the base lodge burned to the ground.

In 1972 Mark Raimer bought the property, built a new base lodge, and was able to open up the ski center in time for the winter of 1972. The center, first called Taconic Trails and then later, Mount Raimer, lasted until around 1980, at which time financial difficulties forced the ski center to close once again and this time forever.

Eventually the abandoned ski lifts were purchased by Channing Murdock of Butternut Basin (a ski center in Massachusetts) and, as the years came and went, traces of the ski center began to vanish as nature reclaimed the land. Today there is little to see of Petersburg Pass's days as a ski center.

From the parking area, walk across Route 2 and follow the blue-blazed Taconic Crest Trail uphill, heading north. You are starting out at an elevation of 2,090 feet. Hikers who come up via spur trails from the valley's floor—frequently through the Hopkins Memorial Forest in Williamstown—have already climbed 1,000 feet.

For hikers uncomfortable with the initial ascent, which involves negotiating a rocky ledge by the road, walk east, downhill, on Route 2 for 200 feet. When you come to a large green-colored sign on your left that states "Welcome to New York. The Empire State," follow a path to your left, uphill, that bypasses the rocky climb and joins with the main trail below the kiosk.

The kiosk is reached in <0.1 mile. From the kiosk and trail register, continue your hike uphill, following the main trail north. Within 100 feet a spur path on your left leads quickly to an open hillside view of the valley below. A plank resting on flat stones provides a nice spot to sit for a moment and take in the views. The path from the viewing area immediately loops east and out to the main trail, a hundred feet up from where you initially turned off for the view.

Continue north on the Taconic Crest Trail, following what was once an old tote road (a road built to haul in supplies, usually for a logging or mining camp). After 0.3 mile the trail descends briefly and then comes back up to regain the elevation lost. At ~0.6 mile you will come to the *Shepard's Well Trail*, which enters on your right. The path eventually leads downhill to the "R. R. R. Brooks Trail" in 1.0 mile, but we will only be following the Shepard's Well Trail for part of that distance.

Follow the blue-blazed Shepard's Well Trail east for ~300 feet and turn left onto a spur path that leads to *Shepard's Well* within 20 feet. Shepard's Well is what remains of an old farm. The well measures ~1.5 feet in diameter and is encircled by a rounded stone wall at ground level. We put a long stick into the opening of the well and found four feet of water with much sediment below.

PART FOUR • TACONIC & BERKSHIRE REGIONS

Shepard's Well is all that remains of the Shepard farm.

Years ago when we first hiked the Shepard's Well Trail, we had to bushwhack through the woods to find the well, which was partially covered by branches to prevent anyone from accidentally stepping into it. The well is very visible now, no branches overlay it, and it is frequently visited, as evidenced by the well-worn spur path. Although we scouted the immediate area, we could find no other traces of the Shepard farm—not a brick, piece of mortar, or plank; nothing.

Continue following the Shepard's Well Trail southeast for <0.2 mile. You will reach a 164-foot-high tower that is part of the Williams College *meteorological site*. In November 2004 a crew from Williams College carried the 2,205-pound tower in sections up to a cleared area and, after assembling it, winched it into a vertical position. The tower has three anemometers to measure wind speed and two wind vanes to gauge the direction of the wind. A thermometer three feet from the ground records temperature. Close to the tower is a small weather station that takes meteorological measurements and transmits the information back to Williams College on a regular basis.

Leaving the tower behind, continue southeast on the Shepard's Well Trail for another 0.2 mile. The trail leads out onto an open hillside with berry bushes. The views are terrific from here. You can see Mt. Greylock and its War Memorial Tower off to the east—the highest point in Massachusetts. Farther south, atop a ridge line, is a series of windmills. A long section of Route 2 is visible below as it wends its way up the mountain, culminating at the Petersburg Pass Recreation Area's parking area. Directly south is Berlin Mountain—at 2,798 feet the highest point on the Taconic Mountain range.

30. SNOW HOLE

From here you could continue on the Shepard's Well Trail for another 0.6 mile to where it joins with the R. R. R. Brooks Trail, named for a Williams College dean who not only cut the path but actually dug out a lower section by hand. For purposes of this hike, however, return to the Taconic Crest Trail after taking in the views from the side of the hill.

Back on the Taconic Crest Trail, resume your hike northward, passing along the shoulder of 2,325-foot-high Jim Smith Hill (presumably named after the James Smith Club, whose only requirement is that you be named James Smith) and reaching the Birch Brook Trail at <1.3 miles.

The 1.5-mile-long Birch Brook Trail descends to join with the Upper Loop Trail and provides another opportunity for a diversionary hike, eventually passing by an old cellar hole dating back to the 1800s. Most of this hike is in the Hopkins Memorial Forest. Much of the forest area at one time consisted of small farms that had been cleared away by Dutch colonists in the 1700s. Life was not easy during those times. In addition to struggling against the elements, the early settlers were in constant danger of attack as Native American war parties periodically swooped down from the Canadian border. It can be challenging to try to imagine how the land once looked, with farmhouses and acres of open fields for farming and cattle grazing. Over the last century the land has been slowly returning to its original state, although the forest has not fully rebounded from the effects of logging and clearing.

But save that hike for another day; for this hike we will not be following the Birch Brook Trail.

A sign here indicates that you still have 1.5 miles to go to reach the Snow Hole.

Continue northward along the Taconic Crest Trail for another 0.7 mile and then climb uphill, eventually emerging into an area of downed trees. It looks like the result of blowdown, but the trees were intentionally cut in 2010. A trail from this general area goes off to the right, leading downhill eventually to a tri-state marker where the borders of Vermont, Massachusetts, and New York meet. Once again, however, that is a hike for another day.

Shortly after you pass by a sign indicating state forest lands, you will reach a tiny oval-shaped spur path to your left. This is White Rocks #1. There are views from here, but some are obscured by forest growth. The name "white rocks" comes from the outcroppings of phyllite formed out of quartz, but you will not see a great deal of exposed rock. Most of it is covered by thin soil and shrubs. This spot makes for an excellent place to stop and rest. Be sure to take along a pair of binoculars, for you will be rewarded with views of the gleaming metallic dome of the Grafton Peace Pagoda on the far side of the valley.

PART FOUR • TACONIC & BERKSHIRE REGIONS

The *Grafton Peace Pagoda* is one of three peace pagodas erected in the United States. The other two are in Leverett, Massachusetts, and in Newport, Tennessee. The Peace Pagoda is an off-shoot of the inspired teachings and peace walks of a Japanese Buddhist nun named Jun Yasuda. In 1978 Yasuda joined with Native Americans on a peace march from San Francisco to Washington, D.C. This march sufficiently inspired a landowner in Grafton to donate a parcel of land with the express purpose that it be used to construct a monument to peace. Work on the Peace Pagoda began in 1985. It is located at 87 Crandall Road, off of Route 2.

Continuing north on the Taconic Crest Trail, you will find that there are excellent views from several spots along the path. In another <0.3 mile you will come to White Rocks #2, which is the best viewing area along this part of the Taconic Crest Trail. White Rocks #2, like White Rocks #1, is a clearing, not an outcrop. The white rocks that you see here are more likely to be just white flakes and small bits of rock lying about on the ground.

Head steadily downhill for 0.3 mile and you will come to an unmarked trail on your right where a sign to your left reads: "Taconic Crest Trail. Route 2, 3.0 mi." The trail to your right is the upper part of a loop trail that takes you down and around to Snow Hole. Although you could take that trail to Snow Hole, the more dramatic approach is from the lower trail, 0.05 mile farther downhill. Taking this into account, continue downhill on the Taconic Crest Trail. Very soon you will see a sign for the Snow Hole. Turn right and follow a road-like trail for several hundred feet to reach the historic crevasse.

Snow Hole has been frequently visited since the mid-1800s.

30. SNOW HOLE

Snow Hole is readily enterable from its west end. The descent is not steep and can be easily negotiated as long as you take your time and proceed with caution. As you climb down into the crevasse, you will begin to appreciate a dramatic change in temperature, particularly if you are visiting in late spring or summer. Even in the absence of snow or ice in the late summer, the earth's coolness thirty feet below its surface is refreshing.

Coming back out of Snow Hole, walk southeast from the crevice, following a well-worn path that is part of the loop trail. What isn't apparent at first is that the deep crevice forming Snow Hole is just one part of a huge displacement in the Earth's crust. A large fault line continues for several hundred feet, with Snow Hole being the northwest extension of this displacement. With the exception of one tiny pit near the east end of the crevasse, however, Snow Hole is the only conduit into the Earth for any significant depth. If you complete the loop, you will return to the Taconic Crest Trail 0.05 mile uphill from where you set out on the lower trail.

We suspect that many hikers who have taken the upper path to Snow Hole may have been initially disappointed, because the first thing they would see is the eastern part of the fault line where there is a sizeable opening into the earth, but without depth. If they continue a couple of hundred feet farther, they will come right up to the back of Snow Hole.

After visiting Snow Hole, it is an invigorating 3.0-mile hike back to the parking area by Route 2.

History: Snow Hole was first described by Professor Chester Dewey of Williams College in 1819, who cited the hole's dimensions as "about thirty feet long, and nearly as deep at the east end," noting that it "ascends to the west, or toward the summit of the ridge, and is from ten to twenty feet wide." Dewey was a botanist, anti-slavery advocate, clergyman, and educator.

In 1822 Henry Dearborn and Thomas Ives wrote an article for the *American Journal of Science and Arts* entitled "Natural Ice House near Williamstown, Mass."

In Clay Perry's *Underground Empire: Wonders and Tales of New York Caves*, published in 1948, Snow Hole is referred to as a *glaciere*, a French word for "ice cave."

In *A Scenic Tour of Rensselaer County, New York*, the author writes "This freak of nature offers abundant snow all year long. Early settlers came here in summer and carried snow back to the valley to cool their food and drinks." This assertion seems a bit dubious to us, however. We find it hard to imagine hardy settlers hiking the long distance to Snow Hole to cart off snow in the summer.

Snow Hole is located on New York State land. Previously it was owned by a municipality that had failed to close its landfill in a timely manner. In lieu of penalties, the municipality deeded this property to New York State.

PART FOUR • TACONIC & BERKSHIRE REGIONS

Snow Hole in the early winter.

Hopkins Memorial Forest is named for Amos Lawrence Hopkins, who acquired great wealth as a railroad magnate. Hopkins died in 1912. His widow, Theresa Burnham Dodge Hopkins, donated the land to Williams College in 1934 to serve as a memorial to her late husband.

Although Snow Hole is not located in the Hopkins Memorial Forest, much of the hike to get to the Snow Hole goes through this forest.

Geology of the Taconics: The rocks forming the Taconic Mountain range were created approximately 440 million years ago when debris and sediment that had come to rest on the floor of an ancient ocean were compressed and hardened. The rock formed was primarily phyllite (a slate-like rock containing minute scales of

30. SNOW HOLE

mica). It is these rocks—the so called "white rocks"—that are visible today in several outcroppings along the trail.

A series of cataclysmic thrust faults and uplifts during the Taconic Orogeny (an era of mountain building) proceeded to raise up the rock bed from the floor of the ocean to great heights. Over millions of years, however, erosive processes eventually scaled the Taconic Mountains back down. Then, starting around two million years ago, glacial advances and retreats further sculpted the Taconic range, scraping the tops and rounding them. Glacial till (an unsorted mixture of sand, gravel, clay, and boulders) was dumped into the valley when the glaciers retreated.

Snow Hole was created through the action of tectonic forces. Extensive cracks formed in the steep slope of the ridge. These cracks were widened and deepened over millennia through the expansion and contraction of ice and the relentless pull of gravity.

The Taconics are not high mountains. Berlin Mountain (south of the parking area) rises up to an elevation of 2,798 feet and is the highest point on the Taconic Crest Trail. ■

Exploring the interior of Snow Hole.

PART FOUR • TACONIC & BERKSHIRE REGIONS

31. FIELD FARM & McMASTERS CAVES

Location: South Williamstown (Berkshire County, Massachusetts)
Massachusetts Atlas & Gazetteer: p. 20, F10
GPS Parking: 42.665470, –73.260358
GPS Destinations: *The Folly*—42.665232, –73.259518;
Jigsaw Rock—42.673538, –73.252412; *McMasters Caves*—42.675253, –73.253999
Hours: Daily, sunrise to sunset
Fee: None, but donations are welcomed
Accessibility: *Caves*—1.0-mile hike; *North Trail* (red-marked)—1.7 miles;
South Trail (yellow-marked)—1.4 miles; *Oak Loop Trail* (orange-marked)—0.8 mile;
Caves Trail (aqua-marked)—0.7 mile; *Pond Trail* (purple-marked)—0.4 mile
Degree of Difficulty: Easy to moderate
Additional Information: Field Farm, 554 Loan Road, Williamstown, MA 01267, (413) 458-3144; *Trail map*—thetrustees.org

Directions: From South Williamstown (junction of Route 43/Hancock Road & Route 7/New Ashford Road), drive south on Route 43/Hancock Road for 150 feet and turn right onto Sloan Street. Proceed northwest for 1.0 mile and then turn right at the entrance to the Field Farm. Bear right into a parking area by the garage before you reach the Field Farm Bed & Breakfast.

Description: The hike takes you through the grounds of a 316-acre estate containing the historic Field Farm, a guesthouse, and 4.5 miles of hiking trails.

Highlights: The Field Farm, owned and maintained by the Trustees of the Reservation • Area of karst, including several caves (suitable only for experienced cavers) • Six-foot-high fractured rock

Hike: From the parking area follow the red-marked "Eastern North Trail" next to the pond north along the edge of a field. In <0.4 mile you will come to the orange-marked "Oak Loop Trail." Bear right and follow the Oak Loop Trail north as it heads into the woods and quickly crosses over a sturdy-looking footbridge spanning a small ravine.

In another 0.2 mile you will come to the aqua-marked "Caves Trail." Once again bear right. The trail quickly takes you north up to the top of a spiny ridge. Along the way you will see a fascinating large rock to your left that has fractured so as to look like pieces of a jigsaw puzzle reassembled, or a pile of pancakes. We call it "Jigsaw Rock."

31. FIELD FARM & MCMASTERS CAVES

In less than 0.2 mile the trail descends. After doing a U-turn, it heads south, paralleling the upper section of the trail from which you just descended.

Within 0.1 mile you will come to the McMasters Caves, a grouping of three small caves that are off to your right. The caves are located by a large depression in the earth where water drains into tiny, shelf-like openings under the trail. In *A Guide to Natural Places in the Berkshires*, René Laubach writes, "Here a small stream flows from the marshland and disappears into one of the McMasters caves, a stony hollow the brook has carved into the bedrock. This scene is repeated at two other places along the path where more streams vanish into the earth." In the March 2008 issue of *Northeastern Caver*, John Dunham writes in greater detail: "The caves themselves are only a few hundred feet long, with some crawls but a surprising amount of walking passage and features including interestingly carved marble and some active flowstone. They receive runoff from adjacent swampland and many sections are extremely muddy with fluctuating water levels." Take note that the caves should only be entered by a party of at least three, and each person should be equipped with three sources of light, a helmet, and proper caving gear. It should also be noted that the caves tend to flood during the winter. These are not the kind of caves that most people will choose to enter, nor should they.

From McMasters Caves continue south on the Cave Trail. When you come to the Oak Loop Trail, bear left and go east. You will soon come to the turn to the Caves Trail on your left that you initially took. Turn right here and proceed

Jigsaw Rock.

PART FOUR • TACONIC & BERKSHIRE REGIONS

south, first on the Oak Loop Trail and then on the North Trail, to return to your starting point.

History: The Field Farm Bed & Breakfast is the former estate of Lawrence "Larry" Hotchkiss Bloedel and Eleanor "Ele" Clare Palmedo Bloedel, who were married in 1924. Undoubtedly some of their money came from the MacMillan Bloedel Lumber Company in Washington State, of which the greater Bloedel family were part-owners.

The Bloedels acquired the land in South Williamstown from two British brothers named Field in 1945 following Lawrence Bloedel's return to civilian life after having served as a machinist in World War II. The main house, completed in 1949, was designed by Edwin Goodell in the American Modern style featuring straight lines and extensive use of glass. Frank Lloyd Wright was originally commissioned to design the house, but he and the Bloedels parted company after Wright refused to design the house the way that Lawrence wanted.

The artwork inside the house is by Wolf Kahn, the German-born American landscape painter. The lawn sculptures are by Richard McDermott Miller, an early

At McMasters Caves, a trio of small caves conducts water into the underworld.

31. FIELD FARM & MCMASTERS CAVES

The Folly—a nontraditional guesthouse.

abstract sculptor who later returned to the human figure to create contemporary art, and Herbert Ferber, a well-known abstract expressionist sculptor. A total of thirteen modern sculptures can be seen in the gardens. The Bloedels insisted on having only modest gardens on their property, feeling that extensive gardens would detract from the view of the pond and the Mt. Greylock massif.

The contemporary guesthouse, whimsically called "The Folly," was designed by Ulrich Franzen, a well-regarded architect known for his "fortress-like" buildings, and completed in 1966. The design incorporates false perspectives, making the cottage look smaller than it actually is when seen from the outside. A portion of the guesthouse resembles a grain silo. The living room has been creatively cut into two distinct sections so that one half is facing the outside. The word "folly" has a number of possible meanings, but the definition "a costly ornamental building with no practical purpose" probably comes closest to what the Bloedels intended when they named the guesthouse. Some of the pieces of interior furniture were designed by Lawrence Bloedel himself.

The pond next to The Folly was used for swimming in the summer and skating during the winter.

Lawrence Bloedel was the librarian at Williams College early in his life. Both he and his wife were avid collectors of modern American art. Their collection included such masterpieces as Marsden Hartley's *Mushrooms* (1940), Alice Trumbull Mason's *Suspension Points: Surface Winds* (1959), Edward Hopper's *Ranch House, Santa Fe* (1925) and *Morning in the City* (1944), and Fairfield Porter's *Screen Porch* (1964). In 1960, the couple established the Greylock Foundation, which allowed them to donate money to artistic and cultural institutions of their choosing.

The Bloedels were generous with their art collection. They would often invite art history classes from Williams College to visit their home and view the artwork.

PART FOUR • TACONIC & BERKSHIRE REGIONS

The Bloedels also had a playful side. On the Fourth of July they would host a festive party that included fireworks accompanied by George Frederic Handel's "Music for the Royal Fireworks."

Lawrence Bloedel died in 1976 at age 74. The property was bequeathed, with endowment, to the Trustees of the Reservation by Mrs. Bloedel upon her death in 1984. You can visit the Bloedels' gravesite, which is located in front of the main entrance to the Field Farmhouse in a tiny fenced-in cemetery.

The Field Farm property continues to grow. In 1990 Nancy Freeman and Sally Foote donated a parcel of land to the Trustees. Then, in 1994, additional lands were purchased by the Trustees.

Peeling back many more layers of the past, the lands in South Williamstown were first traversed by the Mohicans and Mohawks and then, beginning in the mid-1800s, by European settlers who cleared the land for crop fields and livestock pastures.

Geology: The hiking area takes you across what was once the bed of Lake Bascom, a fairly large body of water that formed at the end of the last ice age when an alluvium till impounded glacial meltwaters. The lake rose to as high as 1,050 feet above the valley floor and was easily midway up the shoulder of 3,491-foot-high Mt. Greylock. It encompassed the valleys of Adams, North Adams, Williamstown, Cheshire, Petersburg, and Bennington. The water level was high enough to leave 2,339-foot-high Mt. Anthony in Pownal thrusting up as an island. The lake endured for roughly 800 years until the impoundment broke and the lake waters drained out into the Hudson River.

Lake Bascom was named in honor of John Bascom, professor of rhetoric at Williams College from 1855–1874 and president of the University of Wisconsin from 1874–1887. Bascom was born in Genoa, New York, in 1827 and died in Williamstown in 1912. During his lifetime he was quite a prolific writer, authoring over 30 books.

The Cave Trail follows along the top and then the bottom of a dolostone (limestone-like) ridge. ■

ACKNOWLEDGMENTS

Our sincerest thanks to:

Timothy Albright, coauthor of *John Boyd Thacher State Park and the Indian Ladder Region*, for clarifying some points of uncertainty for us on the John Boyd Thacher State Park chapter.

Audrey Ball, Parks & Recreation Director, Town of Malta, for reviewing an earlier version of Shenantaha Creek Park.

Heidi Bock, Columbia Land Conservancy, for reviewing the chapter on High Falls.

Christy Butler, author, photographer, and explorer, for his input on chapters related to Snow Hole, Dyken Pond, and the Dickenson Hill Fire Tower.

Kristin Casey, for information researched on the High Point area.

Ron Dodson, retired wildlife biologist and educator, for generously sharing his extensive knowledge concerning the history of the Hollyhock Hollow Sanctuary.

Tim Farley, writer, marathoner, and hiker who accompanied us on several of these treks.

Josh French, with Fort Miller in Schuylerville, for help in tracking down a needed photograph for a chapter.

Teri Gay, author and Historian, Town of Malta, for input provided on Shenantaha Creek Park and for reviewing an earlier version of that chapter for accuracy.

Jennifer Greim and the staff of Thomas Cole State Historic Site.

Melanie Hasbrook and the staff of Olana State Historic Site for reviewing the Olana portion of Hudson River Skywalk.

Lisa Hoyt, Director of the Dyken Pond Environmental Education Center, for reviewing the chapter on Dyken Pond and for the wonderful corrections and suggestions made.

Scott Keller, Executive Director, Hudson River Valley Greenway, for reviewing the book and coming up with such memorable and thoughtful words.

Mark King, Executive Director, Mohawk Hudson Land Conservancy, for his help with the chapter on the Hollyhock Hollow Sanctuary and for writing the foreword to this book.

Jill S. Knapp, past Executive Director, Mohawk-Hudson Land Conservancy, for reviewing the Normanskill Farm chapter.

Stephanie Orlando, for her contribution on the Nutten Hook chapter.

Jonathan Palmer, Greene County Historical Society.

Church Porter, retired geology professor, for input provided on caves at the Hollyhock Hollow Sanctuary.

Fredrik M. Realbuto, Director, Audubon Society of New York, for input provided earlier on the Hollyhock Hollow Sanctuary chapter.

David Ross, Vice-President of the Ravena-Coeymans Historical Society, for his valuable input on the history of Joralemon Memorial Park.

Alan Van De Bogart, President, Highland Landing Park Association, for providing background information about Highland Landing Park and Bob Shepard.

Rebecca Walker, Columbia Land Conservancy, for reviewing the chapter on High Falls.

Joe Zoske, for reviewing the chapter on Shenantaha Creek Park and for accompanying us on the Dibbles Quarry hike.

Author Barbara Delaney checking out the Catskill furniture at Dibble's Quarry.

ABOUT THE AUTHORS

Russell Dunn and Barbara Delaney are a husband and wife writing team that has been collaborating for twenty years. Their first two books were *Trails with Tales* and *Adirondack Trails with Tales*, both history-oriented hiking guidebooks. *Paths to the Past* is the third book in the series.

Barbara and Russell are retired New York State–licensed hiking guides. For fifteen consecutive years they led hikes to waterfalls in the Adirondacks. The hikes came to be known as "Waterfall Weekend" and took place annually in early May in the Keene Valley area.

In addition to coauthoring the history-oriented hiking guidebooks, Russell has written a number of other regional outdoors guidebooks to eastern New York State and western New England, including nine waterfall guidebooks, five paddling guidebooks, and seven guidebooks to regional glacial erratics and rock formations. He has also published a series of anaglyph 3-D books.

Barbara has become well-known for her two books of fiction, *Finding Griffin: An Adirondack Novel* and *Follansbee Pond Secrets*.

They live in Albany, New York, and can be reached at Russell's email, rdunnwaterfalls@yahoo.com.

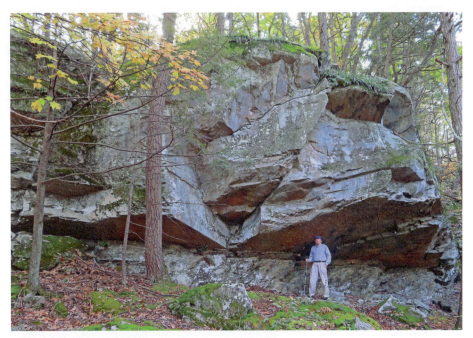

Author Russell Dunn under the rock shelter at Slabsides.

A

Abbt family, 234, 235
Abbt farm, 234
Abbt Farm Road, 235
Abbt Farm Trail, 232–234
Acheson, Lilia, 179
Adams, 254
Adirondack lean-to, 163
Adirondack Mountains, viii, x, 21, 212, 225, 230
Adirondack Northway, 203
Adirondack Park, xii
Adirondack Trails with Tales: History Hikes …, xii, 206
Adkins, Elizabeth, 68
African Americans, 121, 125, 154
Agawamuck, 87
Agawamuck Creek, 82–85, 87–89
Agawamuck Falls, 82, 84, 87
Aircraft Warning Service, 228
Aken, Nelson P., 87
Aken Knitting Mill, 82, 87
Alaska, 42, 200
Albany, Lake, 36, 182
Albany, Port of, 92, 168
Albany City Paper Mill, 175
Albany Common Council, 116, 125
Albany County Helderberg-Hudson Rail Trail, 175
Albany Institute of History & Art, 95, 125
Albany Medical College, 123
Albany Municipal Golf Course, 172
Albany Police Department, 173, 177
Albany Rural Cemetery, 125, 178, 179
Albany Veterans Memorial Monument, 123
Aldine Society of Johnstown, 157
Alexander Street Park, 196
Alfano, Joseph, 19
algae, 213
Algonquians, 75, 100, 219
Alhambra, Order of, 180
Alligator Rock, 80
Altamont, 136, 138, 139, 140, 142
Altamont Historical Society, 137
American Geological Service, 213
American Museum of Natural History, 38
Amtrak, 17, 31, 33, 36, 93, 101
Andes, 97
André, Major John, 6
Andron, David, 80
Andron, Eli, 80
Andron, Jacob, 80
Andron's Mountain House, 80
Anthony, Mt., 254
Anthony Kill, 207
Armsby, M.D., James H., 116, 123
Arnold, Benedict, 6, 218
Arnold's Path, 6
Atlantic Ocean, 21, 104, 180
Audubon Society of New York, 128, 131, 133–135, 256
"Auld Lang Syne," 122
Auriesville, 180
Auriesville Shrine, 180
Ausable Chasm, 52
Austin Glen, 100

B

Bagwell, Vinnie, 16
Ballston Creek, 203–207
Ballston Lake, 207
Ballston Spa, 208
Barberville, 235
Barberville Falls, 235
Barclay Home Products, 193
Barge Canal, New York State, 183, 186, 188
Barnyard, The, 98
Bartow, Maria, 95
Bascom, John, 254
Bascom, Lake, 254
Battaglia, Anthony, 171
batteries (military), 1–4, 6
Battle of Saratoga, 183, 217, 222
Baum, Frank, 175
Baumfree, Isabella, 16
Beach, Charles, 79, 80
Beach, Charles L., 78, 100
Beach, Erastus, 79
Beach, George H., 80
Beacon Institute Weather Station, 170
Beacon Mountain, 78
Beattie, Guy, 183
Beattie, Mary Ann Killough, 183
Beatties Field, 183
Beaver Creek, 124
Beaver War, 93
bedstone, 153
Beecher, Raymond, 73
Beers & Co., J. B., 67
Bell, Chet, 227
Bennington, 195, 198, 218, 254
Berkshire Taconic Community Foundation, 48
Berlin Mountain, 230, 244, 249
Bethlehem, Town of, 171, 175
Beverwijck, 180
Bewitched Caverns, The, 134
Biggerstaff, Colonel Allan, 5
Bikeway, 178, 180
Birch Brook Trail, 245
birds, xi, 103, 126, 135, 166
Black Creek Falls, 42
Blacksmith Shop, 149, 155, 170, 177
Black Snake Bridge, 69, 70, 71
Bleecker Mountain, 153
blockhouse, 154, 155
Bloedel, Clare Palmedo, 252
Bloedel, Lawrence Hotchkiss, 252–254
bluestone, 62, 63, 65–68
boardwalks, 39, 40, 52, 161, 220
Bobby Rock Spring, 146
Boston, 104, 156
Botsford, Thomas, 50
Boughton, George H., 122
Boulder, The, 79
Bowdoin, George, 11
Bowdoin, George Temple, 11, 12
Bowdoin estate, 10
Bowdoin Memorial Farm, 12
Bowdoin Park, 8, 10, 11
Bowdoin Park Historical & Archaeological Association, 10

INDEX

Bowdoin Park Rock Shelters, 9–12
Bozen Kill, 160, 161, 163–165
Bozen Kill Falls, 160, 163, 164
Bozen Kill Gorge, 162
brachiopods, 214
Bradt, Albert Andriessen, 168, 176
Brant, Joseph, 159
Brant, Molly, 151, 154, 158, 159
Brazil, 214
breastworks, 1–3, 6, 216, 220
Briody, Frank, 57
British, 1, 2, 4, 6, 7, 71, 151, 154, 158, 159, 216–219, 221, 252
Bronck House, 79
Brookfield, 188
Brooklyn Bridge, 128, 135
Brooks, R.R., 243, 245
Brown, Frederick, 124
Brown Jr., Thomas E., 78
Buffalo, 93, 185
Burgoyne, General John, 217, 218, 220, 222
Burns, Robert, 116, 121, 122
Burnt Hills, 203
Burroughs, Emily,
Burroughs, John, ix, 33, 39–44, 60, 61
Burroughs, Julian, 39, 40, 42
Burroughs, Ursula, 40
Burroughs Association, John, 38, 41, 43
Burroughs Medal, 166
Burroughs Memorial Association, John, 166
Burroughs Memorial Field, 44
Burroughs Nature Sanctuary, John, 38–44
Burroughs Pond, 41
Butternut Basin, 243
Butternut (Ski Center), 243

C

"cabinet of curiosities," 158
Cairo, 69
calcium carbonate, 11, 211
calcium oxide, 211
Callanan Industries, 129
Call Rock, 17

Calverley, Charles, 122
Cambrian, 212
Canada, 93, 158, 218
Canajoharie, 158, 205
Canajoharie Creek, 205
Canino, John, 20
Cannon Trail, 1, 2
Cape Horn, 75
Capital District Community Gardens (CDCG), 171
Capital Hills at Albany Golf Course, 172
Capitol Reef National Park, 213
Caribbean, 169
Caroga Creek, 158
Carter, President Jimmy, 24
Castleton, 101, 104
Catskill, viii, x, 33, 34, 67–69, 76, 90, 92, 94–97, 99, 100, 114
Catskill Creek, 92, 99, 100
Catskill Day Hikes for all Seasons, 64
Catskill Escarpment, 96
Catskill Front, 75
Catskill Furniture, 62, 66, 68
Catskill Landing, 100
Catskill Mountain Association, 79
Catskill Mountaineer, 72
Catskill Mountain Guide, 64
Catskill Mountain House, 69, 70, 72, 73, 75, 77–81, 100
Catskill Mountain House, The, 81
Catskill Mountain House Trail Guide, 74, 75
Catskill Mountain Railway, 78, 99, 100
Catskill Mountains, 76, 92, 95, 96, 230
Catskill Mountains and the Region Around, The, 71
Catskill Region Waterfall Guide, 71
Caul Rock, 17
Caves Trail, 250, 251
Cayadutta, 153
Cayadutta Creek, 151–154, 158
Cedar Glen, 13, 15, 18, 19, 22
Cedar Grove, 90, 91, 94–96
cedars, 19
Celery Swamp, 39, 40

Certle, George, 65
chain across the Hudson River, 7, 38
Champlain Canal, 184, 197
charcoal, 135, 236, 238
Cherryplain, 236
Cheshire, 254
chestnut blight, 10
Chet Bell Trail, 227
Children's Aid Society, 10–12
China, 185
Chodikee, 40
Choice (cave), 111
Christman, Catherine Bradt, 165, 166
Christman, Henry, 166
Christman, Lansing, 166
Christman, Lucille, 166
Christman, William Weaver, ix, 160, 161, 165, 166
Christman Bird and Wildlife Sanctuary, 166
Christman Memorial, 160, 165
Christman Sanctuary Preserve, 160–166
Church, Frederic, 90, 91, 95, 97, 100
Church, Isabel, 97
Civilian Conservation Corps (CCC), 54, 80
Civil War, 16, 86, 107–109, 218
Civil War Heritage Days, 183
Civil War veterans, 123
Clark, James, 205
Clark, Samuel, 205
Clark & Lindley Oil Mill, 205
Clarke, John M., 214
Claverack, 87
Claverack Creek, 87
Clifton Park, 174
Clinton, Governor Dewitt, 185
Clinton, President Bill, 121
Clinton's Ditch, 178, 182, 184, 185, 192
Clinton's Folly, 185
Cobblestone Courtyard, 154
Coeymans, 110, 113
Coeymans Creek, 130
Coffman, Jane, 205

Coffman, John, 205
Cohoes, 184, 185, 187, 189, 191, 194, 195, 198, 200, 207
Cohoes Falls, 184, 185, 187–189, 191, 194, 208
Cohoes Falls Overlook Park, 187, 194
Cohoes Heritage Trail, 190
Cohoes Mastodon, 184, 200, 201
Cohoes Memorial Hospital, 196
Cohoes Public Library, 200
Cohoes Visitor Center, 187
Cole, Theodore Alexander, 95
Cole, Thomas, 73, 76, 94, 95
Cole House, Thomas, 90, 91, 95
Cole State Historic Site, Thomas, 90, 91
Collins, 240
Collins Construction Co., D. D., 215
colonial wars, 180, 183
Colonie Historical Society, Town of, 178
Columbia Land Conservancy, 87, 88
Comfort, William, 73
Cone, The, 126, 129, 130
Conklin Pass Trail, 227
Conrail, 17
Constitution Island, 2, 7
Continental Army, 3, 7
Continental Corps of Engineers, 3
Continental Village, 4
Cook, Nancy "Nan", 23, 24, 26
Cooper, James Fenimore, 95
Corazon Center Villa St. Dominic, 60
Corning II, Mayor Erastus, 119, 177
Costantino, Claire, 21
Costantino, Ray, 20, 21
Cosy Cottage, 90, 97, 98
Coxsackie, 79, 102, 105
Cragsmoor, 49, 51
Creek Trail, 126, 130–132, 232, 233
Cropsey, Jasper, 96
Cropseyville, 231
Crowley Foods, 177
cryptozoon, 213, 214

CSX Railroad, 17
Cultural Education Center, 201
Cupid's Rock, 52
Curtis, Blanche Desmore, 51
Curtis, Edward, 42
Cushing, H. P., 214
cyanobacteria mats, 213

D

Daddy Longlegs Cave, 147
Dainty Deserts for Dainty People, 156
Dalzell, Clark, 221
dance hall, 103
Danskammer Energy Center, 9
Danskammer Point, 9
Dark Pool, The, 134
Dead Ox Hill, 74, 75
Dearborn, Henry, 247
DeGraff, Simon, 174
Delanson, 7, 178, 160, 163
Delaware, 62
Delaware, Lackawanna & Western Railroad, 5
Delaware & Hudson Railroad (D&H), 208
Delaware Avenue Bridge, 174, 167, 175
Delaware Avenue Turnpike, 174
Deliso, Mr., 243
Delmar, 7, 171
Delorme, 13
Democratic Party, Women's Division of the New York, 45
Denning, William, 4
Denning's Point, 4, 22
Department of Environmental Conservation (DEC), 103
"Devil's Dance Chamber," 9, 10
Devy, Gilbert, 242
Dewey, Professor Chester, 247
Dial Press, 133
Dibble, Edward, 67, 68
Dibble's Quarry, 256
Dickens, Charles, 194
Dickerman, Marion, 18, 23–25, 29
Dickinson Hill, 224, 225
Dickinson Hill Fire Tower, 229, 230

Dion, Mark, 97
Disc-Golf Course, 108
Dodd, Thomas, 68
Dodge, Robert, 5
Dodson, Ron, 131
dolomite, 214
dolomite, Pine Plains, 11
Dominican Congregation of our Lady of the Rosary, 60
Dominican Sisters, 55, 57, 59, 60
Donovan, Tim, 5
Dooley Square, 21
Dover, Town of, 48
Dover Elementary School, 45
Dover Plains, 45
Dover Stone Church and the History of Dutchess County, 45
Dover Stone Church Cave, 45–48
Druid Rock, 79
Duanesburg, 160
Dudley Observatory, 124
Dunham, John, 25
Dunmore, Fifth Earl of, 34
Duportail, General Louis Lebèque, 3
Durand, Asher Brown, 48
Duryee, Samuel Sloan, 5
Dutch, 24, 27, 31, 74, 93, 100, 104, 120, 134, 163, 176, 183, 245
Dutchess County, 9–12, 23, 30, 45, 48, 78
Dutchess County Open Space, 48
Dutchess Land Conservancy, 45, 48
Dutchman's Landing, 92, 100
Dyken Pond, 235
Dyken Pond Environmental Education Center, 231–235
Dyson Foundation, 20

E

Eagle Nest Creek, 196
Eagle Project, Troop 220, 233
Early Settlement of the Town of Hunter, 67
East Overlook Trail, 38
Edison, Thomas, 42
Egerton, William S., 119

INDEX

Eleanor's Walk, 23, 24, 26
Elizabeth, Queen, 28
Ellenville, 49, 51, 53
Ellenville Ice Caves, 53, 54
Ellenville Public Library & Museum, 51
Ellessdie Chapel, 8, 11
Ellett, Helen, 226, 227
Emerson, Ralph Waldo, 42
Emory, Sarah, 73
Empire State Plaza, 120, 177
Empire State Trail, x, 93
England, 4, 7, 26, 28, 45, 67, 76, 104, 131, 185
epidemics, 179
Erie Canal, 135, 174, 178, 182–189, 192, 196, 197, 211, 240; Lock 9, 195, 196: Lock 10, 195, 196; Lock 14, 187, 191; Lock 15, 187, 191; Lock 16, 187, 191; Lock 17, 187, 191; Lock 18, 187, 190
Escarpment Trail, 76
Esopus, 38
Esopus Creek Conservancy, 60
Esopus Island, 33

F

Factory Hill, 88
Falling Waters, 55–61
Falling Waters Preserve, 55
Falling Waters' Villa St. Joseph, 60
Family Magazine, The, 47
Fat Man's Misery, 81
Featherbed Hill, 72, 75
Federal Dam, 21
Federal Footpath, 103
feeder canal, 191, 196
Fennell Memorial Trail, William G., 38
Ferber, Herbert, 253
Fernow, Bernhard, 43
ferry, 4, 92, 103, 104, 174
Feura Bush, 126, 130
Field Farm, xii, 250, 254
Field Farm B&B, 250, 252
Finan, Joe, 222
First National Bank of Saratoga Springs, 213

fish, 87, 103, 118, 135
Fish Creek, 217, 221
Fisher, Donald, W., 213
Fite, Harvey, 68
flaxseed mill, 203–205, 209
Folly, The, 250, 253
Fonda, 153, 158
Foote, Sally, 254
Ford, Henry, 42
Fort Constitution, 2
Fort Hill, 4
Fort Nassau, 176
Fort Niagara, 159
Fort Orange, 120, 180
Fortress, The, 107, 113
Forts and Firesides of the Mohawk Country, 154
Fort Ticonderoga, 183
fossils, 128, 212, 214
"Four Corners", 138
France, 4, 22, 151, 180
Franklinton Vlaie Wildlife Management Area, 99
Franzen, Ulrich, 253
Frasier, Gertrude "Gerdy," 133
Frederick, Susannah Philipse, 4
Freeman, Catherine, 19
Freeman, Nancy, 254
French & Indian War, 159, 179, 123
freshwater tidal wetlands, 103, 178, 180
Fried Chicken War, 80
Frost, Robert, 166
Frueh, James D., 177
Frueh Bros. Farm, 177
Fuertes, Louis Agassiz, 42
Fuller, Samuel, 157
funicular, 78, 238

G

Gardiner, Clyde, 80
Garner, Thomas, 182, 193
Garrison, xii, 1
Garrison, Harry, 4
Garrison, John, 4
Garrison Free School District Board of Education, 2
Garrison School Forest, 2

Garrison School Forest Committee, 6
Garrison's Landing, 4
Garrison's Landing Historic District, 4
Garrison Union Free School District, 5, 6
Gates, General Horatio, 218
gelatin, 155, 156
General Electric (GE), 106
"Geological and Agricultural Hall," 201
Geological Excursions, 213
Geology of Saratoga Springs & Vicinity, 214
George, King, x, 92
George III, King, 218
George VI, King, 28, 29
George Street Park, 195, 197
Ghee, Joyce C., 11
Gildersleeve, Robert A., 74, 75
glacial erratic, 51, 114, 123, 204, 231, 257
glaciere, 247
Glacier National Park, 213
Glasco, 55, 57, 61
Glen Falls, 36, 182
Glenmont, 177
Goat Island, 58
Godyn's Kil, 168
Gonzales, Samuel, 51
Goodale, Major Nathan, 217
Goodell, Edwin, 252
Gould, Stephen Jay, 218
Gouvion, Lieutenant Colonel Jean Baptiste, 3
Grafton, 224, 226, 227, 230, 231, 246
Grafton Lakes State Park, 229, 230
Grafton Lakes State Park, Friends of, 229
Grafton Peace Pagoda, 245, 246
Grafton Trail Blazers Snowmobile Club, 224
Grand Army of the Republic, 123
Grandfather Rock, 231–233
Grand Gorge, 44
Grand Union Hotel, 212

granite, 123, 157, 218
granite, Stony Creek, 122
Grau, Frederick, 53
Great Appalachian Valley, 54
Great Depression, 48, 80
Great Pyramids, 67
Greek, 79, 199, 200
Greendale, 92
Greene County Historical Society, 79, 96
Greene Land Trust, 100
greenfield formation, 214
Greylock, Mt., 242, 244, 253, 254
Greylock Foundation, 253
Grinnell, Irving, 11, 12
Grinnell, Julia, 11
Grossi, Patrick J., 170
Guide to Natural Places in the Berkshires, 251
Guide to the Caves and Karst of the Northeast, 139

H

Hailes, Theodore C., 139
Hailes Cave, 139
Haines Falls, 76
Hale Creek, 154
Hall, James, 213
Hall Creek, 154
Hallenbeck Creek, 93
Hamilton, Alexander, 11, 179
Hamilton Corliss steam engine, 79
Handel, George Frederic, 254
Hang Glider Cliff, 136, 137, 139, 140, 141
Hannacroix Maze, 102, 111, 112
Hannacroix Swamp, 111, 112
Harder family, 175
Harlemville, 82, 87
Harmony, Peter, 192
Harmony Mills, 184, 187, 188, 190–194, 201
Harmony Mills Historic District, 193
Harmony Mills Manufacturing Company, 192
Harriman, Edward, 42
Harriman Expedition to Alaska, 42

Hartley, Marsden, 253
Hartwick College, 37, 66
Havers, Richard, 60
Headless Horseman Bridge, 71
Helderberg-Hudson Grotto, 139
Helderberg-Hudson Rail Trail, 175
Hell's Hole Creek, 62
Henriques, Everton, 20
Henry, E.L., 151
Heritage Baptist Church, 197
Hickok, Lorena, 27
High Bridge, 20
High Falls, 82–89
High Falls Conservation Area, 82, 85, 87, 88
High Falls Overlook, 85, 88
Highland, 15, 17, 21, 38
Highland Landing, 14
Highland Landing Memorial Park, 15, 16
Highland Landing Park Association, 17
Highland Rotary Club, 20
High Peaks, 21
High Point (Altamont), 136-141
High Point (Cragsmoor), 54
High Point (New Jersey), 50
High Rock Knitting Company, 86
Hinckley, 158
Hinkel Hotel, 177
Historic Dover, 47
Hog Barn, 170
Hollyhock Hollow Sanctuary, viii, 126–135
Hopkins, Amos Lawrence, 248
Hopkins, Theresa Burnham Dodge, 248
Hopkins Memorial Forest, 241, 243, 245, 248
Hop-O-Nose, 92,
Hopper, Edward, 253
Horeb, Mount, 119
Horn Point, 7
Hotel Kaaterskill, 67, 78, 80
Howe, Lord, 183
Howe Caverns, 48, 52
Hoyt, Lisa, 233
Hoyt family, 211, 212

Hoyt limestone, 214
Hoyt's lime kiln, 211
Hoyt's Quarry, 210, 214
Hudson, 90, 92
Hudson, Henry, 181
Hudson Highlands, 1, 3, 5, 7, 21, 179
Hudson River, 1–5, 7, 8, 10, 11, 15–18, 20–22, 31, 33–37, 42, 44, 55–57, 59–61, 87, 88, 91–95, 97, 99–102, 104, 106, 168, 176, 179–182, 188, 207, 217, 235, 254
Hudson River National Estuarine Research Reserve, 101
Hudson River School painters, 48, 73, 91, 94, 97, 100
Hudson River Skywalk, 90-98
Hudson Valley, viii, ix, 6, 15, 28, 35, 36, 37, 41, 50, 75, 77, 80, 82, 83, 85, 94, 96, 100, 136, 191
Hudson Valley in the Ice Age, The, 37
Hudson Valley Rail Trail, 21
hummingbirds, 97, 126
Hunt, Richard Morris, 98
hydraulic cement, 185
Hyser, Collins, 67

I

ice caves, 49–54
Ice Caves Mountain, 49, 52, 53
Ice harvesting, 57, 60, 61, 85, 104, 106, 168, 169
Ice House, R.&W. Scott, 101–106
icehouses, 57, 61, 101, 247
Indian Ladder, 136
Indian Ladder escarpment, 147
Indian Ladder Road, 143
Indian Ladder Trail, 140, 143, 145
Indian mortars, 203–205, 207, 209
Indian Pass, 21
Indian Rock (Bowdoin Park), 9, 11, 12
Indian Rock (Sam's Point), 54
Indian Steps, 51
Indian store, 158
Indian Trade House, 152
Inspiration Point, 80

INDEX

Iorio, L.T., 13, 22
Ireland, 159
Iroquois, Six Nations of the, 151, 154, 158, 159, 219
Irving, Washington, 70, 74, 92
Ives, Thomas, 247

J

Jackson & Sharp Co., 79
Jefferson, Thomas, 28
Jefferson Heights, 99
Jennings, Mayor Gerald D., 172
Jenny (African American slave), 154
Jing-Hang Grand Canal, 185
Jogues, Father Isaac, 180
Johnson, Henry, 121
Johnson, John, 158
Johnson, Sir William, 151, 152, 154, 156, 158, 159; gravesite, 150, 151, 158; statue, 150, 151, 157
Johnson Boulevard, 121–123
Johnson Hall State Historic Site, xii, 150–159
Johnson-Iorio Memorial Park, 13–15, 18, 22
Johnson Memorial, Henry, 116, 121
Johnston, David John, 191, 193, 194
Johnston, John, 191
Johnston, R.E., 22
Johnston, Robert, 192–194
Johnston Mansion, 187, 191, 193
Johnstown, xii, 150, 151, 155, 157, 159
Johnstown Historical Society, 156
Joralemon, Frank, 114
Joralemon Cave, 107, 108, 110
Joralemon Memorial Park, 107–114
Joralemon Rock, 107, 108, 114
Joralemon's Back Door Cave, 107–109
Jorn, Father Charles, 56
Jorn Trail, Father C., 55
Jorn Trail Cascade, Father C., 55, 56, 59
Julian's Rock, 39, 40

K

Kaal Rock, 17
Kaal Rock Park, 17
Kaaterskill, Hotel, 67, 78, 80
Kaaterskill Clove, 68, 70, 73, 75
Kaaterskill Clove: Where Nature Met Art, 73
Kaaterskill Creek, 71, 100
Kaaterskill Falls, 79
Kaaterskill High Peak, 63
Kaaterskill Railroad, 78
Kaufman, Uri, 193
Kayaderosseras Creek, 209
Kenwood, 174
Kick, Peter, 64
Kincaid, Trevor, 43
Kinderfold, 11
Kinderhook, 192
King, Rufus H., 119
King Memorial Fountain, 116, 118–120
Kingsford, Helen, 11
kinte-kayes, 10
Knaust brothers, 106
Kneer, Randy, 227
Knickerbocker, 10
Knickerbocker Ice Company, 106
K-9 unit, 173, 177
Knox, Charles B., 155
Knox, Rose Markward, 155
Knox Gelatine Co., 155
Kronk Brook, 236, 237
Kronk Brook Falls, 236, 238, 239
Kurtz, Greg, 108

L

Lafayette, Marquis de, 4
Lake Albany, 36
Lake Champlain, 7
Lake Chodikee, 40
Lake George, 7, 81
Lake George, Battle of, 159
Lake Maratanza, 54
Laubach, René, 251
Legend of Sam's Point, The, 51
Legend of Sleepy Hollow, 71
Lenape Steps, 49, 50
Leni (Lenni) Lenape, 50
Leopold, Aldo, 233
Lester, Esq., Willard, 212
Lester Park, 210–214
Leverett, Mass., 246
limestone, Hoyt, 210, 214
limestone, Manlius, 139
limestone, Onondaga, 110
Lindley, Mr., 205
Little Falls, 205
Little Hoosic River, 239
Little Hoosic Valley, 241, 242
Little River, 180, 181
Little White House, 27
Livingston, Philip, 123
Livingston Cave, 139
Lock Tender's house, Erie Canal, 190, 191, 196
Lofts at Harmony Mills, 193
Lonely Quest—The Evolution of Presidential Leadership, The, 133
Longfellow, Henry Wadsworth, 176
Long Trail, 231–234
Longview, 187, 191, 193
Longview Park, 17
Lookout, The, 150, 151, 155, 156
Lookout Point Trail, 46
Lossing, Benson J., 48
Loveridge, William, 92
Loveridge Patent, 92
Love Rock, 7
Low, Clarence, 57
Lower Loop Trail, 46
Loyalists, 4, 221
Lusk, Elizabeth, 73
Lusk, Gilbert, 73
Lyme disease, xv
Lynch, James, 103
Lynch Hotel, 103

M

Mabie, Robert M., 73
Macmahon, Edna C., 221
Macmahon Hiking Trail, Edna C., 9
MacNeil, Herman A., 122
Magdalen Island, 58
Maguire, Patrick, 221

Maher, Richard Francis, 47
Maine, 94
Mall, The, 120
Malta Trail, 203, 204, 206–208
Mammut, 201
Manhattan Bridge Building Company, 20
Manitou, Great Spirit of, 75, 76
Manitou, Wall of, 73, 75, 96, 100
Manning Paper Company, 235
Maplewood Historic Park, 198, 199
marble, Tennessee, 122
March, Alden, 123
Marcy, Mt., 21
Mariners Harbor Marina & Restaurant, 17
Marist College, 17
Markham, Jared C., 218
Martin, "Smokey" Joe, 229
Martin, T.H., 110
Martin Trail, Amasa, 40
Mason, Alice Trumbull, 253
Massachusetts, 241–246, 250
mastodon, 184, 193, 200, 201
Mastodon Mill, 193
Mathew Creek, 154
Mattison, Job Orlando, 240
Mattison Hollow, 236–240
Mattison Hollow B&B, 240
Mattison Hollow Brook, 236
Mattison Hollow Cascade, 239
Mattison Hollow kiln, 237
Mawignack Preserve, 99, 100
McFalls, Mary Oakley, 234
McFalls Natural History Road, Mary Oakley, 234
McMasters Caves, 250–252
Meals, George, 60
Mechanicville, 207, 208
Medal of Honor, 121
Mellenville, 87
Meltz family, 87
Merchant Ice Company, 106
Merino sheep, 93
Merritt's Cave, 107, 111, 113
Mid-Hudson Bridge, 14, 15, 17, 18, 22, 23
Mid-Hudson Children's Museum, 22

migratory birds, 103
Miller, J.M., 73
Miller, Richard McDermott, 252
millstones, 153
Minelot Creek, 142–149
Minelot Creek Falls, 146, 147
Minelot Pond, 146
Mink Hollow, 63
Minnewaska State Park, 48, 53, 54
Misery Mountain, 237
Modjeski, Ralph, 19
Mohawks, 47, 93, 130, 151, 154, 159, 176, 180, 209, 254
Mohawk-Hudson Land Conservancy, viii, ix, 134, 170, 171
Mohawk River, 21, 153, 157, 158, 185–188, 192, 207
Mohawk Valley, viii, 123, 159, 183, 191, 208, 209
Mohawk Valley Hiking Club, 162–164, 166
Mohicans, 93, 100, 176, 182, 209, 254
Mohonk Mountain House, 56
Moment in the Sun: A Report on the Deteriorating Quality of the American Environment, 133
Moreno, Vito, 20
Morgan, Colonel Daniel, 218
Morgan's Riflemen, 218
Morning in the City, 253
Moseman, Claude, 80
Moses, 116, 119
Moses Fountain, 118, 119
Moss Island, 205
"Mother of the Year" award, 120
Mother's Day, 119, 120
Mt. Ida Falls, 235
Mount Katahdin, 97
Mount Merino, 93
Mt. View Farm, 71
Mudd Quarry, 63
Muhheakunnek, x, 21, 182
Muir, John, 42
Mulford, Charles, 57
Mulford Fire Engine Company, 57
Mulford homestead, 57, 60
Mulford Ice House, 55–57
Murdock, Channing, 243

Murray, Charles Augustus, 34
Mushrooms (statue), 106, 253
"Music for the Royal Fireworks," 254

N

Nardacci, Mike, 139
National Bard, 122
National Environmental Policy Act (NEPA), viii
National Grid, 170, 172
National Guard, 171
National Historic Landmark, 43, 44, 178, 193, 215
National Park Service, xi, 35, 95, 208
National Railroad Passenger Service, 17
National Register of Historic Places, 20, 103, 165, 187, 193, 221, 230
Native Americans, 92, 125, 152, 155, 178, 180–183, 188, 203, 205, 209, 219, 222, 246
Nature Conservancy, ix, 53, 54, 133; Eastern Chapter, 160, 166
Nelson, Cornelius, 4
Nelson family, 4
Netherlands, 100, 120
Netherwood, 11
Newburgh, 36, 182
New Hamburg, 8, 11, 12
New Jersey, 50
Newman's Ledge, 50
New Paltz, 13
Newport, Tennessee, 246
New Salem, 136, 142
New Year's Eve, 122
New York City, 5, 11, 20, 35, 47, 50, 67, 93, 94, 104, 164, 192, 225, 229
New York State Education Building, 201
New York State Environmental Quality Review Act (SEQRA), viii
New York State Museum, 200, 213, 214
New York State Police, 229
New York State Register of Historic Places, 103

INDEX

New York State Thruway, 13, 55, 69, 90, 172
Niagara Falls, 97, 185
Norman, 167
Normanside Country Club, 171
Normans Kill Cascade, 167
Normans Kill (creek), 167, 168
Normans Kill Dairy Farm, 167
Normanskill Farm, 167
Normanskill Farm, Friends of the, 167
Normanskill Farm Dog Park, 171
Normans Kill Gorge, 175
Normanskill Viaduct, 175
Normansville, 163, 167
Normansville Community Church, 167
North Adams, 254
Northeastern Caver, 251
North Lake, 69, 70, 73, 75, 76
North Mountain, 75, 76
North Pond Overlook Trail, 38
North Redoubt, 1–4, 6
North Road, 90, 93
North-South Lake, 70, 75, 80, 81
North-South Lake Campground, 70, 80
North Trail, 250, 252
Norwegian, 168, 176
Nutten Hook (*Newton Hock, Nutten Hock*), 101–105
Nutten Hook Preserve, 106
Nutten Hook Reserve, 101
Nutten Hook Unique Area, 103

O

Oak Loop Trail, 250–252
Obama, President Barack, 121
Ockawamick Creek, 87
Ockawamick Hosiery Mills, 86
Office of Parks, Recreation and Historic Preservation, NYS, 19, 48, 213, 229
Of Snuff, Sin, and the Senate, 133
Olana, 90, 91, 93, 94, 97, 98; greenhouse site/Church's studio, 97; kitchen garden, 98
Olana Partnership, 91, 96
Olana State Historic Site, 90

Old Mountain Turnpike, 69, 70, 73, 75, 77, 79
Olton, Jean, 179
O'Neil, Mary E., 133
O'Neil Educational Center, Mary E., 133
O'Neil House, 126, 130, 131, 133
Onesquethaw Creek, 126, 130, 131
Onteora, 75
Open Space Institute (OSI), 16, 179
Opus 40, 68
"orange wonder," 120
Osborn, General Frederick Henry, 5
Osterhoudt, Oscar, 57
Otis, Charles Owen, 78
Otis Elevating Railway, 70, 73, 75–77, 78, 81, 100
Otis Elevating Railway Summit Station, 69, 76, 79
Otis Elevator Company, 78
Otter Creek Trail, 232, 233, 235
Our New Life with the Atom, 133
Overbaugh, Peter, 60
Overlook Mountain, 67, 68
Overlook Mountain Road, 67

P

Paint Mine Area, 142, 143
Palenville, 67–69, 75, 79, 100
Palenville Overlook, 68, 69, 75
Palisades, 21
Pancake Rock, 142, 143, 148, 149
Pappalau, Edward, 169
Pappalau, George, 168
Pappalau, Harry, 168
Pappalau, Vincent, 168
Pappalau, William, 168
Pappalau Ice House, 167–169, 176, 177
Parker, Margaret K., 131
Park Playhouse, 118
Peace Pagoda, 245, 246
Peck Hill State Forest, 154
Pecoy Notch, 62, 63, 66
pedestrian footbridge (Washington Park), 117, 118, 125

Peebles Island, 188
Peninsula Rock, 116
Peninsula Trail, 40
Pennsylvania, 50
Pequot, 47
Perimeter Trail (Thacher Park), 137, 141
Perry, Clay, 139, 247
Pershing, General John, 121
Petanock, 168
Petersburg Pass, 230, 241–243
Petersburg Pass Recreation Area, 241, 244
Petersburg Pass Ski Center, 242
Petrified Sea Gardens, 210, 212, 215
Petrified Sea Gardens, Friends of the, 215
Philip, George P., 85
Philipse, Adolphus, 4
Philipse Patent, 4
Philmont, 82, 87–89
Pine Bush, 49
Pine Orchard, 69, 75, 79
Pine Plains dolomite, 11
Pinksterfest, 120
pitch pines, 51, 52; barrens, 52
Plant, Doris Saunders, 162
Plant, Henri Treadwell, 162
Plantation Trail, 164
Plant Bridge, 162
plate tectonics, 214
Platte Clove, 62–64, 67, 68, 75
Ploughman, The, 122
Poconos River, 71
Poe, Edgar Allen, 175
Poesten Kill, 235
Pollinator Pavilion, 97
Pond House, 38, 40
Pond Trail, 250
Pond Trail, North, 40, 41
Pontiac, Chief, 154
Pontiac's War, 154
Popular Forest, 28, 229
Porter, Fairfield, 253
Port of Albany, 92, 168
Poughkeepsie, 9, 13–15, 17, 21–23, 30, 102, 104, 212

265

Poughkeepsie Halfway up the Hudson: Images of America, 11
Poughkeepsie-Highland Railroad Bridge, 20
Poughkeepsie Railroad Bridge, 18, 20
Poughkeepsie Railroad Station, 22
powder house, 125
Powell, Arthur James Emery, 48
Power Canal Park, 187, 192
powerhouse, 101, 102, 105, 106
Pownal, 254
Promenade, The, 120–122
Prospect Hill Cemetery, 216–219
Prospect Mountain, 78
Pullette Stone Co., 215
Pulpit, The, 46, 47
Putnam County, 1, 4

Q

Quarryman's Museum, 68
quicklime, 211

R

rail-trail, 14, 16, 21, 175, 176, 208
Rail-Trail Hall of Fame, 21
Raimer, Mark, 243
Rambles to Remarkable Rocks, 114
Ranch House, Santa Fe, 253
Ravena, 107
Ravena-Coeymans Historical Society, 114
Ravena Fish & Game Club, 107
redoubts, xii, 1–6
Redoubt Mountain, 4
Reese, Franny, 22
Reese State Park, Franny, 13–15, 17, 18, 22
refrigeration, 106, 168, 169
Rensselaer & Saratoga Railroad, 208
Rensselaer Plateau, 229, 235
Rensselaerswyck, 182
Reservoir, The, 85
Revolutionary War, 1, 3, 4, 74, 100, 158, 159, 179, 180, 218, 222
Rexford, 207

Rhind, J. Massey, 119
"Rhine of America," 21
Rickerson, 79
Ridge Trail, 39, 40
Ridgway, Robert, 43
Rienow, Leona Train, 132
Rienow, Robert, 128, 133, 134
Rienow House, 133, 134
Rienow Memorial Building, 130, 134
Ring Rock, 231, 233, 234
Rip's Ledge, 74
Rip's Rock, 69, 71, 74
Rip Van Winkle, 89
Rip Van Winkle Bridge, 90–92, 95
Rip Van Winkle Brook, 70
Rip Van Winkle House, 69, 70, 72, 73
Rip Van Winkle Trail, 70
Ritchie, Robert F. 215
Ritchie Park, 215
Rivenberg, Charles, 183
River and Estuary Observation Network, 170
Riverby, 40, 42, 44
Riverside Trail, 55, 59, 60
Rivers of Mystery, 52
"Road to Stone Arabia" ("Road to Stoneraby"), 155
Roaring Brook, 63, 65
Roaring Brook Trail, 63
Roberts, Dr. Charles H., 19
Robinson, Beverley, 4
Rochefontaine, Captain Etienne Bechet de, 3
Rock City, 210
Rock Garden, 231, 233
Rockwell, Charles, 71
Rogers, Robert, 51
Rogers Island, 91, 93
Roosevelt, Eleanor, 23–26, 28, 29
Roosevelt, Franklin Delano, 18, 26, 48
Roosevelt, Theodore, 42
Roosevelt National Historic Site, Eleanor, 23
Ross, David, 114, 256
Round Lake, 203, 207

Rounds, Kevin, 108
Round Top, 63, 74
R.R.R. Brooks Trail, 243, 245
Ruedamann, R., 214
Ruhle Road Park Committee, 209

S

saber-toothed tigers, 200
Saint Andrew's Society, 122
St. John's Episcopal Church, 151, 158, 159
St. Lawrence Valley, 209
Sam's Point, 49–51, 53, 54
Sam's Point Dwarf Pine Ridge Preserve, 52, 53
Sam's Point Mountain House, 50
Sam's Point Overlook, 49
Sam's Point Visitor Center, 49
Sand Lake, 238
Santvoord, Alfred Van, 78
Saratoga, Battle of, 183
Saratoga Battlefield, Friends of, 209
Saratoga Monument, 216–218
Saratoga Monument Association, 218
Saratoga National Historic Park, 209, 216, 222
Saratoga Railroad, 208
Saratoga Springs, 158, 209, 210, 212–216
Saratoga Victory Manufacturing Company, 221
Sassacus, 47
Saugerties, 55, 62, 68, 69
Saw Mill Road, 142–149
Saxe, Frederick, 70, 71, 79
Saxe, Ira, 73, 79
Saxe's Farm, 70, 79
Scenic Hudson, ix, 19, 22, 60, 100
Scenic Hudson Land Trust, 103
Scenic Tour of Rensselaer County, New York, 247
Scheafe estate, John Fisher, 12
Schenectady, 17, 162, 180, 205, 207
Schnackenberg family, 87
Schoharie County, 48, 99, 131
Schoharie Creek, 64

INDEX

Schoharie Turnpike, 160, 166
Schroeder, Fred, 137
Schroeder Memorial Kiosk, Fred, 137
Schroeder Memorial Trail, Fred, 138, 139
Schuchert, Charles, 214
Schuff, H.A., 73
Schumer, Senator Charles, 121
Schuyler, General Philip, 179
Schuyler, Philip Pieterse, 183
Schuyler, Pieter, 183
Schuyler Burying Grounds, 178, 179
Schuyler Flatts Archeological District, 178, 183
Schuyler Flatts Cultural Park, 178–183
Schuyler House, 178
Schuylerville, xii, 213, 216–218
Scotland, 122
Scott, Robert, 105
Scott, William, 105
Screen Porch (painting), 253
Secret Cascade, 142–144
Secret Caverns, 52
Sentinels, The, 231, 234
Share Corporation, Frederick, 92
Shawangunk conglomerate, 49, 54
Shawangunk Ridge, 54
Shenantaha Creek Park, 203–209
Shepard farm, 244
Shepard Highland Landing Memorial Park, Bob, 13–17
Shepard's Well, 241, 243, 244
Shepard's Well Trail, 241–245
Sherwood, Dana, 97
Shingle Gully Ice Caves, 54
Shoreline Path, 235
sinkholes, 126, 129, 130, 138, 140, 141, 147
Slabsides, 38–44
slaves, 125, 154, 155
Sleeping Alligator (cave), 111
Sleepy Hollow, 70, 71
Sleepy Hollow Brook, 71
Sleepy Hollow Horse Trail, 70
Slingerlands, Teunis C., 176

Slipsteen Island, 58
Sloan, Samuel, 4, 5
Sloan Mountain, 5
Sloan's Tower, 2
Sluiceway Falls, 84
Smith, Benny, 149
Smith, Matthew, 17
Smith, Zimri "Zim," 209
Smith Club, James, 245
Smith Hill, James, 245
Smith's Corners, 149
Smith Trail, Zim, 207, 208
Smokey Bear, 228, 229
Snow Hole, 236, 241–249
Soldiers & Sailors Monument, 116, 123
Solitary Rock, 142, 143, 148
Song of Hiawatha, The, 176
Song of the Helderhills, 166
Song of the Western Gateway, 166
Sons of the Revolution, 123
South Lake, 69, 70, 75, 76, 78, 80, 81
South Long Pond, 235
South Pond, 38, 40, 41
South Redoubt, 1–6
South Redoubt Reclamation Project, 5
South Trail, 250
South Williamstown, xii, 250, 252, 254
Sparkill, 57, 60
Sparkill Infirmary, 56
Spaulding, Gilbert, 60
Spence, Joan, 11
Spindle City, 187
Spindle City Historic Society, 187
Sprague Electric Company, 242
Springwood, 26
Spruce Bog Trail, 227
Staehle, Albert, 229
Starks Knob, 213
Starr, Jonah, 205
State Cabinet of Natural History, 201
State University of New York, Albany (SUNYA), 133
Stevens, C.P., 176, 177

Stevens, Mark, 176, 177
Stoller, James H., 188, 213
Stone Church Brook, 46, 47
Stone Church Cave, 45–48
Stone Church Cave, Friends of the Dover, 48
Stone Cottage, 23, 24, 27, 29
Stonehenge, 67, 136, 137
Storm King Highway, 2
Storm King Mountain, viii, 2
Strates, James E., 183
stromatolites, 210, 211, 213, 214
Stuyvesant, Peter, 10
Sugar Loaf Hill, 4
Sugarloaf Mountain, 62, 66
summer theater (Washington Park), 118
Summit Knitting Mill, 82, 85, 86
Summit Lake, 82, 85, 89
Summit Lake Dam, 85
Summit Reservoir, 82
Sunnycrest Nursing Home, 183
Superintendent of Indian Affairs, 151
Suspension Points: Surface Winds (painting), 253
Suto Road, 146
Swartekill, 16
Swartekill Creek, 16
Syracuse, 174

T

Table Rock, 54
Taconic Crest Trail, 236, 237, 241, 243, 245–247
Taconic Hiking Club, 241, 242
Taconic Mountain Range, 241, 244, 248, 249
Taconic Orogeny, 249
Taconics, 21, 230, 241
Taconic Trails, 243
Talbot, Silas, 159
Tannersville, 62, 76
Tawasenths (Normans Kill), 168, 176
Teller's Point, 6
Tenant House (Normanskill Farm), 170
Ten Commandments, 119
Thacher, Emma Treadwell, 136

Thacher Park, John Boyd, 136–149
Thompson Lake, 138, 145
Thomson, John, 94, 95
Thomson family, 95
ticks, xiv, xv
Ticonderoga, 183
Tin Horns and Calico, 166
Titus, Robert, 37, 67
Tivoli Bays, 58
Tivoli Lake Preserve & Farm, Inc., 177
tobacco, 168
Todhunter, Winifred, 27
Todhunter School, 27
tolls (Erie Canal), 189, 199
Toombs, Henry J., 27, 28
Top Cottage, 23–28
Tories, 123
Tortuga Foundation, 56
Trackside Homes, 155
Trails with Tales: History Hikes ..., xii, 80, 97, 136, 213
Tribes Hill, 158
trilobites, 214
Tri Municipal Sewer Plant, 12
tri-state marker, 245
Troy, 21, 195, 198, 208, 230, 235, 238, 242
Troy County Fair, 201
Trustees of the Reservation, 250, 254
Truth, Sojourner, 16
Tulip Festival, Albany, 119, 120
Tulip Queen, 120
tulips, 119, 120
Turco, Peggy, 11
turning runner stone, 153
Turret Room, 65
Twin Mountain, 62, 64, 66

U

Ulster County Chamber of Commerce, 16
Unbottled Scotch, 133
Underground Empire: Wonders and Tales of New York Caves, 139, 247
Union Army, 16, 86, 123
Union Bridge Company, 20

Union College, 213
United States Department of Interior and National Park Service, 208
Untillable Hills, 166
Untold Story of Helen Ellett, The, 227
Upland Trail, 55, 58, 59, 60
Upland Trail Cascade, 55
Upper Hollow, 174
Upper Landing Park, 18, 21
Upper Loop Trail (Dover Stone Church Cave), 46
Upper Loop Trail (Snow Hole), 245

V

Val-Kill, 23–28, 29
Val-Kill Industries, 24, 27
Van Curler, Arent, 180, 182
Van Leuven, 60
Van Rensselaer, Kiliaen, 180, 182
Van Rensselaer, Richard, 183
Van Santvoord, Alfred, 78
Van Vechten, Dirk Teunisse, 100
Van Vechten House, 99, 100
Van Wagonen, John, 80
Van Winkle, Rip, 70, 71, 72, 74
Van Winkle Bridge, Rip, 90, 91, 92, 95
Van Winkle Brook, Rip, 70, 71
Van Winkle House, Rip, 69–76
Van Winkle Rock, Rip, 74
Van Winkle Trail, Rip, 70
Van Zandt, Henry, 147
Van Zandt, Margaret, 149
Van Zandt, Roland, 72, 79, 81
Van Zandt, William, 149
Vassar College, 9
Vastrick Island, 93
Verkeerderkill Falls, 54
Verplanck's Point, 6
Victory, village of, 221
Victory Mills, 221, 222
Victory Mills Packing Company, 222
Victory Woods, 216–222
Vietnam War, 22
View of the Catskill Mountain House, New York, 75

View of the Two Lakes and Mountain House, Catskill Mountains, Morning, 76
Village One Apartments, 181
Villa St. Joseph, 59, 60
Vischer Ferry Nature & Historic Preserve, 174
Vita Nova Woodworking, 87
Voorheesville, 175
Vrooman, John J., 154
Vulture, The, 6

W

Walks and Rambles in Dutchess and Putnam Counties, 11
Walkway over the Hudson, 13–18, 20, 21
Walkway over the Hudson (organization), 20
Wallace, Dewitt, 179
Wallkill, 16
Wall of Manitou, 73, 75, 96, 100
Wall Street Canyon, 52
Walton, 140
Wappinger Falls, 8, 11, 14
Wappinger Greenway Trail, 9, 11
War Memorial Tower, 244
Warm Springs (Georgia), 27
Warraghegagey, 159
Warren, Peter, 159
Waryas Park, Victor C., 17
Wash House (Johnson Hall), 153
Washington, General George, 3, 6, 35
Washington Park, 116–125; burial site, 125
Washington Park Conservancy, 116
Washington Park Lake, 16, 117, 124
Washington Square, 125
Waterford Flight of Locks, 188
Water Lot 1, 4
Watervliet, 178, 198
Watervliet Reservoir, 163, 168
Water Watch, 131
weather station, 170, 244
weighlock, 198, 199
Weisenberg, Catharine, 158

INDEX

Wells, John E., 159
West Canada Creek, 158
Westerlo, 176
West Park, 33, 38, 42, 44, 61
West Point, 1–4, 6, 7
West Saugerties, 62
wetland plants, 180
wetland pond, 147
Whipple, Squire, 174
Whipple Bowstring Truss Bridge, 167, 173, 174
White, Canvass, 185
White, Carol, 64
White, Dave, 64
White, J. Russell, 118, 124
White Lily Pond, 227
White Lily Trail, 227
White Rocks, 241, 242, 245, 246, 249
Whitman, Walt, 42, 166
Wild, Alfred, 192

Wild Pasture Pine, 166
Wilhelmina, Queen, 120
Willett, Marinus, 123
Willett Rock, 116, 123
Williams, George W., 91
Williams College, 241, 244, 245, 247, 248, 253, 254
Williams College Center for Environmental Studies (CES), 241
Williams Park, Tony, 21
Williamstown, xii, 241, 243, 247, 250, 252, 254
William III, King, 4
Wilson, Francis, 242
Wilson, President Woodrow, xi
windmill, 19, 244
Windsor Hotel, 212
Winne, Pieter, 176
Witches Hole, 147
Wizard of Oz, The, 175

Wolcott, C. E., 214
Woodchuck Lodge, 44
Woodstock, 55
Works Program Administration (WPA), 48
World's End Gun Club, 141
World's End Sinkhole, 141
World War I, 121, 122, 169
World War II, ix, 20, 29, 80, 252
Wright, Frank Lloyd, 252
Wynd brothers, 139
Wynd Brothers Robber Cave, 139

Y

Yahweh, 119
Yasuda, Jun, 246
Year of the Eagle, The, 133
Yellow Brick Road, 167, 173, 175, 177
Yellow Brick Road Bridge, 173, 175

ALSO BY DUNN & DELANEY

TRAILS WITH TALES
History Hikes through the Capital Region, Saratoga, Berkshires, Catskills & Hudson Valley

By Russell Dunn & Barbara Delaney • foreword by Karl Beard, National Park Service • Paper, 6" × 9", 304 pages, photographs, illustrations & maps • ISBN 9781883789480 $19.95

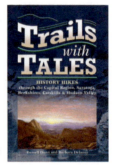

Thirty nature treks, selected for their natural, stand-alone beauty, are enhanced by tangible silhouettes of a fascinating past, from early Native Americans and Colonial settlers to the Industrial Revolution and Victorian-era grand hotels. Hike to waterfalls, mountains, escarpments, lakes, sculpted rocks, ponds, rivers, islands, caves, balanced rocks, geysers, and deep gorges while visiting the sites of famous battles of the Revolutionary War, ghostly industrial ruins, a Moorish-style castle, views and vistas made world-famous by America's greatest painters, vanished Shaker communities, great estates of the Gilded Age, a working lighthouse, and New York's Mount Rushmore.

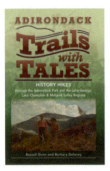

ADIRONDACK TRAILS WITH TALES
History Hikes through the Adirondack Park and the Lake George, Lake Champlain & Mohawk Valley Regions

By Russell Dunn & Barbara Delaney • foreword by Joe Martens, President, Open Space Institute • Paper, 6" × 9", 320 pages, maps & photographs • ISBN 9781883789640 $19.95

Hike, paddle, bike, or cross-country ski along beautiful trails through sites made famous by Adirondack guides, artists, writers, entrepreneurs, colonial settlers, and combatants in the French and Indian and Revolutionary Wars. Visit abandoned iron mines and the ruins of tanneries, famous Adirondack great camps and old resorts, lost villages, Native American battlegrounds, and the homestead of John Brown, catalyst for the Civil War. Visit the scene of America's first naval battle and marvel at geological wonders like Indian Pass, Canajoharie Gorge, Chimney Mountain, and the tufa caves of Van Hornesville. Detailed directions, maps, photographs, and vintage postcards.